MIKE HARDEN

road songs

For Christian, my grandson

Acknowledgements

I am grateful to *The Columbus Dispatch* for permitting me to reprint the following columns in a bound collection. I am also most appreciative of the newspaper's support of this project.

Road Songs was aided immensely by the painstaking work of Aaron Harden, my son. For generously giving his time to this project, I am most appreciative.

Thanks to Tim Revell for the cover photo and to Jen Hoffer for the inside shot of Christian Aaron.

Mike Harden,
April, 2001

ISBN 0-9710730-0-7

Wing & Prayer Publishers
First Printing: April, 2001

Contents

BOOKS BY MIKE HARDEN

Passage to America

First Gathering

Playing Favorites

Fight for Life

Homegrown

Heartland Journal

Among Friends

Road Songs

The Last Days of George Corley Wallace

April 12, 1998

MONTGOMERY, Ala. - Inside, past the steel-fretted storm door, the uniformed guard and the security cameras dangling like somnolent bats from the eaves of the house, former Alabama Gov. George Wallace rested uneasily at the momentarily slack end of a slim tether to the living.

From the mute box near the hospital bed in his home, the blinking images of Fred and Wilma Flintstone danced toward him.

Fate has piled Parkinson's disease atop the paralysis from the assassination attempt and thrown in arthritis and deafness for good measure. The man, a bantamweight boxer in his youth, now wears the look of an old fighting cock pressed to too many rounds in the spurs and the dirt and the blood.

A strong right paw greeted his visitor with a firmness almost disquieting, like an unexpected hand on the shoulder of a lone vigil-keeper deep in the night of an Irish wake.

Upon a hospital tray positioned across the bed there resided an ashtray the size of a hubcap, holding the cold remains of a Gran Primio cigar.

It is a tricky thing, an awkward *pas de trois*, to conduct an interview with the man who once flung racism's smudged gauntlet in the Alabama dust, proclaiming, "Segregation now, segregation tomorrow, segregation forever."

Questions must be printed on a tablet, then positioned before him by an aide.

Answers issue forth in husky, unsyncopated grunts, like the fits and starts of a car engine that refuses to let go after the ignition has been shut off.

"Did good," Wallace said when asked, hypothetically, what words he would have were the visitor at his bedrail not a Yankee journalist but Dr. Martin Luther King Jr.

"Forgave him," he rasped when quizzed about Arthur Bremer, the would-be assassin whose spray of bullets in a Maryland shopping center in 1972 consigned him to a wheelchair and ended his national political aspirations.

After the shooting, Wallace became a supplicant for the same acquitting remittance he has accorded Bremer, his contrition laid before the congregations of black churches all over Southern soil.

Some forgave the man who, after a defeat in the 1958 Alabama gubernatorial race by a Klan-courting opponent, had pledged that he would never be "out-niggered" again.

Some dismissed his pleas for atonement as might the kin of the victim when the author of their torment undergoes a jailhouse religious conversion.

One savvy observer of Southern politics in general, and George Wallace in particular, recently offered, "There are plenty of people in this world who have done some pretty terrible things and never raised a voice in apology. At least George Wallace said he was sorry."

Funny thing. He was more readily forgiven by the Alabama blacks who knew the imprint of his heel than by Northern whites. To them he was but a remote tyrant, an odd little cipher whose signal appearances on the evening news were like a TV test pattern designed to remind them of why they found the South so deplorable.

Wallace, turning away from his interviewer, thumped the heel of his palm on a worn scrapbook half-concealed among his bedclothes.

"He wants you to see the pictures," the aide at his shoulder explained.

There, in the book, are the glossies of Wallace posed with every notable from JFK to Ronald Reagan, from Jimmy Carter to the pope.

It was the gritty populist manifesto of Wallace's presidential bids that drew working-class Democrats away from traditional voting habits. Still, he was only their catechist, their Moses.

The heir to the promised land was Ronald Reagan.

In newspapers all around this nation, canned obituaries for the 78-year-old Wallace stand at the ready, awaiting only the flick of a cursor each time some new infectious assault sends ominous dispatches from Montgomery.

"He doesn't normally watch The Flintstones," the aide at his side protectively noted. "He usually watches CNN or The History Channel."

In the room where Wallace insists upon continuing to hold court for visitors he is too sick to see, black angels come and go, ministering to their fragile patient.

It is a curious enterprise, the bathing and the lifting, the arranging of the sparse and graying mane.

They have been a long time at their tender mercies.

When they began, the prisoner of Montgomery's Fitzgerald Road still seemed, at least a little, like a statue of some feisty Confederate general they were polishing for out-of-town company.

It has reached the point that their ablutions and scourings have so worn away the paint from this sad, little lawn jockey of a man that it is impossible to tell what color he is.

She said, "Yes"

April 27, 1999

LITTLETON, Colo. - Ray Zander sat on the blue folding chair with the rigid bearing of a West Point plebe at dinner. His shoes were the homely, frugal variety one might expect to be uniform issue to parolees. The sport coat and slacks were slightly mismatched, but when you're pushing 80, the relevance of fashion and the price of upgrading can be bothersome.

The funeral for Cassie Bernall was about to begin when he whispered to his seatmate that he had come all the way from Delray Beach, Fla., for the Columbine victim's service.

"I didn't know this young girl," he nodded toward the face on the monitor, "but when I heard the news I wept. When I heard the news that this girl faced a gun muzzle for her faith, I had to come. I wanted to meet the parents."

He wanted to tell them that their 17-year-old daughter had died a martyr.

The story of each of those slain at Columbine is different.

Bernall's distinguishes itself because, as she crouched in Columbine's library, she was asked by the gunman, "Do you believe in God?" When she answered "Yes, I believe in God," she was shot.

"She did something that one of the thieves did when Jesus was on the cross," praised her schoolmate, 16-year-old Joshua Lapp.

Ray Zander thought that was about right, so he packed some warm clothes and bought a plane ticket for Denver.

It didn't get him a seat in the sanctuary. He was packed down in the basement with the overflow at West Bowles Community Church.

As a tape-recorded hymn accompanied the scurrying of late arrivals, Zander leaned to his neighbor and said, "That is *I Will Sing of the Mercies of the Lord*," smiling as though he might have had a hand in writing it.

When a fellow in the row ahead of Zander shot a censuring glance his way, he fell silent, though he continued to nod and whisper, "Yes," when the pastor hit a respondent chord.

He nodded, "Yes," when Pastor Dave McPherson said, "Jesus fed 5,000 with five loaves and two fishes. Cassie fed the world with one word: Yes."

McPherson recalled that Bernall had told friends that April was the month of the year in which she hoped one day to marry, then added pointedly to those in attendance, "Jesus said, 'I come for my bride.' So why are we crying? Because we weren't invited to the wedding."

Zander's chin dipped again, and he squinted at the tiny figures on the distant screen singing:

From the mountaintops,
To the depths of the sea.
I will always trust in you.
Though the world
May label me a fool,
I believe in you.

"More good will come of this than we will ever know," Zander whispered.

"We are here to celebrate the graduation of Cassie with honors," the minister said of the slain Columbine junior. "She graduated a little early, Lord."

When the service had ended, Zander made his way up the steps and out to the drive where the hearse awaited.

As the casket and Cassie's family emerged from the church, Zander fished an instant camera from his pocket and snapped a picture. Security was too tight for him to offer them his hand. He snapped another photo as the casket was swallowed by the yawning hearse.

"In the prime of her life," he whispered, though he no longer had to worry about anyone shushing him. "If she had not answered, 'Yes,' she'd be alive today."

He walked across the parking lot to the sidewalk and stood there for a while, pressing into the palms of passers-by tiny cards printed with the message of John 3:16.

When the crowd was gone, he nodded and smiled, then turning stuffed the remaining cards in his pocket and headed down the sidewalk toward the distant and snow-dappled Rockies.

The Courting Flute

Oct. 27, 1999

LAME DEER, Mont. - If the clouds passing over the face of a new moon made a sound, it would be the melancholy vibrato of the Cheyenne courting flute.

If the ache of love unrequited had voice, it would be the smoky soughing coaxed from this short staff of sundance cedar.

No one recalls who taught the Cheyenne Turkey Legs to craft the flute. Yet when arthritis began to gnarl his knuckles, he passed the knowledge down to Wolf Voice. Wolf Voice, in turn, taught Black Bear.

"It was about 1940," Black Bear guessed of the time of his encounter with Wolf Voice. "He came to me and he said, 'I'm going to give you something. You will be the next flutemaker. When you get too old to make them, hand it down.'"

And so it has gone.

Seven years ago, when Black Bear began to feel his years, he called aside his grandson, Jay Old Mouse.

Old Mouse remembered, "He asked me, 'Would you like to learn to make the flute?' I said, 'Yes.' He said, 'Then let's go down to the river and look for the wood.' "

Traditionally, the flute's lone purpose was to assist a young man in winning the heart of the woman he hoped to marry. At night, the suitor would draw near the tepee or lodge of the young woman's family to begin his guileless recital.

"On a clear night, you could hear it far, far away," Black Bear said. All the families in all the surrounding tepees would hear and know.

Roger Old Mouse, Black Bear's son-in-law, explained, "It could be a day, it could be a couple days that he would have to sit there and play."

When the elders of the family of the Cheyenne maiden determined that the song of the flute was earnest, they would emerge from the lodge to negotiate a dowry.

In Cheyenne culture, the male provided the dowry to the young woman's family.

"Maybe three horses, three buffalo robes, three guns," Roger speculated.

Once the flute had served its purpose, it was put away and never again played. With the passage of time, though, the flute and its silver song became a part of other benchmarks in life -- from birthdays to funerals.

"When I play at a funeral," Jay Old Mouse said, "I am asking the creator to pity the family and help them accept the death and continue living.

"When I play for the birthday of a child, I play so that she will grow to an old age."

When Jay's grandfather, Black Bear, learned to make the flute, the instrument was crafted with the most basic of tools -- a knife, a rasp, a swath of sandpaper.

His grandson employs lathe and router to do the same.

That seems to matter less to Black Bear than that his grandson, Jay, understands certain truths about the courting flute.

"It is a powerful instrument," Jay recited. "You should respect it. My grandfather told me, 'When it is finished, whatever notes it gives you, make your music from that. Don't ask the flute to give you the musical scale.' "

Black Bear is pleased that there is a young flutemaker to carry on the tradition among the Northern Cheyenne.

"We all want to hold onto the old ways," said Jay. "We are trying our best to hold on to our language, but we know that we can't survive if we don't adapt. I'm just a person trying to hold on to two worlds."

By way of example, he notes that although he was married in a Catholic church service, he stood by the Cheyenne tradition of providing a dowry to the bride's family.

"I gave my father-in-law a tepee and poles, three horses (a bay, a sorrel and a palomino) and three blankets."

That is the old way, just as flutemaking is part of the old way.

"I handed it down to Jay," Black Bear said. "He will hand it down to his son or to someone close to the family."

Jay brought the flute to his lips and closed his eyes. When he had finished playing, the room was silent until he spoke.

"What the flute means to me is what the church means to other people."

A Guy Named "Studs"

Sept. 13, 1999

CHICAGO - A barefoot Studs Terkel answered the door of his north Chicago home, flinching when he spied my colleague's camera.

"Oh, pictures," he said, massaging his chin with his fingers. "I should shave. What do you think? I could shave. I look like a bum. Do I look like a bum?"

Dissuaded from fetching a razor, the irrepressible Terkel lowered himself into a patio chair and began to re-create a robbery he endured recently.

"Burglars are not like murderers," he said as he launched into his story. "They don't want confrontation."

Neither did Terkel.

On the evening of the crime, Terkel had just tucked himself into bed when, he recalled, "The light goes on in the hallway. There's a guy walking into the bedroom." I said, 'What's going on?' He said something, but my hearing aids were in the bathroom. I go to the bathroom."

By that time, Terkel could tell that the impatient burglar was getting a little jumpy.

"I tell him, 'Take it easy. Take it easy.' "

Vintage Terkel: an 87-year-old man in his underwear trying to soothe the intruder who's robbing him.

"My pants are on the chair," Terkel continued. "I reach in my pants pocket. I had about $280. He took it."

At that instant, Terkel realized that he had been taken for all the money he had in the house. He called to the retreating thief, "Hey, I'm broke. How about $20? He gives it to me without saying anything."

He continued, "That moment was an epiphany for me. This is what unregulated free enterprise is all about. He was doing his job; he got his money. He gave me $20, so now he's a philanthropist."

Terkel threw back his head -- crowned with a cockatiel's coif of spun angel hair -- and cackled at remembering the scene.

Had the burglar stayed, Terkel said, he might have hauled out his tape recorder and interviewed him. After all, he has held a microphone under America's nose for decades.

Through sweat, grace and intelligence, Terkel made his bones as oral historian and author. What pushed him in that direction, though, was being pilloried with another, and less desirable designation: suspected communist.

In 1949 and 1950, he had hosted his own Chicago TV show until sponsors learned that he had signed petitions pressing for price and rent controls and abolishing Jim Crow laws.

Producers were willing to give Terkel a way out. If only he would say that he had been duped into signing those petitions, he could save his TV show.

He refused.

"Stud's Place was knocked off the air," he said.

That led him to a one-hour interview show on Chicago's WFMT radio that lasted more than four decades. During that stretch, he turned out a dozen books. The oral histories among those volumes explored how we dealt with hard times and war, issues of race, our working lives and our dreams.

In this era, Terkel thinks it essential that we understand the century's prevailing currents that have carried us to 1999. He worries that we don't seem to care.

"We're suffering from a national Alzheimer's disease," he complained of the present dearth of historical perspective. "There is no memory. We're more and more into communications and less and less into communication."

A charter member of the lead-pencil club, Terkel shuns the computer.

"When people talk about software, I think of linens, pillowcases, Turkish towels. Hardware? I think about hammers, nails, pots and pans.

"I use an electric typewriter. That was a big advance for me. I'm a primitive."

He never learned to drive, relying on his wife, Ida, to steer him to interview subjects when his work required him to hit the road.

His latest book project is a trio of compilations of interviews and commentary. The first volume is titled *The Spectator.*

The work encompasses Terkel's interviews with everyone from Buster Keaton to Arnold Schwarzenegger.

The second book of the trilogy will be *The Listener.* In it, Terkel will talk about music and offer up the transcripts of interviews he did with those who make music.

The third one, *The Reader,* will do the same thing, only with writers.

Terkel speculates that he will be 94 by the time he finishes the trilogy.

"What will we do then?" he asked his publisher.

That issue will be discussed once the trilogy is finished, he was told (and assumes that Terkel will live to 94).

The man who has done more to illuminate the stories of those he calls the "anonymous many" (for his life's work has largely been about everyday folk) seems ill at ease with compliments.

He handles praise in the same manner a Buddhist monk might discourage a mosquito -- with a gentle wave of the hand that prevents the welt yet preserves the pest.

"It's a matter of passing history down," Terkel said of what he already has done. "I try to capture certain moments."

He has no intention of stopping.

"I'll retire with my toes turned up," he said, chuckling. "I'll go out raging against the dying of the light."

He wishes that he could have interviewed Picasso, Charlie Chaplin, George Bernard Shaw.

Good subjects all.

He wishes also that he could have interviewed the burglar who robbed him.

"How did you get in?" he asked the departing thief, by way of introducing himself to a fellow who seemed a good prospect for an oral history.

It may have been the only moment in the life of America's best interviewer that the subject couldn't stay long enough to respond.

Trust God Brake & Clutch

Sept. 4, 2000

ACCRA, Ghana - "Trust God," I read on the side of a taxi after arriving in this west African nation in August -- only to discover that my luggage had not made it.

Trust God, I thought.

Every stitch of clothing I had packed for an 18-day trip was gone.

I had to trust God; I wasn't sure whether I could trust either Ghana Airways or United.

Moreover, I was profoundly moved by the stunning display of faith in the almighty exhibited by Ghanaians regarding the most secular of concerns.

"God's Time Is the Best Tailoring," read a sign above a shop on the outskirts of Accra, the capital.

My new friend, Efo Kodjo Mawugbe, explained, "The owner may have struggled in life while all of his friends made it.

"He bided his time until he got his shop. He finally got his shop, and he knows now that God's time is the best."

When the smiling baggage clerk at the Ghana Airways desk suggested that my suitcase might be aboard a later flight, I reminded myself that, in God's time, I would recover it.

It unsettled me that hidden in a shoe in my missing luggage was a tiny bag holding a portion of the cremains of a departed friend. I had secreted the ashes in a loafer to get them past customs agents so I could spread them on the waters of the Gulf of Guinea.

Now they were missing.

Two days passed in the African heat. I sensed that I might be able to grow mushrooms under the arms of the polo shirt I'd worn since boarding the flight from Columbus. (Perhaps God wanted me to have a seat by myself on the bus).

Again and again, out the window of the rolling vehicle, I found continuing encouragement to leave my concerns in the hands of a higher power:

God Will Provide Shoe Repair
Apostolic Manicure
God First Video Library
The Name of the Lord Is a Strong Tower Enterprises, Inc.
Jesus Saves Coca-Cola
God Is My Helper Salon
Living Springs Meat Shop
King of Kings Electrical Works

By the third day, though my faith in God had not dimmed, I looked for a clothing store. Ask, "Where will I find a men's clothing store?" in Koforidua on a Sunday and the Ghanaian you are addressing will smile in the indulgent manner of an airline baggage clerk before replying, "Come back tomorrow."

I was only hours away from covering a formal reception at Koforidua's royal palace. In desperation, I purchased a dashiki of scintillating metallic orange.

I could fit both of my ham hocks into one leg of the matching pants. The suit included a hat (of a style made of paper in the United States) that I could not wear without feeling compelled to ask, "Did you want two scoops of

Rocky Road or just one?"

The bus lumbered through Koforidua toward the palace. I reminded myself that God was working on my lost luggage even if the airlines were not. I needed to steel myself with the faith that had produced Christ Is the Answer Paint Store.

Four more days passed. My notebook filled with the names of Ghanaian enterprises in Kumasi, Accra, Elmina:

> Don't Give Up Christ Is King Art & Sign
> My Redeemer Liveth Market
> The Secret of Christ Rasta Hairdo
> Be With the Lord Gas
> God of Wonders Furniture Works
> For Christ We Live Brake and Clutch Lining
> Higher Ground Fastfood

In Accra, I could not help but notice that nearly every passing taxi was painted with a message of faith. "Trust God" I read. "God Provides."

Along the Gulf of Guinea, near the Ghanaian city of Cape Coast, I spied a boat christened, "Even Jesus Had Enemies."

This sent the translator into a fit of giggles. He ventured, "This fisherman has said, 'It doesn't surprise me that people don't like me. Even Jesus had enemies.' "

I tried to laugh, yet small children were beginning to make fun of my clothes. Even Jesus had enemies, I thought. He probably had his luggage, though.

My luggage was gone, and with it the ashes of my friend. Suppose a cokehead, luggage thief had come upon that tiny bag of white powder hidden in a loafer? He could be snorting a line of Tom. I shuddered.

One week had become two, then stretched toward three. I scribbled the name of each new eye-catching shop in my notebook. How I longed to approach the baggage counter at Ghana Airways to confront a sign announcing "Jesus Has the Answers, But We've Got Your Samsonite."

It was not to be.

I wrote on:

> Envy No Man Furniture
> No One Is Perfect Except the Lord House of Lotto
> With God Motors
> God Never Fails Leather Works
> God's Able Brake Shop
> Blessed Is He Who Considers the Poor Tire Repair
> God Is Love Meat Shop
> No Jesus No Life Furniture

Perhaps I could launch a traveler's-rescue charity mission to dole out used clothing to desperate tourists. I could call it No Jesus, No Life, No Luggage.

I was pondering that possibility when I stepped from the curb onto Accra's Independence Avenue without checking traffic. A cabbie roared by. Careful, I reminded myself.

I could be killed in Ghana, I thought. I could be bowled over by a runaway taxi and left for dead in the street -- wearing an orange dashiki.

"Can you describe the vehicle that hit you?" a policeman would inquire, leaning an ear to my lips as life ebbed away.

With my dying breath I would whisper, "It was blue.

"And, oh. I almost forgot. On the trunk someone had painted "God's Will Be Done."

An Invincible Spring

Feb. 27, 2000

I trudged out to the woodpile last Sunday and loaded the split ash and oak into a waiting wheelbarrow.

The old dog, her dimmed vision making a shadowland of her world, paced and sniffed the wind as I worked.

Gathering wood against a Buckeye winter is a Sisyphean act. The task usually is conducted in air so brittle and beneath skies so ominous that the sole solace comes in reminding oneself that Ohio only seems like a Siberian gulag.

I am sick to death of winter -- sick of roadside snow hummocks whose brows have been blackened by the spewn exhaust of passing cars.

I am weary of storm warnings, tired of TV meteorologists whose euphemistic talk of "that white stuff" makes TV-viewing cocaine addicts twitch with longing.

"These are the desolate dark weeks," wrote Wiliam Carlos Williams in *These*:

The year plunges into night
and the heart plunges
lower than night

Long before Williams penned those lines, Emily Dickinson confessed:

There is a certain slant of light,
Winter afternoons --
That oppresses, like the heft
Of cathedral tunes.

No, it weighs heavier even than cathedral tunes.

Beneath winter's gray-flannel clouds, failure and loss, the ache of thwarted chance, induce an unrelieved keening, a rue bitter as any myrrh.

Several days ago, I sat at the bedside of a dying woman. Her whispering husband confided his prayer that she would live until Valentine's Day. I prayed that she would make it till spring. How cruel to spend one's measured last days staring at brown grass and barren limbs, to be put away beneath chill-wilted roses in ground as hard as granite.

T.S. Eliot was wrong. April is not "the cruelest month." It is the kindest. Nothing matches the brutality of February.

Somewhere in my basement there resides a book titled *Wisconsin Death Trip*. The recountings of life on the frontier prairie chill the reader with descriptions of the homicidal mayhem of settlers driven mad by isolation and the unrelenting howl of the February wind.

Antarctic explorers, sequestered for months, are said to develop a frightening strain of cabin fever called "big eye." It is a counterpart of what combat veterans call the 1,000-yard stare. It is the unseeing cast of eyes too tired to endure any more, a catatonic stupor induced by the heart's pining for warmth.

When I was a schoolchild, I chafed at my fifth-grade teacher's attempts to force me to memorize *Trees* and *I Wandered Lonely as a Cloud*, to lift my Alfalfa-like singing voice to the strains of *When It's Springtime in the Rockies.*

These are the days I would trade a year of my life to glimpse, newly sprung from thawing ground, the saffron trumpet and corona of a daffodil.

In February, I am a road-weary pilgrim whose Lourdes is April, whose grail is the cup of a blossoming crocus.

I sit in the half-lit dining room holding the bound script of an old Archibald MacLeish verse play titled *J.B.* The drama is a contemporary version of the Bible's story of Job. It is a piece as bleak and cheerless as the arctic blast that shivers the panes not far from my chair.

In a moment when the life of the play's protagonist seems too full of anguish to weather another blow, a voice -- seeking to comfort him while avoiding false cheer -- consoles:

The candles in churches are out
The stars have gone dark in the sky.
Blow on the coals of the heart
And we'll see by and by.

In the midst of cruel winter, I am blowing on those coals and yearning for an invincible spring.

Bill and Sally

Feb. 14, 2000

Tough guys always stare at their shoes when they feel themselves getting choked up.

Last week, I caught Bill Cooke doing that a couple of times.

He was sitting on a footstool near the end of Sally's bed when talk turned to Valentine's Day.

Reverie led him into an ambush, and he swallowed hard against the last half of a sentence he couldn't finish.

Then he stared at his shoes.

After a while, he said, "The first time I saw her, I was 15 years old. She was coming down the street between her two sisters. She had dark hair down to her shoulders. Blue eyes. Peaches-and-cream complexion. And could she wear a sweater."

At that, Sally pulled herself up against the side rail of the hospital bed.

She studied her reflection in the wall mirror, joking, "I was going to look in there and see who that woman was."

"That's my girlfriend," Bill assured her, rising to kiss the tips of her jaundiced fingers with the mock courtliness of a supplicant at the queen's throne.

When he closes his eyes, he can almost imagine it is the summer of 1944. He was a deckhand on the river, shoving crude oil from Baton Rouge to Ashland Oil's Kentucky refinery. America was at war.

In the dead of night he could see the lights of shipyards where graveyard shifts labored to build landing craft to carry the fight to the enemy.

The Allies were winning, God was in his heaven and Bill was dating Sally Rutledge, the belle of Ironton, Ohio.

"If you had a boyfriend," Sally remembered, "and his car ran, you held onto him. It was a little peer status."

"It wasn't easy to keep this woman," Bill said. "There was a lot of competition."

The first time they danced, the jukebox at Ironton's Tiger Grill was playing *Moonlight Becomes You.*

"The hand on my back," Sally said of that dance, "I could feel it all the way down to my toenails. I don't think his hand ever stopped shaking."

On Valentine's Day, he brought her chocolates from Staley's drugstore and flowers.

When the Army took him, Sally was yet a high-school junior. He wondered, thousands of miles away in the Philippines, whether she would be waiting when he came home.

He borrowed $300 from a buddy for the diamond he bought her in the spring of 1948. When they married, he was 20 and she was 19.

They scraped through his GI Bill college days. He went to work as an elementary school teacher. They had four children.

Valentine's Day never slipped his mind.

"I never missed," he said. "She always got candy or something. Later on, I used to buy her jewelry, a little necklace from down at Lazarus."

As this Valentine's Day approached, he found himself bringing her morphine, feeding her.

The cancer had wasted her down to 80 pounds. Both of them know it won't be long.

In January, she mustered enough strength to attend her granddaughter's wedding in Texas. She and Bill danced. His hand didn't tremble.

By the time they returned to the Holiday Inn, though, she was disturbingly weakened by the ordeal. She fell in the room. It took 15 stitches to close the laceration above her eye.

"She's got the best nurse in the whole world," Bill boasted from the foot of her bed last week. 'Smilin' Bill.

"I keep a cloth damp on her forehead. Sometimes she wants it cold. Sometimes she wants it warm."

Love, even amid the soul-killing treachery of a cancer battle, manages to hold the days together.

"All the old cliches," Sally said, "they really work. The warmth is there. You can say, 'I love you' over and over. I mean it as much today as I did then. Those feelings, they don't die out."

I was long gone from Bill and Sally Cooke's North Columbus home when an unasked question crossed my mind.

On the telephone, Bill obliged the inquiry. We made a little small talk. "Her eyes are giving out on her," he said. So, he reads to her.

Lately, she has asked for Elizabeth Barrett Browning's *Songs From the Portuguese.*

"Doesn't that include *How Do I Love Thee*?" I asked.

"Yes."

"How do you get through that last line?" I asked (. . . and, if God choose, I shall but love thee better after death).

"I cry, damn it," he blurted. "I cry. It's the only line that gets me."

Somehow I knew he was staring at his shoes again.

Next Exit, Breezewood

Sept. 10, 1997

BREEZEWOOD, Pa. - The mutant spawn of America's love affair with the automobile, Breezewood lurks in an Allegheny hollow just waiting to ambush travelers trapped halfway between "Are we there yet?" and car sickness.

To call it a town would be a lie. Though the billboards announce "The Town of Motels," only a few dozen residences occupy the bluff overlooking a patch of turf where a pair of Siamese-twin freeways join at the McDonald's.

Three dozen gas stations, motels and fast-food joints are crammed cheek-by-jowl where I-70 collides with the Pennsylvania Turnpike and -- as the locals like to say -- America begins.

It is a middle-of-nowhere, neon hangover consigned to be remembered by those who shake hands with its self-serve gas pumps or yawn in the faces of its fast-food clerks.

It is a place where rows of morose and road-weary truckers hunker paunch-to-pay-phone, discoursing with dispatchers halfway across the country.

Behind Breezewood's Gateway Plaza, the collective thrum of scores of idling diesel engines vibrates the air.

On the second floor of the Plaza, his door open to the truckers, chaplain Bruce Maxwell sits at a small desk, not far from a stack of paperback New Testaments whose covers are adorned with a sketch of an 18-wheeler.

Phone to his ear, Maxwell instructs a caller, "Let me get some information on you, and we can get you $10 for gas to help you on your way."

It is a stranded driver out of money, gas and luck in Breezewood, a spot where 2.6 million travelers and truckers exit each year.

Maxwell, supported by the Pennsylvania Council of Churches, is there for any in need of his spiritual counsel, though he deals mostly with truckers.

"In most instances," he observed, "I meet a person once in their life."

Many of the non-truckers he advises have just lost a job or are headed for divorce court. Choosing flight over fight, they hit the highway. It may be something ingrained in the psyche of a nation of highly mobile people.

"The road becomes for many a place for grieving, a place for healing," he said.

Sooner or later, they end up in Breezewood.

William Swartzwelder, a native of the area and a volunteer firefighter, is no stranger to the trouble brought Breezewood's way by the coming of the roads. Crashes on I-70 or the turnpike long ago became routine fare.

Swartzwelder's frame home sits on a hill that overlooks the commercial sprawl and the maw asphalt motorists traverse getting into and out of Breezewood. From his back yard, he can see the land that once held a four-room school he attended.

It now holds an Exxon station.

"It's a gold mine for the tax base," he said of the glut of businesses, "but a pain for the residents."

He and his wife, Anna, drive school buses. Attempting to negotiate the stretch of Rt. 30 where turnpike and interstate converge is a recurring nightmare.

And Breezewood never shuts down.

"This place is open 24 hours, seven days a week, 365 days a year," Maxwell said, "and there are many things to be tempted by out there on the road."

Among them are "lot lizards," trucker vernacular for the hookers who ply their trade among the sprawl of parked diesels at truck stops.

The same restless wanderlust that entices men -- for most of them are -- to become long-distance drivers often exacts a ransom in loneliness and estrangement.

Maxwell knows all about that.

"There's a bit of wanderer in me," he allowed, explaining that when he finished his theological training several years ago in Dayton, he sold his few belongings and set out to see the West in a wheezing Subaru, $186 in his wallet.

When the money ran out, he knocked on doors, asking people if they needed any odd jobs done. He ate in a few soup kitchens, slept in a shelter or two.

After he returned East, the chance to become Breezewood's St. Christopher was thrust his way. He didn't hesitate.

He sees a little of everything.

A young woman, only 13, who -- along with a 15-year-old girlfriend -- had run off with a trucker, used Maxwell's office phone to tell her father, "Dad, I'm scared. I want to come home."

There has been at least one suicide on the back truck lot.

Maxwell has conducted two marriages.

"It's a unique ministry," he stated of the obvious. "Very transient."

After all, no one comes "to" Breezewood, just "through" it.

It is here and gone, leaving its imprint chiefly on gas credit card receipts and asking no questions more difficult than, "You want fries with that?"

Forgotten But Not Gone

July 23, 1997

When I learned that singer Julius LaRosa was scheduled to perform in Columbus last week, I was ecstatic.

It was an ecstasy unrelated to his talent. I was simply pleased that he wasn't dead.

LaRosa is one of those fringe-of-oblivion celebrities I had mentally dispatched to the morgue several years ago.

Cruel though that sounds, it was totally without malice, and I have a sound theory on why I keep killing off obscure notables and sending Christmas cards to dead ones.

When Andy Warhol -- who is now actually as dead as he looked alive -- issued his universal fame manifesto entitling everyone to a quarter-hour of celebrity, it suddenly became much more difficult to keep track of who had or hadn't kissed the floor.

Compounding this problem were the advent of cable TV and the proliferation of syndicated reruns. Television, they say, is the ultimate reality, a truth that deludes the beholder into believing that if Donna Reed is still stirring the cake batter on cable TV, she must still be around (which she is not, right?)

One of the best examples of reruns showcasing the dead has to be Hollywood Squares, the TV game show that, at one time, was recycling segments in which two "Xs" and an "O" already were dirt-napping.

Urban legends occasionally throw a wrench into my efforts to keep straight who's worm food and who's not. For years, otherwise intelligent individuals tried to persuade me that Jerry Mathers had been killed in Vietnam. He hadn't been. Ken Osmond (who played Eddie Haskell) I could have believed. His TV persona was well-suited to the most-likely-to-be-fragged mold.

Actually, Osmond is yet with us. I think he runs a combination funeral home and mail-order distributorship.

Sometimes, I unconsciously move celebrities from the "forgotten" file to the "gone" bin simply because of their actions.

I've listed Oral Roberts as dead for a decade now because -- for so long --he kept threatening to die unless his followers cleaned out their savings accounts and sent him the certified checks.

You see? It is hard to keep it all straight.

I owe a tremendous debt of gratitude, however, to the manufacturers of dog food, denture adhesives and Depend undergarments for helping me keep things straight.

I theorize that if a silver-screen has-been is hawking Alpo, he or she most likely is still breathing. When Lorne Greene suddenly stopped pitching dog food, I knew he was headed for that Ponderosa reunion in the ultimate Big Sky country.

Ditto Martha Raye when she disappeared from ads for denture cleaner.

Those who go gentle into the good night of obscurity do me no favors. They end up wandering about in some fog-shrouded swamp in the back of my mind, and I never hear the splash when they finally buy the farm.

My list of these characters is a long one.

Is Loretta Young still kicking? How about Ernest Borgnine?

I asked the copy desk about Borgnine. He was voted dead by a 3-0 margin, though I believe he is still alive.

The vote on Victor Borge was 2-1, but I can't recall whether it was two votes for "dead" and one for "alive" or two votes for "dead" and one for "who cares?".

The confusion over all this complicates my job. It is terribly insensitive to make sport of the freshly dead. Yet there is no good way to call the William Morris Agency and inquire, "Is Slim Whitman dead? If he isn't, I'd sure like to say in my Wednesday column that he is one of the most ridiculous-looking country performers alive."

Then there are Guy Madison and Arlene Francis and Skitch Henderson and Victor Mature and Vera Miles and. . . .

Ah, forget it.

Trailer Trash

March 4, 1994

The Olympics are over. Nancy Kerrigan is dancing with Mickey Mouse. God is in his heaven, and all is well with the world.

At the closing ceremony in Lillehammer, Norway, the good Munchkins defeated the evil trolls as the torch was extinguished.

Most Americans who viewed the Winter Games witnessed a few moments that made their hearts swell or chins tremble.

As for me, I'm glad that, even though her dirty laundry is still in the presoak cycle, I won't be seeing Tonya Harding each time I switch on the tube.

It's not that I dislike the skater; it's that each time I look at her I see myself.

I see myself back on the playground during recess at Highland Elementary School, being taunted for wearing a hand-me-down girl's blouse that even my mother's best efforts as a seamstress couldn't disguise.

Seeing Harding reminds me of the times my skin tingled and burned from hearing the epithet "White trash!"

I still feel the same way in a discount store when I watch a grim-faced mother grab a wet-nosed child by the arm and hiss, "Chuckie, if I gotta tell you one more time I'm gonna knock you halfway into next week."

In a long-vanished five-and-dime on the Hilltop, I lolled about the aisles with a weekly allowance of three pinched nickels clutched in a sweating palm.

The store was patrolled by a pair of spinster clerks who -- shoulders hunched like vultures waiting for road kill -- had a way of sneaking up on children they suspected to be empty-handed paupers and demanding, "Something I can help you find, young man?"

The inquiry, sourly propelled by denture breath capable of stunning a monkey, was enough to make a 6-year-old wet himself.

The only "something" that the clerk wanted to help me "find" was the exit.

Eat enough shame as a kid, and you always carry it with you, just below the surface, as an adult. Separate Harding from the crime, in which the courts must yet determine her role, and you have a woman-child who, by turns, shows an in-your-face pugnacity or a brink-of-tears frailty -- the former ever the mask that hides the latter.

The Rev. Jesse Jackson said of Harding: "Her mother married six times; she grew up in a trailer home, was called trailer trash, was called a white nigger. Abused child, abused wife. Her insides must look like broken glass, but she keeps smiling and keeps skating."

A *Dispatch* reader from Canal Winchester wrote, asking, "Can we not reserve some pity and love for someone who has walked in shoes that never fit but in skates which always fit perfectly, like Cinderella's?

"She is America, with all its flaws. And we have many.

"Ask a Kennedy -- any one of them."

I don't know that Harding "is America." But neither do I think that Kerrigan truly represents us as much as she does an idealized version of that to which we aspire.

Kerrigan is the notion that the Olympic Games mirror the real world; Harding is the real world.

Before this column incites a raft of no-tears-for-Tonya mail, let me say that I wish neither to diminish Kerrigan's achievement nor to apologize for what part, if any, Harding had in the ugly little plot to knock Kerrigan out of the Olympics.

Harding will have to face the music on that one.

While Kerrigan was skating for the final time Friday, Harding was somewhere in the bowels of the ice rink, in tears, trying to watch on television while vomiting into a wastebasket because of a coughing jag triggered by her asthma.

It is at such moments that the world's Tonyas always half-expect to be grabbed by the arm and threatened, "If you don't get back in that trailer where you belong, I'm gonna really give you something to cry about!"

Kolumn Korner

Sept. 10, 2000

I'm thinking of changing the name of this column from In Essence to Kountry Korner. I spied that klever khristening on a greasy spoon somewhere near East Roothog, Tenn.

Actually, I've glimpsed it in Lost Switch Engine, Ala., Abnormal, Ill., and Big Udder, Wis.

Once every four minutes in the United States, a half-dozen people spontaneously exclaim, "I've got it! We'll call it Kountry Korner."

Each will think himself the first on the planet to have brainstormed such an eye-popping bit of marketing genius.

Smalltown folk love to throw around that "k." However silly that inclination, I want to be among the first journalists on the scene when someone unveils a new sign for Karl's Korpse & Kasket.

Actually, that could never happen here because the Ohio Revised Code requires that funereal enterprises employ the last name of a licensed mortician. It keeps someone from opening a Stiffs-R-Us, for example.

I digress.

No, I likely will not change the name of my column to Kountry Korner.

I might try Just Columns. Retail merchants who want you to know that they're serious about a product will name the business Just Plutonium to keep browsers from wandering in and asking for a cheeseburger or a bong.

Just Columns might not work. Sometimes I write a series or feature. I dabble in doggerel when the spirit moves me and occasionally have served up recipes. No, Just Columns won't get it. It would be like naming the column Just Pathos. I'd never be able to try humor again.

I could append the name of the title with & More. Columns & More. It might work. If I called it Columns & More, I could write four pieces a week, groom teacup poodles and sell discount toilet-tank floats.

Columns Plus has possibilities. This name, too, is nonconfining, although Plus frequently is used in conjunction with shops that sell clothing (such as Wandalene's Plus Fashions).

Railroad themes were big for a while, as in Home Depot or Frame Station. Column Junction might do.

Large discount operations gravitate toward names that suggest a boundless inventory -- Warehouse or Unlimited. Such names also imply huge savings, and that carries an undeniable appeal.

If, as my mother has warned, I should poke my eye out, I'm staying away from replacement businesses that sound like upscale law firms (Cartier, Vandervoort & Dehavilland). I'm taking my business to Eyes Unlimited or The Eye Warehouse, checking the phone book to see whether there is a factory outlet at the Jeffersonville exit.

I could go with an off-the-wall name. Three decades ago, while I was yet a journalism student at Ohio State University, an entrepreneur christened his N. High Street record store Magnolia Thunderpussy.

"I'll give it a month," I said then of that outrageously named enterprise. The place is still going strong.

A cue to follow?

What out-of-left-field name could I hang on the column -- something that has nothing to do with newspapering? How about Druid Warts or The Varicose Penguin?

Nah, casual readers would be baffled by the title and expect me to write about plutonium or bongs or teacup poodles.

Besides, I'd get angry letters from offended members of support groups or an organization taking me to task for taking its pet cause too lightly.

Were I to title the column Nonstop Drivel, I would (within a week) receive a scathing letter chastening, "You insensitive moron. My 9-year-old son, Colon (we named him after that general), suffers from Shweiger-Foonman Syndrome, which causes uncontrolled drooling. If you could have seen that brave little guy onstage in the Nativity pageant with the other shepherds around him trying to keep their footing, it would have broken your heart. In the future, I suggest . . ."

Yeah, yeah, yeah.

I guess I'll stick with In Essence. That conclusion might tempt me to think that today's column is a waste of space. Not totally. At least I'll get a few letters from the 90,000 readers who think it really should be called Nonstop Drivel.

The View from Medicine Bow

Sept. 28, 1997

MEDICINE BOW CURVE, Colo. -- Up the switchback two-lane we climbed, through drizzle and fog bank.

Old notions of the Rockies, shaped by pictures on bank calendars and in beer commercials, sloughed off like the skin of a rattler as Trail Ridge Road wended through ponderosa pine and fir, wearing patches of autumn-yellow aspen like a prom boutonniere.

This is the season when the mountains wrest nature back from the hands of camera-wielding tourists.

The elk and bighorn sheep are moving down from the upper reaches. A volunteer at a ranger station on the east face of the mountains conceded that the road at Medicine Bow Curve might close if the rain at the park entrance became snow at the summit.

An ascending wall of mist marched up the canyon walls like a wake of dust trailing a phantom cavalry advance.

At times, among the thickening brume, the faint-hearted become secretly grateful to be denied a glimpse at what plunges frighteningly downward only a few feet from roads unguarded by rail or wall.

Where the trees give way to tundra, the rain gives way to sleet, then to the whisper of snow.

A printed guide to the peak points out that to match the dramatic meteo-
rological caprice from base to summit, a traveler would have to go from
Denver to the Arctic Circle.

Tourists, giddy and babbling at the base, fall ever more silent at each new
elevation marker, as thinning air and blossoming majesty reduce frivolity to
awe.

At the pull-offs near the summit, they step from their cars into a mare's
tail of mist, stupefied by nature like stunned heifers, forgetting momentarily
that they have even brought cameras or why.

If a man standing below the apex of the Rockies were suddenly smitten
with the revelation that his future -- after the mountains -- held only a
despairing and protracted end, he could do far worse than to walk out into
the peaks and pines and die peacefully where the West strains to brush
heaven's cheek.

Somewhere between Lava Cliffs and Gorge Range, more than 2 miles
up, in embarrassment I closed my reporter's notebook, convinced that it was
a fool's errand to try to reduce to words a scene only experience could make
fathomable.

Down past Medicine Bow Curve, the tendril of asphalt reached the
Continental Divide. At this point, Beaver Creek drains to the Colorado River,
which will flow through the Grand Canyon and eventually spill into the Gulf
of California.

On the other side, Cache La Poudre waters cascade into the Platte, then
the Mississippi, before arriving at New Orleans and the Gulf of Mexico.

A geological sword of Solomon, the divide splits the hemisphere and the
flow of rivers from Alaska to Cape Horn.

Descending the back slope of the Rockies, travelers screeched to the
berm at the sight of a bull elk only a few yards off the trail road.

Rutting the moss from his rack of antlers against tree bark, he had come
down from the high ground to mate.

His bugling, a fluted keening whose message was incomprehensible to
humans, alerted elk cow in the meadows below of his arrival.

He stared hard at the spectacle that lay before him and between the herd
he would mate as though tourists in Subarus might be some strange pre-
tenders to the title of his domain.

The Shawnee called him wapiti or white coat for the lightness of his spring
coat. But now, in autumn, his fur had gone dark and he stood poised to battle the other bulls to claim his harem.

He flinched momentarily at the camera flash but refused to retreat, nibbling at the roadside foliage as though a gesture of nonchalance would be
enough to make the intruders move on.

At the foot of the western face, where the Green Mountain trail head gives
way to kitschy lodge-motels, bars and souvenir shops, dusk fell.

On the wall of a guest room of a cheap knotty-pine hostelry hung a fading print of the Rockies.

Road weary, I studied it, this panorama many glimpse only from the windows of commercial flights.

Snow fell at the summit during the night, leaving the Continental Divide dappled with scallops of white at dawn.

The bull elk, glimpsed at roadside in late afternoon the day before, had moved on.

From time beyond the bounds of memory he has come down from the peaks in autumn to mate.

Only recently, in the temporal scheme of the cosmos, has he been forced to wait to do so until the tourists leave.

Exodusters

Sept. 24, 1997

NICODEMUS, Kan. -- Grass rises through the pavement of a main street that dogs cross without looking.

Empty lots, like gaps between teeth in a rueful smile, sprout weeds where houses once stood.

A field of ripening milo, its windrows thick with foxtail, separates most of the homes from the county road and a small museum whose photographs and archives tell the story of a place that only 35 people yet call home.

Fred Switzer, who holds the Maytag-repairman job of mayor, carries a deputy's badge in his wallet just in case he needs to prove to anyone that he is also the long arm of the law in Nicodemus.

He wags a finger at locals who run stop signs, even though there is nothing for them to hit when they do.

"All I do is keep the peace and come around and look in on the older folks," he said. "If a tornado comes, I go and warn the people."

He warns them, that is, unless the twister arrives on Wednesday afternoon.

Wednesday afternoon he bowls in the next town over.

On the Great Plains are many winnowed hamlets whose rotting houses and fat graveyards tell a story to which no one listens.

What separates Nicodemus from the others, and what has earned it the honor of being declared a National Historic Site, is the true-grit saga of how it came to be.

Nicodemus was settled by "exodusters," newly freed slaves who -- 15 years after the Emancipation Proclamation -- were learning, as the song goes, that freedom's just another word for nothing left to lose.

For a mere $5, promoters promised them 40 acres and a mule if they wanted to start a new life on the Plains.

The first arrivals, in 1877, had neither seed nor tools nor money. The mules never materialized.

They made dugout homes in the prairie earth, covering the holes with small igloos they crafted from mud and straw and sunflower stalks.

Ora Switzer, the 94-year-old mother of Nicodemus' mayor, recalls that her grandmother's dugout home was completed barely in time for the woman to give birth to the first baby born in town.

The first winter, a few of the fresh migrants got jobs working on the Kansas Pacific. Those who didn't gathered and sold buffalo bones.

Despite the hardships, by 1880, Nicodemus was a town of 400.

The colonies of other "exodusters" did not fare as well. Disease, malnutrition and the brutal winters took a heavy toll.

Somehow, Nicodemus survived.

The former slaves built an academy to educate their children, formed a town band, started a newspaper called *The Western Cyclone*.

Nicodemus was still thriving when the Dust Bowl days of the Depression hit.

"I had six little fellas," Ora Switzer said. "We had to hang wet sheets up to the windows to keep out the dust."

"We'd leave home for school with one hand over our eye," her son said. "We ate a lot of dust."

During those years, his mother was Nicodemus' midwife.

Whenever the call came that a woman had gone into labor, off she would trudge, through dust so thick it made midnight of noon.

Two or three of the children she delivered, now old enough for Social Security, are still in town.

"I had one come out feet first," she recalled. "That like to scared me to death. But I made it, and the baby made it."

She could tie off an umbilical in her sleep.

She talked about the year the grasshoppers came in swarms so thick they made shadows, how no one in Nicodemus harvested anything that autumn.

She talked about her son, Veryl, who went off to college and then to the Green Bay Packers.

The hands that reared six children and ushered several more into this world at Nicodemus are gnarled like cypress roots.

They no longer play *Love Lifted Me* on the piano at the Baptist church next door.

Once a year, on Founder's Day, scores of former residents and descendants of Nicodemus families return to celebrate the spunk and gumption that built a thriving town out of mud, straw, sunflower stalks and undiluted courage.

Then they go home.

When they are gone, it is once again possible to hear the soughing prairie wind cutting through the tree boughs, a sound now louder than the heartbeat of Nicodemus.

The Punch Heard 'Round the World

Nov. 23, 1997

It didn't seem odd that the man from West Chester, Ohio, should be interested in directions to Woody Hayes' grave.

Football season usually brings a considerable number of visitors to Union Cemetery and the black granite marker that, fittingly enough, faces a lane named for Civil War Gen. William Tecumseh Sherman.

"Michigan week is the heaviest," volunteered Herschel Green, an office worker at the cemetery.

The marker is etched with the late coach's name and, below that, an inscription that is strikingly tender for a man who built a career on toughness:

And in the night of death, hope sees a star, and listening love hears the rustle of a wing.

Charles Bauman, the fellow from West Chester, said he planned to be in Columbus on business last week.

Maybe, he said, he would stop at the grave.

Bauman is regional manager for Sommer Metal Craft, a custom wire products manufacturer with plants in Indianapolis and Crawfordsville, Ind., and Auburn, Ala.

His professional title and credentials, though, are likely less important to Ohio State University fans than his unique distinction in Hayes' coaching career.

"I hear about it every day," Bauman allowed. "People introduce me as the guy who got hit by Woody Hayes."

Bauman was a Clemson sophomore middle guard in the 1978 Gator Bowl.

It was Danny Ford's first game as Clemson head coach, and it was the last game for OSU head coach Woody Hayes.

"It didn't hurt me," Bauman said of the punch Hayes threw after the Clemson middle guard picked off an Art Schlichter pass and ran out of bounds near the Buckeye bench.

Woody knew that.

"I didn't hit him to hurt him," Hayes told a reporter several months after the career-ending incident. "It only hurt me. But you can't always explain everything. Some things are beyond you."

The fate of the pivotal characters in the sad drama at the 1978 Gator Bowl is intriguing.

Danny Ford, only 30 in 1978, notched the distinction of being the last coach to beat Woody Hayes.

From that night forward -- as though rising from the ashes of his disgraced adversary -- Ford's coaching fortunes soared. He posted a 96-29-4 record at Clemson, snaring a national championship in 1981, six league championships while at the school and a 6-2 bowl record.

His record has not been as impressive at Arkansas, where he took over in 1993 as head coach. His best season with the Razorbacks to date is 8-5.

Schlichter, who threw the pass Bauman intercepted, is in prison in Indiana.

Arrested in 1996, only a month after being released from the U.S. penitentiary in Terre Haute, Schlichter is said to have forged a pair of $25,000 checks stolen from his employer.

Authorities say he took the checks to pay off gambling debts.

The judge who sentenced the former OSU and NFL quarterback in July on two counts of forgery and one count of theft agreed to suspend six years of the 16-year sentence.

Hugh Hindman, the former OSU athletic director who had to fire Hayes after the Gator Bowl, is dead.

When Hayes died 10 years ago, his service was conducted by two men who knew more than a little about public humiliation.

Former Watergate conspirator Jeb Stuart Magruder was minister of First Community Church, where the funeral was held. Former President Richard Nixon was eulogist.

Charles Bauman played out his two remaining years of eligibility at Clemson.

"I tried out for the Miami Dolphins," he said, conceding now that his failed attempt to make the NFL likely was propelled by his heady success as a college middle guard.

"I knew I had to come off that cloud. I knew my playing days were spent."

He has been asked -- given their star-crossed fates -- whether he ever could have played for Hayes.

"I probably would (have)," he said. "He knew how to motivate his players. He knew how to push them beyond their means. And they knew he loved them."

But that is all history by hypothesis.

Football, and "the punch heard 'round the world," become more indistinct in Bauman's rearview mirror with each passing year.

"I really don't even follow sports that much," he said last week.

"I couldn't tell you who is ranked No. 1 today."

An Honest Furrow

July 23, 1995

FREDERICKSBURG, Ohio - I heard David Kline before I could see him.

The jangle of shackles hitching the trio of Belgians he was leading home from mowing drifted past the corncrib to the garden, where I waited for him to finish his labor.

By the time I made it over to the barn, he was ready to feed and water his team.

"This one," he said, nodding toward the younger of two geldings, "he would give his soul for oats."

Despite a broken mower blade, the day had been a productive one: Kline had finished a cutting of alfalfa and timothy.

A bold sun and steady breeze assured him that it would dry well.

For a few seconds, he regarded without comment the aerobatics of a squadron of cliff swallows whose gourd-shaped mud nests hug the eaves of his barn. Then he moved inside to hook feed bags onto the Belgians.

Kline is an anomaly in the profession of my calling.

He might not even mention his ties to the wordsmith's craft unless a stranger inquired, for it certainly does not have top billing in the "old-order" Amish realm that is his world.

First and foremost, he is husband, father, farmer, churchman and worthy friend of nature and neighbor alike.

True, he fills a once-a-week column for *The Daily Record* in nearby Wooster with his quiet, unadorned yet powerful observations on the commerce of the natural world around him. He does not, however, possess the urge, ego or stomach to become a public persona.

Kline, who turned 50 this month, for years crafted elegantly simple essays on the turnings of nature for a Canadian Amish publication, *Family Life*. When a publisher suggested that the collected pieces be bound as a book, he reluctantly agreed.

Book critics were unprepared for the quiet naturalist whose work most had not seen before. They tripped over one another in their rush to heap hosannas upon *Great Possessions: An Amish Farmer's Journal* when the book was published five years ago.

A critic for *The New York Times Book Review* called it "a quiet paean to things lost, a set of values we've put in the attic."

The reviewer for *The Washington Post Book World* marveled that it is "a generous and erudite book that gives great pleasure."

Shocked by the acclaim and unwilling to become a literary celebrity, he retreated to his farm and, for three years, didn't write for publication.

"I was just scared," he said, shaking his head and looking off toward the sprawling silver maple in the yard near his porch. "Maybe it was some of those demons writers wrestle with."

Nature was his life, but writing was certainly not his livelihood.

He had apprenticed himself for the latter from childhood, not because he dreamed of fame but because he stuttered.

"I could read things and write things I couldn't say," he bluntly admitted.

He spent the seven years of school that Amish children are accorded before being turned out into the workaday world under the inspired tutelage of an Amish teacher named Clarence Zuercher.

"He was a naturalist," Kline explained. "We had seven years of education we just didn't want to end. He gave us a sense of awe about our world."

Kline laughs today at the strikingly Spartan entries he wrote in a diary he kept as a youngster, recounting two days' worth of his recorded childhood:

"Went to school. Played ball.

"No school. Hauled manure."

"When I was 18," he said, "I began keeping a more reflective diary."

After he reached draft age and -- because of his faith -- appealed for alternative service, he kept a busy journal during his two years as a surgical orderly at a suburban Cleveland hospital.

He returned to Holmes County and the family farm that his grandfather had bought at a sheriff's auction in 1918 and began the work his hands were meant to perform.

"I write by ear," said Kline, quoting the late E.B. White, "and I'm never quite sure what is going to come out."

His narrative style is earnest, unornamented, free of the adjective's elaborate embroidery.

Among a bushel of essays glimmers a striking piece titled *Hunger Moon* about walking the fields behind his house when the earth sleeps beneath a fresh mantle of snow and nature's creatures paint a snowscape with their tracks.

"To understand what is happening," Kline wrote of one January walk, "one has only to venture outdoors after a snowfall. The experience is almost like reading a book. Not only do the wild creatures tell who they are by their tracks, but they'll also likely reveal what they were up to. . . . Frequently I'd come upon the tracks of a white-footed mouse, which look like two rows of stitches across a white quilt. The mouse, forced by hunger, ventured from the safety of the woodpile in search of wild seeds. Often the tracks ended in a depression in the snow where a great horned owl had surprised the unsuspecting mouse. The evidence was plain: the impression of an owl's wingtips and several crimson spots in the snow."

Of a late-spring cold snap and days of pelting rain that chilled the cliff swallows in the eaves and temporarily dwindled the insect supply on which they feed, he wrote:

"After the weather cleared and things returned to normal, I noticed that the entrance to a cliff swallow's nest was plugged by one of their dead. We set up a ladder and checked the nest. We were surprised at what we found: 11 dead adult swallows and four eggs. Apparently they had crowded together for warmth, and when the one in the entrance died they all perished."

Kline writes in a small cabin behind his farmhouse -- a fittingly simple, one-room affair built during Andrew Jackson's first term in the White House.

Beside his writing table is part of his grudging concession to electronic journalism: a 12-volt car battery to power the Smith-Corona word processor on which he knocks out his column.

When the column is done, he sends it off to Wooster from the shop of a nearby pallet maker who has a fax machine.

At first, when the Wooster newspaper entreated him to write, he balked, fearing that it wanted a "cutesy Amish" column for those who look upon his kind with the gaping, ignorant curiosity they otherwise inflict upon costumed characters at Disney World.

He continually battles to maintain a simple life amid the burgeoning technocracy around him.

When his family hires a van so Kline's wife and children can shop at the Wal-Mart in Millersburg, he stays in the vehicle.

"I'm not going in there," he tells them. "It is a one-man revolt."

What he may not tell them is that, while they are in Wal-Mart, he has been known to wander over to the neighboring McDonald's to make sure that the place is giving customers their money's worth.

He knows that the world of the English -- as the Amish call those who are not -- is pervasive, sometimes insidious.

His life's task is to carve an island of simplicity and sanity for his family, to cut an honest furrow and see to the stewardship of the natural world around him.

If he has time when he's done, he may write about it.

Christian Aaron

Dec. 6, 1998

Christian Aaron, on the night before you were born, a bone-china moon, radiant with a halo of haze, drew your mother to the window.

Superstition would have me believe that the moon whispered your name then, telling you it was time.

I could be wrong. That whispering might have been the toppings on the pizza she had eaten a few hours earlier.

You waited awhile before setting up the ruckus that heralded your birth Thursday at 12 minutes past noon in the 12th month of the year.

I was three cups of coffee into the waning pages of Carrie Young's *The Wedding Dress* when your grinning father, Jim, popped into the maternity waiting room to announce your arrival.

"What's it gonna be?" son Aaron asked, draping an arm over my shoulder. "Grandpa? Gramps? Grandfather?"

For nine months I have been listening to the question, "How does it make you feel that you're going to be a grandfather?"

Just fine, Christian Aaron. Just fine.

They say the reason grandparents and grandchildren get along so well is because they have a common enemy.

I suppose I'll be getting a bellyful of advice and counsel on this new role.

Grandparenting, I think, must be a little like doing stand-up comedy on open-stage night, a role defined as much by the wit and improvisational skills of the practitioner as by the patience of the audience.

I'll try not to bore you.

Grandparents are pretty good teachers about the things that matter in life.

There is, of course, a reason for that.

As people grow older, they often rediscover the commonplace wonders of the physical world around them; first snows and dogwood blossoms, the smell of rain on the wind, the frolic sculpture of Orion on a clear night.

You lose sight of those things for a while when, ironically, you are consumed with rearing your children, making ends meet, keeping up appearances.

They come back to you, though, at just the right time when fate gives you a grandchild.

Not coincidentally, it is the same time you begin to realize the petty folly, shallowness and predictability of much of what you once thought mattered.

A person fritters away a frightening number of years clawing and sweating for success and recognition only to realize, as Roger Miller once observed, that no matter how big you become, the size of your funeral is still going to depend, more or less, on the weather.

You realize that, in this changing world, not much really changes.

Your mother, Christian Aaron, was born the year of the Nixon impeachment hearings. You enter the world during the Clinton impeachment hearings. There was unrest in the Mideast when she was born and unrest now. When your mom was born, we were worried about Russia and nuclear weapons. Now we are fretting over North Korea and nuclear weapons.

We still consume too much, waste too much and neglect too often the people who have the least to consume, much less waste.

If I can teach you anything about being humane and compassionate, I will be doing more than I could ever hope.

But just now, Christian Aaron, I'm not thinking about all that.

I'm trying to remember which box in the basement *Curious George* is hiding in and the lyrics to the third verse of *Hobo's Lullaby*.

In the country of your mother's birth, your grandfather would be going to the temple now to thank the Buddha of compassion for a son born under a full moon in the Year of the Tiger. Your mother would be happy with your swift, uncomplicated delivery, for it would portend obedience and deep affection for her. In the weeks ahead, when you are a little older, she would spread a table with various symbolic objects -- a pencil, a toy, a book of poetry and watch to see which you reached for first. It would tell her of your inclinations in this life as well as the one before.

And she would say, "Child, this is your grandfather."

But it isn't that country, Christian Aaron, and all I heard when your mother held you up for me to see was, "How come you're crying, Dad?"

Aunt Gracie: Air Methane

April 2, 2000

My Dear Nephew Mike,

I should warn you that Buster Etlow is none too happy that you didn't make it down to your old hometown to cut the ribbon at Port Methane International for the opening of his new airline.

The grand opening was quite a nice little soiree. I kind of like the ring of Air Methane. Buster came up with it right after he got his degree and his commercial pilot's license from Ironton Tech. (He minored in bartending and telemarketing.)

He managed to pick up an old DC3 from a Meigs County fellow doing 3-5 for aggravated cultivation.

Buster rented a billboard out on Two Pig Run but couldn't decide on a message. He asked me what I thought.

"Buster," I said, "what is it about your operation that sets it apart?"

He said, "We're the only commericial airline with two nonstop flights to Circleville."

I told him, "Hell, Buster, you're the only commercial airline with one non-stop flight to Circleville. And besides, if it wasn't nonstop from Methane to Circleville, where would you be stopping anyway? Knockemstiff? You're gonna have to do better than that."

He thought it might be kind of special that his is the only airline that does crop-dusting during regularly scheduled flights. I told him that wasn't likely to sell too many tickets.

Finally, he settled on a billboard message that reads, "Air Methane. Two packs of salted peanuts."

What can you say? It is original.

Dewey, from over at Mudgett's Funeral Home and Bed & Breakfast, volunteered to sign on as co-pilot. He said he calculated that flying a DC3 was pretty much like driving a 50-year-old hearse with wings. In exchange for Dewey's time, Buster is letting him pass out business cards to passengers, but only after the plane has landed.

That still left Buster with two flight attendant positions to fill. The Nutter twins, Ruth and Iny Rae, thought they'd be perfect since they are always down at Dillman's Pic-N-Save, handing out them little toothpicked samples of turkey kielbasa.

Well, the first flight was set for last Monday morning. Buster had to do it that way since Port Methane International reverts on weekends to Methane Drag Strip, and on Tuesday and Thursdays the Highway Patrol uses it for driver's license exams.

Buster spent two days before the first flight painting the plane yellow.

That plane looked like Big Bird on Monday morning. The mayor, J. Harold Sizemore, was supposed to christen the DC3 with a magnum of champagne, but when the time came, no one could seem to find the bottle.

Everyone got a little frantic trying to find something to substitute. The veterinarian had a quart of udder balm, yet that didn't seem right. Finally, the airport snack bar loaned them one of those big glass gallon jugs of ketchup.

J. Harold gave her a whack. Unfortunately, the ketchup left a huge red circle on the side of the aircraft.

Buster got the old plane off the ground and made a beeline out toward Oney Rice's farm.

What happened next I didn't find out until later. Seems that Oney had been having some trouble with foxes in the chicken coop. He had hauled a chair out by the henhouse and was sitting there with his rifle. I guess he had nodded off to sleep a bit. God knows what he had been dreaming (you know Oney saw a lot of action in the South Pacific during WWII).

The sound of Buster's engines approaching startled him half-awake, and he looked up in the sky to see a big yellow plane with a huge red circle on its side. He started blasting away. It got one of the plane's hydraulic lines. Buster swung it around to make an emergency landing at Methane, even though the passengers had seen only two minutes of the in-flight movie, *Ernest, Scared Stupid.*

He was coming in on a wing and a prayer when he noticed Marcilene Harshman's '89 Duster out on the runway with her in it practicing parking for her driver's license exam the next day. He was in too steep to pull up.

Marcilene saw that plane coming in trailing smoke and she was a deer in the headlights. She couldn't have no more moved that Duster than she could have moved Mount Rushmore. At the last minute, she flung herself out the door and out of the way.

A DC3 can push a Duster a long ways, and there wasn't much left of what Chrysler built when the plane finally stopped.

No one was hurt. Marcilene decided she didn't want a driver's license after all.

Buster gave all the passengers a third bag of peanuts (which they all enjoyed) while he drove them up to Circleville in a bus he borrowed from the Two Pig Run Church of the Risen Lord.

Air Methane will be out of business awhile.

You might want to drop by after the plane is fixed.

And repainted.

My best to your momma.

Love,

Aunt Gracie

The Poet of Derry

Sept. 22, 1999

DERRY, N.H. -- Robert and Elinor Frost brought their grieving hearts to the farm at Derry in autumn of the new century's first year.

Elliott, the couple's 3-year-old son, had died of typhoid fever less than three months before the move to New Hampshire. The guilt-tortured poet blamed himself for the death, having endured an excoriating rebuke from the physician he'd summoned too late to save his dying son.

Frost hoped that the consuming tasks of running the farm in Derry would distract both him and his wife from the ache of fresh loss.

Here he tended cattle and poultry and looked after the orchard. Elinor ran the household and, in time, schooled the couple's four children.

"He was a highly unusual farmer," observed Kate Lackey, a volunteer guide at the old Frost farm in Derry. "His neighbors thought he was crazy.

He used to milk his cows at noon and midnight."

He tended the farm not according to the biological clocks of his Jerseys and hens, but by his own.

Frost wrote fictionalized accounts of the adventures of his Wyandotte hens. He sold the works, earning $5 for each tale the poultry journals found worthy of printing.

Most important, during the 11 years he spent here, Frost hurled himself at the task of finding his voice as a poet.

"To a large extent, the terrain of my poetry is the Derry landscape, the Derry farm," he would later tell a friend. "Poems growing out of this, though composite, were built on incidents and are therefore autobiographical. There was something about the experience at Derry which stayed in my mind, and was tapped for poetry in the years that came after."

Deep into the predawn of New England winter nights, Frost would ensconce himself in an old Morris chair and prop his writing paper on a shelf that he'd borrowed from the closet.

"Robert called this the seedbed of his poetry," Lackey said of the farm. For it was at Derry that he immersed himself in nature, the turning of the seasons, the ritual chores that, at once, exhaust the body and invigorate creativity. One can forgive the scythe the blisters inflicted if the wielding of it yields the exquisitely crafted lines of *Mowing*:

There was never a sound beside the wood but one,
And that was my long scythe whispering to the ground.

At Derry, Frost luxuriated in the years that were kindest to his children.

He frolicked with the four youngsters and imbued them with all he knew of botany, astronomy and literature.

He would think often and lovingly of those days at Derry when his children's lives as adults would come to grief or recrimination.

His son Carol, at 38, committed suicide with a deer rifle.

Daughter Marjorie, who had long battled depression, died of complications stemming from a postpartum infection.

Daughter Irma's battles with mental illness eventually led to her admittance to a state hospital in Concord, where she would remain until her death in 1981.

Daughter Lesley accused her father of having ruined her mother's life by his selfishness. She refused to take him in when Elinor's death made him a widower.

"Cast your eye back over my family luck," Frost told a friend, "and perhaps you will wonder if I haven't had pretty near enough. That is for the angels to say."

Though celebrated by his nation and exalted with four Pulitzers, Frost never quite outran the family heartbreak that dogged him, nor his own mind's torment.

"He was manic-depressive," tour guide Lackey pointed out.

When Frost wrote, "I have been one acquainted with the night," he was not speaking exclusively in the literal but of a figurative night, the furthest reaches of a moonless soul. That was the dark he was perhaps trying to hold at bay when he wrote *Winter Storm*, another Derry poem.

After 11 years at Derry, Frost essentially had written his first two collections of poetry -- *A Boy's Will* and *North of Boston*.

He had hoped that the New York publishing industry might find favor in his verse, though he would later recall for an audience at Amherst, "The literary world didn't want to hear from me when I was a farmer in New Hampshire. I had mud on my shoes. They could see the mud, and that didn't seem right to them for a poet."

Frost would leave Derry and, shortly thereafter, move his family to England, where his first two volumes of poetry were published.

World War I brought him back to the United States and his beloved New England, which continued to shape his maturation as a poet.

Robert Penn Warren mused of Frost, "It's as though he were dropped into the countryside north of Boston from outer space, and remained perpetually stunned by what he saw."

Much of what he saw, he beheld at Derry.

When Elinor died, he had hoped to honor the wish that her ashes be scattered along Hyla Creek adjacent the Derry place. Unfortunately, the new owners were unenthusiastic. Frost was compelled to inter her cremains in Vermont.

That was one of Frost's last visits to Derry.

Blessedly, he did not see the place in the 1950s when it became Frosty Acres Junkyard.

What had been the orchard in Frost's day was a staggering array of gutted Buicks and Chryslers by 1961. That year, the state acquired Derry and began a long and painstaking restoration.

Out behind the barn where Frost milked at the witching hour, a natural trail winds through the undergrowth to the Hyla Creek bed. Between the creek and barn runs the stunted, broken remains of a wall built by piling stone upon stone.

A sycamore has taken firm root where a portion of that wall once stood. Time and the elements have wrought their own havoc on the stone hedge.

Yet, even in its ruin, the old barricade whispers the lines of *Mending Wall* to passers-by.

"I am both a wall-builder and a wall-destroyer," Frost would one day claim.

At Derry, by penstroke, he began putting boulder atop boulder, essentially creating the poet he would become.

In the tragedy-beset years that followed, he may have wondered whether it was at Derry that he had sold his soul.

Homer Hickam, Rocket Boy

June 13, 1999

COALWOOD, W.Va. -- The serpentine two-lane switchback that leads to Coalwood is so narrow that a motorist confronting the sign warning "Jesus is coming" hopes it is not from the opposite direction and with a wide load.

Cradled between the shoulders of flanking mountains, the little town sits atop the Pocahontas seam, one of the richest veins of "high coal" in the nation. At one time, almost 5,000 miners worked the seam at Coalwood and neighboring Caretta. At the peak of operations in Coalwood, three shifts extracted enough coal in a day to fill 125 railroad cars.

When the nation's steel industry went to rust and ruin, it took Coalwood down with it.

Ernest "Red" Carroll knows the particulars.

Seated at a picnic table inside Coalwood's Country Corner general store, he mused, "I've lived in Coalwood -- what's today, the 7th? I've been here 81 years, four months and three days today.

"At one time, there were four schools, four stores, an ice plant, a pop-bottling plant, a theater, bakery and library. I've seen the best of it and I've seen the worst of it. The worst was during the Depression. Wasn't nobody working then. The best was during World War II, and another war is about the only thing that would bring it back.

"A lot of people left Coalwood and were almost ashamed to say they were from here until the book and movie came out. That's the only thing that put us back on the map."

The book, *Rocket Boys*, and the movie it spawned, *October Sky*, tell the story of six local boys who, in the post-Sputnik days of the waning 1950s, used rocketry to propel themselves past daunting odds and demeaning stereotypes to win the National Science Fair's most-coveted award -- the silver and gold first place.

Homer Hickam Jr., the ringleader of Coalwood's "Rocket Boys" and author of the memoir recounting their exploits, seems mildly amazed at the acclaim generated by his published recollections and the movie.

"*Rocket Boys* to me has been one miracle after another," Hickam said last week, when he returned to southern West Virginia for a homecoming welcome from Coalwood and a reunion with the four surviving members of his old high-school launch crew.

Lingering over his breakfast at the Bluefield Holiday Inn, Hickam -- recently retired as a NASA engineer -- observed of *Rocket Boys*, "It ended up touching a lot of people at a visceral level. They come to me and say, 'You have told my story.' " Some think *Rocket Boys* is about fathers and sons and the prickly, porcupine waltz that relationship sometimes engenders. Some think it a revenge-of-the-nerds tale about loving science in an era when doing so branded one as geeky. Teachers praise it for its exaltation of their calling. Residents of Hickam's beloved home state have a particular fondness for it.

"For a change, this area has been portrayed in a positive light," said Clarence Justice Jr., a former classmate of Hickam's at Big Creek High School, where he now teaches English. "Seems like we're always portrayed as though we don't wear shoes."

"I almost missed telling this story," Hickam said. "I didn't see that this was a story that needed to be written down."

In its first incarnation, *Rocket Boys* was a brief essay for a magazine published by the Smithsonian's National Air and Space Museum.

The popularity of that short piece goaded Hickam to finish the book, though not without reluctance.

"This book really got dragged out of me," he said. "It wasn't something I was really burning to write. Memoirs are tough. You've got to dig down deep as you can in your soul. If you don't dig down deep and bring up the truth, the readers are going to know it. Being a West Virginian, stoic and stolid -- all the things we tend to be -- it was not that easy."

The finished product quickly caught Hollywood's eye. Film rights were negotiated, and, in early 1998, 56-year-old Hickam found himself a technical adviser on the set of *October Sky*.

He wrestled with the screenwriters over dramatic flourishes they added that didn't square with the memoir. He won some, lost some.

"The biggest one I lost," he said, "is the scene where I quit high school to work in the mines. I detested that scene. There is no way I would have quit high school."

In *October Sky*, Hickam is portrayed descending into the bowels of the mine at Coalwood to help the family make ends meet.

"My family would have lived in a tree before they would have let me quit school," he said.

He also was alarmed at some of the dialogue.

"There were just so many 'you-alls' in there," he explained. "That wasn't West Virginia."

He persuaded the filmmakers to hire Athens, Ohio, speech pathologist Emily Sue Buckberry, another classmate from Big Creek High, to coach the cast on dialect.

"She has actually worked with some people over the years to rid themselves of that dialect," Hickam wryly noted.

Hickam had hoped that the producers of *October Sky* might choose his native state for the shooting, but Tennessee won out. Coalwood and McDowell County got the bragging rights, though none of the Hollywood capital they could use.

McDowell County, whose mine operations once gave the area one of the state's largest tax bases, has never quite recovered from the shutdown of operations such as those at Coalwood and Caretta.

"There is not a single mile of four-lane highway anywhere in the county," Clarence Justice said. "In the McDowell County School System, probably 70 percent of the families of students are on some form of public assistance."

Justice's boss, Big Creek principal Hobert Muncey, doesn't see any prospect of a major industry delivering the area from its economic torpor.

"GM is not going to come to McDowell County," he said. "We don't have the flat land or the water for major industry. You can't put housing developments on the side of a mountain."

This year, Big Creek High graduated 72 seniors, compared with 197 graduates in 1960, when Hickam received his diploma.

Muncey estimated that only 30 percent of this year's graduates will go on to college and that many others will have to leave McDowell County to find employment.

One hears talk that the planned Coalfields Expressway through the area might provide an economic boost, as might the Hatfield-McCoy Trail project, a recreational byway styled after the Appalachian Trail.

"What I would like to see," Hickam said, "is some high-tech industry come into southern West Virginia. They need to stop exploiting the natural resources, clear-cutting timber and tearing the tops off mountains to get what little coal there is."

Without economic revitalization, Hickam sees a grim future:

"I just have a sense of time slipping away in Coalwood. Another decade or two and there is not going to be anything there."

The only recent business venture has been a small museum and gift shop across the street from Hickam's boyhood home.

Visitors can purchase ballcaps bearing the legend "Home of the Rocket Boys. Coalwood, W.Va.," or admire the mining artifacts and the desk at which Hickam's mine-superintendent father worked.

Across from the museum last week, locals were erecting a sign welcoming home the Rocket Boys.

The five men -- who as high-school students operated Cape Coalwood on a slag dump outside town -- were reunited in Bluefield the night before the Coalwood homecoming.

"I'm a different person because all of this happened," Hickam told a dinner crowd of almost 1,000 at the Brushfork Armory near Bluefield.

Looking on were not only the other Rocket Boys and Hickam's mother, Elsie, but also the sister of Freda Riley, the physics teacher who pushed the Rocket Boys to enter the science fair.

"She was not an easy teacher," Hickam recalled of Riley, "and she took the measure of us boys quite quickly."

Riley battled Hodgkin's disease during Hickam's last years at Big Creek, though she continued teaching until so weak that she had to be carried to class. She died in 1969, at 32.

On Wednesday, Coalwood turned out to honor the men who Carroll says put his little corner of West Virginia back on the map.

Even Gov. Cecil Underwood showed up. Townsfolk could not recall another governor who had set foot in Coalwood.

Following Wednesday's events, Hickam, who lives in Huntsville, Ala., began preparing for a book tour that will launch the publication of *Back to the Moon*, a "techno-thriller" novel he wrote. He is also at work on a sequel to Rocket Boys titled A *Coalwood Christmas*. And there is talk of a TV series about the Rocket Boys, which -- if it materializes -- Hickam hopes will not become a Walton's Mountain with Wernher von Braun.

As for the little town Hickam left almost 30 years ago, it likely will continue to indulge the strangers with out-of-state tags who chug up the hill to see whether Coalwood really exists.

Carroll will show them the abandoned mine buildings, point out Hickam's boyhood home, maybe sell them a Rocket Boys ballcap.

Then they'll move on.

Someone always seems to be saying goodbye to Coalwood.

Jesus Comes to Roswell

July 7, 1997

ROSWELL, N.M. -- Lanny Harris' cross, fashioned from 2-by-4s and colored with redwood deck stain, rested on the sidewalk outside a storefront tabernacle downtown.

"I'm waiting until it cools off a little," he said, holding a shading palm above swim-goggle spectacles and pondering an unforgiving sun that had punched thermometers to 104 degrees.

A paunchy 6-footer with an ungainly Baby Huey bearing, he looked like a man who might have once played center for his science club's intramural basketball team.

Down from Provo, Utah, to save the masses from the scourge of UFO madness, he made no bones about the peril he thinks will remain after Roswell has swept up the confetti and watched the last of the tourists fade into the sunset.

"I believe in aliens," he allowed, "but I look at them as demons. I believe this whole thing is very demonic, very satanic.

"People have a void. We all have a void. Some use Bigfoot, vampires, UFOs, but the only way you can fill that void is with Jesus Christ."

The vagabond preacher is not alone in his concern about the potential for spiritual corruption he believes has been abetted by Roswell's huge anniversary celebration.

"It's almost turning into a religion," said Jim Suttle, pastor of Roswell's Calvary Chapel. "You can see it. You can feel it. Fifty-eight percent of the people in this country believe in UFOs."

Suttle took solace in the fact that part of Roswell's big show included a Saturday event titled "Alien Encounters," which provided the clergy the opportunity to offer tourists a pastoral perspective on the notion of visitors from outer space.

Pastor "Bear" Barker, a "biker minister" who runs a storefront church on Main Street called Body of Christ, has taken the tack of engagement rather than confrontation.

A hand-lettered sign in the sanctuary downstairs from his cubbyhole office reads: "Jesus, the only alien that died for you."

"I've heard pastors here in town saying this thing is evil," he said. "I was kind of with them until I thought, didn't God make everything? How selfish of us to think we're the only form of life existing.

"We're supposed to love each other, and that includes aliens."

He doesn't think that belief in extraterrestrials is incompatible with belief in the teachings of Christianity.

"I'm not going to judge people," he added. "That's God's job to do."

But even as he spoke, local minister Weldon Frazor, who calls himself "The Country Preacher," was stuffing fliers under the windshield wipers of tourists' cars, urging them to get right with God before it is too late.

"There's 141 churches in this area," Barker observed, smiling wryly as he added, "and most of them are religious."

Each evening of Encounter '97, he sat in an open storefront door, strumming a 12-string guitar and preaching a low-key message of tolerance and acceptance. He seemed content to let the throng come to him.

"This is not a problem," he said, nodding toward the sidewalks where visitors trudged past his church. "This is an opportunity."

But outside, Lanny Harris wasn't so sure.

He looked up at the setting sun, then down at the burden to which he had affixed both his faith and a lawn-mower wheel, the latter for easier pulling, the former for reasons only he knows.

It was time to move out and start saving a few souls.

The Greatest Generation

Aug. 27, 1995

My mother is reading *Grit, Good Old Days* magazine and a slender hardback penned by a pair of centenarian sisters of the South.

A glance at her coffee table reveals this as I sit waiting for her to finish with her makeup so we can leave for the funeral home.

Grit I recall from my adolescence and the entreaties in *Boy's Life* magazine to sell the tabloid and grow rich. it is a newspaper filled with ads for cheap hearing aids and White Cloverine Salve, alongside stories (with Paul Harvey bylines) that cynical journalists love to dismiss as "warm fuzzies."

We are off to Lancaster, my mother and I, to pay our respects at the casket of the second brother she has lost since spring.

Not unlike the earlier death, this loss has triggered an avalanche of memories.

I have come to call these sessions with my mother "Remedial Family History 101."

Though her health is good, my mother lately seems beset by a need to reckon langsyne accounts -- to chronicle for me the stories I may not yet have heard.

I don't know whether the stories are spilling out because the deaths of her siblings have occasioned intimations of her own mortality. It makes little difference. She is holding court, and I am a willing listener.

My father, she tells me, once hatched a plan with his brother and a cousin to strike out for Venezuela, where they had heard there was an abundance of roustabout jobs in the oil fields. Like many of my father's schemes, it never panned out.

Her mother, she continues, slept the last few years of her life on three dining room chairs pushed together, the seats lined with pillows. Grandma was an unrepentant hoarder and, after the old girl had drifted off to sleep, her children would tiptoe to the windows with bound stacks of old newspapers and fling them out onto the lawn for the rag man.

An uncle I scarce recall once kept more than 250 pet birds in his north side home. In a fit of pique one morning, he tried to gas or drown them all and was discovered in the basement dunking canaries in a No. 2 washtub.

The smile of my mother's sister is crooked, mom informs me, because she was struck by a car while playing hide-and-seek. My mother had secreted herself in the empty rain barrel in the back yard when she heard the heart-stopping scream out on Duncan Street.

Mom's uncle Mike, my namesake and the bank-robbing black sheep of the clan, was a roguish Robin Hood. He helped keep the family in clothes and shoes during lean times and -- even in the midst of the depression -- always dressed like a million bucks (albeit someone else's million).

I ease the car into the funeral home parking lot, and we enter through a side door.

"Who are you here to see?" the funeral director politely inquires.

"Elmer Hand," mom volunteers with a certain pride of kinship.

A folded American flag has been tucked against the lid of the open casket not far from the brow of a man who fought from Sicily to Germany in World War II. The late war hero Audie Murphy was in my uncle's infantry unit.

I have been told -- though not by my uncle -- that he was in on the liberation of at least one concentration camp. He had snapshots of that experience, though not for the eyes of children.

I deposit my mother at her apartment and start for home before, in a mildly epiphanic awakening, I suddenly connect what previously seemed disparate -- though recurrent -- influences in my life lately.

The death of my mother's brothers (both World War II veterans), her recent reading list and the catharsis of her life remembered is entwined with much of what I have been writing about for the past few years.

Lately, newspaper readers with little interest or no familial connection to World War II may have thought journalism overtaken by a confederacy of war-obsessed anniversarists.

But the teller is nowhere without the tale, and stories by the score have been carried to my newspaper and others by men and women who -- like my mother -- press onward down a dimming path into woods unknown.

This is their last hurrah.

My mother never got a medal for all the purple hearts turned out by the factory in which she worked during World War II. She doesn't expect one. but her time is passing, and there are so many things to be told.

Not all of it is war-related, as my mother's scattershot recollections bear witness. All of it, though, must be told.

She and her contemporaries, their stories floating like feathers in a melancholy wind, simply want someone to hear and remember.

Always, Patsy Cline

Dec. 28, 1994

In 1963, the year in which America said goodbye to Camelot's slain prince, the death of a hillbilly singer from Winchester, Va., didn't count for much.

Back then, when country wasn't exactly cool, Patsy Cline probably was regarded by folks outside country's influence as just another mournful Nashville whippoorwill who would be replaced before the government could sort out the wreckage from the small plane in which she died.

Cline's death was an earthquake, however, to people such as Louise Seger, a Houston fan whose abiding love of Patsy's music and correspondence with the artist eventually shaped a musical titled *Always . . . Patsy Cline*.

Why Patsy touched the Louise Segers of this world is not much of a secret: Seger's idol was an immense talent of such raw vocal power that her voice had to be double-baffled during recording sessions, and a singer who could make misplaced or unrequited love ache with a stunning finality.

A spurned lover listening to Cline's *Faded Love* for the first time was well-advised to hide the razor blades.

Anyone left dazed, disillusioned or wounded by love could identify with Cline. Not surprisingly, that alone garnered her a legion of devoted fans.

I remember one of them -- a waitress at a West Jefferson, Ohio, diner called Higgins' Restaurant -- reacting in a tearful rage when a handful of high-school boys dared to snicker and guffaw at a jukebox tune lamenting Cline's untimely passing.

The youths, too caught up in their worship of talents such as Connie Stevens and Brian Hyland, thought it morbidly hysterical that anyone would record a song whose pivotal lyric whines:

Three country stars, in heaven now they shine,
Cowboy Copas, Hawkshaw Hawkins, Patsy Cline.

Copas and Hawkins had been killed with Cline.

We -- yes, I was a part of the irreverent bunch -- laughed at the sappy ditty until we cried. Then we played it again just to have another good laugh.

We were still absorbed in our hilarity when the waitress stormed over to our booth from her perch on a counter stool.

Arms crossed, she stood silently before us as if daring us to chuckle just one more time. Her jaw was set in unconcealed rage; tears brimmed in both eyes.

Had she been another one of the restaurant's waitresses or even the owner, the incident could have been passed off with an apology followed by a few teasing gibes to save face.

This woman, though, was not among the regulars who thrived on fencing and parrying with us. No, this one was quiet, a little melancholy.

The husband who picked her up when her evening shift ended had little to say to her, forever grunting monosyllabic replies to her how-was-your-day inquiries. He sat sullenly over his coffee until she had punched out.

I always felt a little sorry for her. When the dinner rush was over, she always stuck a handful of change into the jukebox and refilled the creamers and sugar shakers to a succession of Patsy Cline heartbreakers.

"You boys ought to be ashamed of yourselves," she said, struggling to keep her anger in check. "Suppose that had been someone you cared about."

At that moment, I felt as if I could sit on a dime and swing my legs.

My buddies and I stared at our hands. We couldn't slink out in shame; she was blocking our exit from the booth.

"You really disappoint me," she said with a tinge of pitying sadness.

Then, turning on her heel, she strode back to the kitchen.

I long ago outgrew the rock stars I idolized in high school, coming full circle back to the country music with which I grew up -- even though I had mocked it in my adolescence.

The waitress quickly forgave us our unfeeling irreverence. She kept playing Patsy on the jukebox, and we kept our mouths shut.

I don't know whom she thought about when she played *Why Can't He Be You* or *I Fall to Pieces*.

I hope she stuck around long enough to see Cline's legend reach its fruition. And, for all the endearing sensitivity I demonstrated at age 16, I hope she forgot I exist.

What's Another Word for Thesaurus?

Nov. 20, 1994

This autumn marks the 125th anniversary of the death of Peter Mark Roget.

The milestone might have passed unnoticed if not for the recent discovery, at a Kings Road antiques shop in London, of a half-dozen journals kept by Uriah Penniweather.

Penniweather was a faithful aide and personal secretary to the famous lexicographer and physician for threescore years. He wrote prodigiously of his employer and friend.

Sadly, he reveals that which has escaped most historians: Roget was a medical practitioner of suspect skills, a dismal failure at love and, in the end, a man who established his niche in history only by enduring a lifelong, neurosis-driven need to express himself with irreproachable precision.

In 1809, while Roget was a physician at Malvern Infirmary, Penniweather chronicled the doctor's battles with the fixation that plagued him while ministering to gravely ill patients.

He detailed the incident that led to Roget's dismissal for incompetence:

Sept. 6 - Dr. Roget and several students were about the business of medical rounds when they approached the foot of the bed of Lord Henry Athington. The good doctor inquired, "And how fares my lordship today?" Athington responded with a sudden lurch, clawing at his chest and beseeching the doctor's eyes with a stare of plaintive helplessness. Turning to his students, Roget observed: "This man is having an attack! Well, no, actually you could call it a paroxysm, a coronary seizure, perhaps an ictus or a spasm. Some might call it a fit. I think it rather serious because he is beginning to turn blue, cerulean, actually more azure than indigo. One might describe it as ultramarine, though it intensifies by the second. It also appears fatal, mortal, if you will. Or would it be deadly, deathly or deathful?" By then, Lord Athington was colder than a mackerel.

Penniweather, a companion of heroic patience, tried various methods to relieve Roget of his annoying fetish. His efforts went unrewarded and, on at least one occasion, produced painful results:

Feb. 6 - This evening, I prevailed upon the doctor to take in an alehouse near Charring Cross, thinking, perchance, that spirits might dull his horrible verbal propensity, keep it at bay for a few hours of jollity. My supposition seemed to prove itself valid, for, as his cheeks pinkened in the mild embrace of the spirits, his lips fell blessedly silent. Unfortunately, we had barely stepped out into the brisk night air and begun to make our way down the cobblestones when a brigand appeared from a darkened alcove and thrust his form squarely before the doctor. The muzzle of a pistol was clearly visible, its nose peeking out from the robber's greatcoat. I'm sure the doctor could see the gun and knew what business the man was about. Eager to draw as little attention as possible to his crime, the fellow, while waiting for Roget to hand over his purse, remarked, "Rather chilly night, isn't it, milord?" He had made a terrible mistake. "I think 'brisk' might aptly describe it," the doctor replied, "or perhaps 'crisp,' 'nippy' or 'raw' - maybe even 'brittle,' though not 'frigid.' " The impatient robber then shot Roget through the boot. He will recover, though I dare say that he shall miss the toe when hiking."

In a moment of candor, the doctor conceded to Penniweather that he had been cast aside by his wife on the couple's honeymoon.

She had asked in the receding heat of ardor, "Was it good for you?" His inability to let stand, uncontested, the vague descriptor *good* spelled the demise of the pair's brief marriage.

Penniweather's last journal entry, in 1869, was written after the undertaker had removed the 90-year-old Roget from his deathbed in West Malvern.

Sept. 12 - 'Tis a sad day, indeed. Milord has gone to his reward, and, alas, his final confession must wait to be heard by his maker. For, as the priest drew his chair nigh the failing doctor's bed, Roget began, "Bless me, Lord, for I have sinned." He paused a second, though not because he was aware that I was behind the dressing screen scribbling down every word. Then he continued: "Actually, Father, 'sinned' is awfully heavy with the freight of moral turpitude and rottenness. It might be more correct to say that I have 'erred' or 'offended.' A more precise word might be - urgh!" That was it; the poor man died with a half-bestial utterance on his lips - a word I dare any man to find in a thesaurus.

Cowboy Poetry

Oct. 3, 1997

ELKO, Nev. -- I swept into the cowboy poetry capital of the Free World with a headful of stereotypical notions and an empty notebook. I was half-expecting to find a bunch of cussin', spittin' cowpokes hunkered around a campfire (a la *Blazing Saddles*), using air biscuits to punctuate schmaltzy skeins of iambic pentameter about ropin' and ridin' and the wild coyote's call.

Rod McQueary, a third-generation Nevada rancher and poet of considerable gifts, shrugged and smiled, pushing himself away from his desk at the Western Folklife Center. "People assume that you're a semi-wild, uncivilized soul," he allowed. "I think that Western poetry is generalized as rhyme-and-meter balladeering. There is a lot of rhyme-and-meter balladeering to it, but you also have poets such as Buck Ramsey writing poetry in the style of Pushkin."

You also have South Dakota native Elizabeth Ebert composing *The Tea Set*, about spousal abuse on the ranch, or McQueary himself writing not about his 46 years of ranch life in Ruby Valley, but about the imprint of his Vietnam experience in a poem titled *White Wall*:

There ought to be another wall
White, bright, pretty
In a grove of trees
with picnic tables,
dance floor, and a
Viet vet ragtime band.
A happy place where
Folks could go to laugh
and dance and argue
Football teams and candidates.
On the White Wall, there would be
A tremendous list of those
Who didn't die.
Behind each name,

a little heart . . . for a fulfilling marriage
a little happy face . . . for a well-adjusted child,
a little diploma . . . for a valuable education,
a rewarding life.
Everyone is welcome here,
To cool drinks, rummy games,
To meet interesting people who
Talk, laugh, have fun, wander off.
Live.
To celebrate our survivorhood.
Not mourn our stolen martyrdom.
There are some who will
Have to be shown
The White Wall.
Taken to their own name
and told
"There, by God, is proof."

McQueary also writes about the West and about ranch life, as does poet Sue Wallis, to whom he is married.

Wallis grew up on a ranch in Recluse, Wyo. During her days of helping with the roping and calving, she acquired the wisdom of life's truths that would one day beg for the sweet distillation of poetry's voice.

One of the poems in her book *Another Green Grass Lover*, was featured on a PBS series titled *The United States of Poetry*. In that series, Wallis represented Wyoming with her poem *Timothy Draw*:

We pause at the top of Timothy Draw
Look down the country for stray cows
He cocks his head
Stands in the stirrups
Hands on the horn
Relaxed and easy and graceful
He moves with a horse
Like few men can
In one brief, quick space
I love him more
Than I will ever love again
Like passion, but not of sex
Like Life without death
Like the nudge and the tug and the sleepy smile
Of a too-full child at your still-full breast
Something that explodes from your toes
But flows through your bones
Like warm honey
More powerful than violence
I lift my reins
Our horses sidestep

And we slip on down the draw.

Each January, the population of Elko swells by almost one-third when 8,000 people come to town for a week to take in the Cowboy Poetry Gathering.

They come certainly to hear the traditional Western voices of cowboy poets such as Baxter Black and Wallace McRae, men whose poetry is somewhere between Robert W. Service and Shel Silverstein.

But they come also to hear how voices such as those of Sue Wallis and Elizabeth Ebert interpret life in the West.

"The standard of reciting and the standard of writing have improved," McQueary said of the event, now in its 12th year. "Writers and reciters are held to a higher standard than they have ever been."

To a mind that has never known much of the world west of Manhattan or Miami, the experience of growing up in Nevada or Wyoming is something so alien that it might as well have taken place on one of the moons of Jupiter.

At the Western Folklife Center, they know that.

They also know that if the Wall Street broker or the Philadelphia systems analyst are ever to understand the West, it will have to be through the Esperanto of the soul, poetry, the official language of Elko.

A Mini-mall at Auschwitz?

April 15, 1996

Listen, Rachel.

Hear me, Chaim.

Demonstrators from the Polish city of Oswiecim have marched in protest to the gates of the nearby Auschwitz extermination camp.

Had they come to protest the Nazi outrage against you -- though more than a half-century too late -- it would at least have been a step in the right direction. But they came carrying signs reading, "Jews, thieves stay away from the government."

They are angry because they have been blocked from building a mini-mall and fast-food restaurant across the road from the spot where you and more than a million of your brothers and sisters perished.

They had big plans to beautify the saddest, bleakest, most horrible parcel of land on this globe with a tree-lined promenade and a hamburger stand. The deal, they said, had been made fiscally sound by the solid backing of a German financier. How apropos.

The Nazis always wanted you to think that Auschwitz was a warm and welcome place to visit. That is why, in the early years, they gave you lovely picture postcards to send home to relatives -- postcards preprinted with the message: "We are doing very well here. We have work and are well treated. We await your arrival."

How they wanted Auschwitz to be a place that wouldn't frighten you. They gave you towels and soap to persuade you that you were being subjected only to delousing showers. Only after the door was bolted and the guards prepared to drop cyanide or Zyklon B into the "showers" would those yet gullible among you notice that the showers had no drains.

They wanted to make Auschwitz pretty then. Amid neatly trimmed grass and flower beds fertilized with the remains of those who had come before you, a small orchestra of young women serenaded your march to death.

An SS man counseled, "No harm will come to you. You just have to breathe very deeply. That strengthens the lungs. Inhaling is a means of preventing contagious diseases. It's a good disinfection."

When you were safely locked inside the Badeanstalten, the same SS officer would shout to the guards above, who controlled the drop of the poison crystals: "Now give them something to chew on."

The SS thought it all so neat and efficient. Appearances were as important to it as they apparently are today to the Polish nationals who want a buffer zone of boutiques and birch trees around the camp.

Make Auschwitz a showplace?

Do you hear that, Rachel?

Are you listening, Chaim?

It has been done already.

In March 1943, when the new crematoria were opened, top military officials and Berlin high society were invited to Auschwitz for a special "program" inaugurating the new equipment. A line of them waited eagerly for their turn at the specially fitted peephole on the gas-chamber door.

To impress that crowd of top brass and highbrows with the glory of Auschwitz, 8,000 Krakow Jews were put to death.

Now they want to scrub Auschwitz of its awful stain?

With what?

I have seen the recipe for soap the Nazis left behind: 12 pounds of human fat, 10 quarts of water. Add 8 ounces to the pound of caustic soda. Boil for three hours, then cool.

Those remains not used as fertilizer or soap were thrown into the Sola River.

Beautify Auschwitz? Why would such a model of production efficiency need the ornamentation of arboreal splendor or cute and clever mini-mall shops?

This is the place where the SS showed that killing only 200 Jews at a time -- as the Treblinka camp did using carbon monoxide exhaust from idling tanks and diesel engines -- was antiquated.

Auschwitz could kill them 2,000 to a chamber -- packed so tightly that there was nowhere to fall once they were dead.

Sleep on, Rachel.

Rest quiet, Chaim.

For now, a government order has temporarily banned the planned mini-mall and fast-food outlet next to the place where you died.

The financier is probably upset.

Thank God he has yet only a small voice in the affair.

This Little Light of Mine

April 16, 1995

When a Sunday morning visitor asked the Rev. Frank Flemister how he had come to preach the gospel, the minister looked down thoughtfully, as if he might find the answer in the culinary architecture of a half-eaten Egg McMuffin in his hands.

"When God lays something on your heart," the 77-year-old pastor explained gently, "that job is yours to do."

The gas heater in the storefront church, a cinder-block sanctuary at Joyce Avenue and Hudson Street, strained against the chill of an April morning.

Flemister, wearing a trench coat, braced himself with intermittent sips of coffee as he sat facing the sparsely occupied pews 10 minutes before a scheduled service.

The minister is a courtly man, striking in a studious way, with unlined skin the color of pecan shells and with hands whose delicacy belies the fact he was a swing grinder in a steel foundry for decades.

Outside his church, motorists clad in their Sunday finery whizzed past. They clearly were heading for houses of worship where stone and stained glass invite a solace not evoked by a 6-foot chain-link fence crowned by triple strands of barbed wire, which makes up the front of Mount Pisgah Baptist Church.

"People go to church for the saving of the soul," Flemister observed, "not for the building."

His church seems a bit down at the heels because he has pieced it together from ecclesiastical leftovers of other tabernacles.

"I was a scavenger," he admitted. "Whatever things I could pick that they were throwing out, I did."

He launched Mount Pisgah Baptist Church -- so named for a prominence cited in the book of Joshua -- years ago in the basement of his home on E. 22nd Avenue.

"I put up two chairs and a pulpit," he remembered. "I invited some of the neighbors."

He started the church for his wife, who died 20 years ago, because arthritis limited her mobility.

In time, he moved the church to a building on E. 3rd Avenue, where he would rise at 6 each Sunday morning in winter to tend the woodburning stove, carrying with him a blanket and pillow to catnap on the floor after the fire was built and before a service began.

A few years ago, he moved Mount Pisgah to its present location just around the corner from My Mama's Sweet Potato Pies and across the street from Jordan's Live Bait.

A carryout and bait store once occupied the church's building. Tacked to the door of the walk-in cooler that once chilled beer and night crawlers is the small metal sign "Pastor's Study."

"Let's turn to 132, *Amazing Grace*," Flemister said when he stepped to the pulpit after finishing his fast-food breakfast. "You'll have to help me with it."

No pianist sat at the bench to his right.

The five members of Flemister's congregation who had shown up gave their all to the old hymn. When they had finished singing, one of the flock picked up the thread of a melody of another gospel standard and sang out:

This little light of mine, I'm gonna let it shine.

This little light of mine, I'm gonna let it shine.

Though soft, the voice was full of earnest conviction.

Flemister, holding a tambourine, slapped out the beat against his leg.

"I wish I could be active and holler like I used to," he told the congregation as he gripped the sides of the pulpit, acknowledging the slight stroke he suffered when he was descending from the roof of the church after making repairs a year or so ago. "I thank God for sending me on and delivering me here. I thank him that I could beat the devil running.

"King said: 'I've been on the mountain, and I've seen the Promised Land. I may not get back to go there with you. But we will be there together.'

"This is what Jesus meant when he said, 'Go out into the fields and gather the grain, bring in the sheaves.' I turned to the Lord when I turned 25 or 26. His calling was not for me to go out there and try to be the biggest and the best. I started out in my home."

His observations were greeted with affirming nods, soft murmurs of "Yes" and "Amen."

Then he swung into the meat of his sermon.

"Paul said, 'In the last days, perilous times will come,' " Flemister said. "I've seen the cruisers and I've seen a sheet covering the body, and it breaks my heart.

"In Revelations, it tells me that the four horsemen have been loosed upon the earth. Just look around you: They are riding in Bosnia and Somalia.

"Africa, when you see those children with flies on their lips and not enough strength to wipe them away," he said, shaking his head. "Babies cry for milk, but mothers don't have any milk to give them because they haven't had anything to eat."

Lillian Bonner, Flemister's assistant minister, read from the Gospel of Mark. She spells the pastor during services so he can try to obey his doctor's insistence that he limit his activity.

"He would never tell you he's tired," church secretary Glendara Clayton said. "But you can tell."

Clayton joined the church in 1980 when she came to Ohio from Mississippi. She handles the sparse offertory, often of loose change; she knows that Flemister routinely dips into his retirement income to help cover the $300 monthly rent and utilities for the converted bait store.

He doesn't discuss such sacrifices.

For communion, Clayton fetched a white enameled basin from the back of the church and stood with a ready towel as Flemister ceremonially cleansed his hands.

The hands have sold newspapers on street corners, pushed brooms, ground burrs from cast metal - all for the chance to be folded in a prayer of thanksgiving for the gift of such a life.

As Flemister dried his hands, Clayton lifted her voice, a stunning instrument of grace and power:

One day when I was lost,
He died upon the cross.
I know it was the blood for me.

Not for money does she sing or he preach. Generous though the congregation may be, a flock of five doesn't pay anyone's salary.

And not for the comforts of ostentation does Flemister push on, as his health resists.

"He said, as long as his health prevails, he wants to do it," Clayton sighed.

"I made a vow to the Lord," he said.

The service over, Clayton watched as Flemister fumbled with the lock on the front door.

He glanced to the side of the storefront tabernacle at a placard on which he had earlier chalked, "Come to church Sun."

He looked up at noon skies that had begun leaking an intermittent and chilly drizzle.

Behind him, and inside, were the hand-me-down pews, the plastic lilies, the 3-D re-creation of the Last Supper. Outside, near his shoulder, hung a pair of crude crosses fashioned from furring strips and a fading sign: "Mt. Pisgah."

In Joshua, Mount Pisgah is the peak to which God leads Moses to show him -- lest he despair of his often-disheartening efforts to lead the chosen ones -- the lush gardens and vineyards that await his people in the Promised Land.

"Bless the pastor of the fold," Bonner had prayed during the service. "Bless him and keep him and give him the strength to run on and do what God would have him do."

Clayton echoed, "For as long as he has breath."

Tinker Creek Ethics

Jan. 15,1996

KEY WEST, Fla. -- Annie Dillard stepped to the lectern at center stage in the splendidly restored opera house that is home to San Carlos Institute and the annual Key West Literary Seminars.

Dillard, author of the Pulitzer Prize-winning *Pilgrim at Tinker Creek*, had been selected to give the John Hersey Memorial Reading to open the seminar.

She seemed an excellent choice, given this year's theme -- ``American Writers and the Natural World'' -- and Dillard's reputation as scholar and guru of the scribe's mysterious craft.

Her book, *The Writing Life*, has earned a permanent place on my night stand, a niche where others might keep a volume of daily meditations.

``Touch her hand for me while you're there,'' *Dispatch* Book Critic George Myers Jr. requested, perhaps only half in jest.

At the opera house, the assemblage of beards and Birkenstocks rose for the playing of the national anthems of the United States and Cuba. The tradition is an acknowledged homage to the life of Jose Marti, the revolutionary and poet who once read his works from the opera house's stage.

Nodding her appreciation of the crowd's generous applause, Dillard began reading from the opening passage of *Pilgrim*, a personal recollection that won for her the 1975 Pulitzer for non-fiction:

``I used to have a cat, an old fighting tom, who would jump through the open window by my bed in the middle of the night and land on my chest. I'd half awaken. He'd stick his skull under my nose and purr, stinking of urine and blood. Some nights he kneaded my bare chest with his front paws, powerfully, arching his back as if sharpening his claws, or pummeling a mother for milk. And some mornings I'd wake in daylight to find my body covered with paw prints in blood: I looked as though I had been painted with roses.''

Had Dillard read on from the engaging beginnings of *Pilgrim*, she would have asked, ``What blood was this, and what roses?'' And she would have answered the question, ``I never knew as I washed, and the blood streaked, faded and finally disappeared, whether I'd purified myself or ruined the blood sign of the passover . . . I still think of that old tomcat, mornings, when I wake.''

Instead, she read from *Living Like Weasels*, a portion of her work that she implied was intended to use nature (and the weasel) as analogy for the dedication required to live the writing life.

Finishing her readings, Dillard opened the floor for questions.

Quite innocently, a cat fancier in the front row asked about the tomcat that had tattooed Dillard with blood roses.

Without batting an eye, Dillard admitted that the incident was not an experience she could legitimately claim as her own. She had heard the tomcat story from another aspiring writer, a graduate student, if memory serves.

If the question about the cat, innocently posed, had brought her to a sudden ethical reckoning before a crowd of contemporaries and wanna-bes, she showed no sign of it.

She said she had asked the fellow who had actually lived the tomcat story whether he minded that she borrow it. Apparently, he had no objection.

Thus was a deal struck for the compelling beginning of a work that Pulitzer judges regarded as worthy of their highest accolade for non-fiction.

A naive part of me half expected that one of the seminar's luminaries, seated upon a crescent arrangement of folding chairs behind the lectern -- like priests at a concelebrated High Mass -- might rise and take offense with the confession of journalistic fraud.

Not a whisper of outrage was raised.

Dillard suggested that it was time for seminar participants to proceed to the cocktail reception at nearby Key West Wreckers Museum.

I had every intention of asking Dillard about the purloined cat story at the reception, but the line of aspiring writers waiting for her autograph on copies of *Pilgrim* was two abreast and 15 feet long.

I reminded myself that we learn as much by disillusionment as by inspiration.

It no longer seemed important to stick around long enough to touch her hand.

Shuttering the Shore

Sept. 7, 1997

SEASIDE HEIGHTS, N.J. -- The motels strung along the barrier island of the Jersey shore have the look of decadence ill-used, like a middle-aged hooker with a broken nose.

Cinder-block motels with Caribbean names and minimum-wage clerks nuzzle dunes that are largely nude save for patchy goatees of sea grass.

Dumpsters yawn. Rusty anchors are twined with strands of miniature lights.

Spartan rooms for rent, slathered with institutional beige semi-gloss, exude the sort of faded tawdriness that makes guests want to check the headboard for the carved initials of Joey Buttafuoco.

On the boardwalk, an occasional jogger slogs past sour-smelling trash barrels.

Midway carnival games -- Frog Bog, Shoot the Geek and Whack the Cat -- are shuttered against the rain. Unattended is a game-of-chance booth whose sign beckons, "Big Hearted John's -- I'd like to give 'em away, but my wife won't let me."

Out on a broad pier piled huggermugger with amusement-park rides, an unoccupied Ferris wheel turns listlessly beneath scud.

Volunteers have abandoned a kiosk dedicated to helping Our Lady of Perpetual Help sell enough raffle tickets to give away a 1997 Corvette.

Yet even in the chill drizzle of Labor Day's aftermath, the tourists come -- like Christmas card shoppers on Dec. 26 -- carrying a calculated willingness to partake of joy as long as it is marked down 50 percent.

"People save up for this vacation and, dammit, they're going to go on vacation," Chris McDowell said from his perch in the lifeguard headquarters of the Seaside Heights Beach Patrol. "In the pouring rain, you'll see an entire family come out here on the beach. Spread a blanket. Joey Bag-of-doughnuts gives a shovel and bucket to the kids and goes out in the ocean, no matter what the temperature. For a lot of these people, this is the biggest body of water they see outside their bathtub."

A lifeguard for 10 years at Seaside Heights, McDowell speaks with the weary cynicism of one who long ago passed his quota of pulling drunken revelers out of the surf.

Though his station's stretch of sand is but 1 mile long, he pointed out, "Per square foot, this is the most crowded beach on the East Coast."

Just to keep things exciting, the same mile is occupied by 32 liquor license-holders.

On the cusp of autumn, McDowell is feeling relaxed. As he explained, New Jersey state statutes specify, "After Labor Day, we cannot be held liable for anything."

Posted on a bulletin board at his right hand is a list of summer court dates at which he and his contemporaries made appearances in conjunction with citations they issued for every offense from alcohol on the beach to disrobing in public.

Most of that is behind McDowell.

After Labor Day, the Seaside Heights Beach Patrol is cut from 30 lifeguards to five.

Those who remain will scrape and paint the lifeguard stands and rescue boats, dry-dock the Jet Skis and, essentially, put the beach away for winter.

With most of the tourists gone, year-round residents of the area -- a full one-third of them retirees -- will once again venture out to stroll the boardwalk or cast in the surf for striped bass and blues.

Students from nearby Ocean County College will straggle out with Nietzsche and Coppertone to catch a few rays of the waning afternoon sun.

At a food stand not far from beach patrol headquarters, Eleanor Kurzynowski peered out at the morning rain.

"When it's like this, they just kind of lay around in bed," she said of the late-summer tourists.

As she spoke, the drizzle sprinkled a nearby food stand, its sign advertising calzones, zeppoles, pork rolls and Philly cheese steaks.

No engraver was present at Your Love Note Handwritten on a Grain of Rice in a Bottle.

A few miles north, at Normandy Beach, a determined out-of-season vacationer lounged on a plastic recliner positioned precisely, though likely inadvertently, upon the unmarked latitude of 40 degrees north.

Following the lazy arc of that line across the Atlantic, a mariner would make landfall at Figueiro da Foz, Portugal.

It seemed almost as far away as the beginning of next summer on the boardwalk at Seaside Heights, N.J.

P.T. Barnum Was Right

July 6, 1997

ROSWELL, N.M. -- Sheep rancher Hub Corn saw the yellow school bus approaching on the ridge long before it groaned to a halt and disgorged a load of tourists.

Each new arrival had paid $15 to be ferried 20 miles from downtown Roswell to Corn's ranch to gaze at the site where believers swear a UFO bit the dirt in 1947.

The Corn family keeps sheep and beef cattle on the 15,000-acre spread. The ranch is on rolling, semi-arid land, dotted here and there by oil wells whose nodding pump jacks resemble giant narcoleptic mantises dipping their heads rhythmically toward the ground.

One generation or another of Corns has farmed the land north of Roswell for a century. Yet the real estate encompassing the "crash site" was not acquired by Hub Corn's father until 1976. The property did not become the most productive parcel of land until a little more than a year ago.

That was when the family graded the road and cleared a parking site, erected four sandstone pillars and generally tried to make the middle of nowhere look like the Holy Grail of ufology.

At the fringe of the parking lot, not far from a booth selling roasting ears and soda pop, Corn hauled in the rusting carcass of a Depression-era Chevy pickup.

"It kind of adds a little character," he said.

Lean and sun-weathered, the rancher, 36, was born 14 years after the Roswell Incident. He has studied the literature and researched various accounts. He says he believes. At $15 a head, he'd be a fool not to.

"The craft was coming out of the northwest," he began telling a fresh knot of the curious. "It ended up there.

"There were supposedly three bodies inside the craft, one half in and half out that died at the base. There was one sitting on that rock when the military came upon them."

Corn stabbed a finger toward the rock -- unaware that he was striking one of the most cliched poses ever associated with UFOs: a farmer pointing to a spot where something isn't.

It is wholly unremarkable.

The site, located on the rim of an arroyo, is a patch of limestone outcropping flanked by mesquite and hackberry and a small bush Corn calls "sheep marijuana."

Another family member planted a small American flag where Corn says the craft hit.

"If they could have cleared that ridge, they might have made it another 5 or 6 miles," he told the tourists.

He listened politely as a few people interjected their notions of what happened, shopworn conjecture and none of it as engagingly fresh as the theory of Kristin, Corn's 14-year-old daughter.

"I think there was a mother ship up in outer space," she said, "and like today, a bunch of teen-agers stole a UFO and went out for a joy ride and that joy ride just happened to crash to Earth."

The requisite makings for an alien *Teen Angel* song.

She toyed with the hair scrunchie on her wrist, paused to gather her thoughts, then continued: "It'd be neat to have had them all live . . . and to have the UFO, if it hadn't crashed, to study and things."

Her father conceded that he is sometimes uneasy when confronted by tourists who are emotionally overcome at the "crash site" as they stand next to the sandstone tablet engraved:

We don't know who they were.

We don't know why they came.

We only know they changed our view of the universe.

"Some of those that claim to be abducted want to tell you their whole life's story," he said. "They'll keep you out here an hour and a half telling you everything that happened to them.

"Yesterday we had a woman get right down and start crying."

Corn loosed a squirt of Skoal juice in the general direction of the draw and the "crash site."

In the cloudless sky above, a loose formation of turkey buzzards wheeled and turned as though trained by the Corns to add the crowning touch of sentimental punctuation to the tableau.

"They're always there," Corn's wife, Sheila, said of the birds.

Not far away, a hard-core believer muttered, "It's the government."

I'm OK, You're OK, Damnit

Dec. 17, 1993

"I think I finally may have found a home," said "Phyllis," her voice catching on the last word as she filled a coffee cup in the basement of a northwest Columbus church and watched other members of her support group take their seats in a small circle of folding chairs.

Phyllis and the half-dozen others who gather each Monday night at Church of the Lesser Martyrs are members of one of central Ohio's newest support groups: Adult Children of Functional Families.

"My parents were actually pretty boring," Phyllis confessed, as those seated around her rose for the "group hug" with which members open each meeting.

"They worked, paid their taxes and tried to rear us in the most wholesome, loving environment they could provide," she continued. "They never got drunk and fell into the Christmas tree, never forgot a promise to take us to the circus.

"They were Ozzie and Harriet, Ward and June. It was a terribly predictable way to live.

"They had their arguments, sure; every couple does. But it was silly stuff, small stuff: Should the toilet paper roll from the top or the bottom? Potatoes or Stove Top stuffing? Most of the time, they got along disgustingly well.

"I can't think of a school pageant or athletic event they missed unless it was absolutely unavoidable.

"Every night at 5 o'clock, I knew I could count on my father coming directly home from his job as a mail carrier. It was sickening. He was a gruntled postal employee.

"I recall lying in bed one night and seeing my entire future unfold before me. It was summer, and the couple next door was having a knock-down, drag-out fight. You could hear it all. They were screaming at each other and throwing small appliances and frozen poultry. Their children had run outside and were hiding in the bushes, waiting for it to blow over. Meanwhile, the neighbor on the other side had come home drunk again and run over the bicycle his kid had left in the driveway.

"There I was in the middle. It was quiet. And I knew it was always going to be quiet.

"Do you realize what this can do to you when you're grown? You have absolutely nothing to talk about at parties. Everyone but us has horror stories to tell about their parents.

"Think about it: Can you name 10 friends about whom you can say with absolute certainty that they do not belong to some kind of support group? If they are not bulimic, they are children of bulimics or children of bulimics who gambled.

"We are a society of victims, and all we are trying to do with Adult Children of Functional Families is make sure we get our full measure of public concern and sympathy for our plight.

"Until this group, we had nothing we could join that would truly make us feel a sense of oneness with the other members.

"There were a few obscure support groups to which I could have belonged if I'd pushed the issue. I could be meeting with Children of Skylab those young adults with post-traumatic stress because of the uncertainty they experienced as children, not knowing where parts of the disintegrating Skylab satellite were going to fall to Earth.

"My husband restores classic Mustangs, so technically I could have joined Women Who Love Men Who Love Cars.

"But, no, I belong here. I've taken the steps. I've had to realize that as a child my life was manageable and I was powerless over the quiet mediocrity of my parents.

"Still, the burden of my upbringing is awesome. If I screw up as an adult, I have absolutely no one to blame but myself. What a terrible thing to face.

"This group helps. There are still times, after I mess up something royally, that I think it would be nice to say I did it because someone whacked me up 'side the head when I was 9 or because Dad got drunk and barfed on my homecoming date.

"I just have to realize that I'm always going to feel more or less OK for the rest of my life. Now I have friends who understand."

The Man in Black

April 11, 1999

I stared at the photo of Johnny Cash for a long time.

More than once during the past year, the supermarket tabloids have had him on his deathbed. Shy-Drager syndrome, a neurological disorder, has been chewing away at his system like weevils in grain.

Yet there he was onstage in Manhattan singing *I Walk the Line* to the woman who helped him learn to toe it.

When I close my eyes, I can remember the first time I heard his voice.

I was 10, rolling along in the back seat of the old man's Buick. It had to be a Sunday because we were headed back to Columbus on Rt. 40 after a weekend at my grandfather's fishing cabin on the Muskingum River.

The radio was blaring, but I paid it scant attention until I heard that voice. Some people say that God probably sounds like James Earl Jones. I'll put my money on Johnny Cash. His voice rumbled up from somewhere down in his boot, picking up grit and gravel as it moved up into his throat.

The song, of course, was *I Walk the Line*.

Cash was 24 and doing a little bit of everything except walking the line. He had come a long way from dragging a 9-foot cotton bag through the fields of Dyess, Ark., and singing along with WMPS High Noon Roundup.

I Walk the Line would stay on the country charts for 43 weeks. That kind of success can make a man think he's invincible. For a long time, Johnny Cash thought he was.

It wasn't enough to burn the candle at both ends. He wanted to light it in the middle, too. The dexedrine would keep him awake for three or four days. Thorazine would bring him back down when he needed to crash. The speed parched his throat, often leaving him with a whisper and a lame excuse to the audience about "laryngitis."

June Carter was touring with him then -- in the '60s -- trying to hide the pills when sleep finally overtook him.

On the night he was fired from the Grand Ole Opry, he walked off the stage smashing footlights with his microphone stand. That also was the night he borrowed June's Cadillac, drove it into a utility pole and watched, bleeding, as the downed electrical wires snake-danced sparks around the car.

Cash recalled in his autobiography, "I was in and out of jails, hospitals, car wrecks. I was a walking vision of death, and that's exactly how I felt."

Although he says there was something instinctive that always helped him navigate the tricky shoals that separate "almost" from "fatal," by 1967 he was ready to die.

He was sick from the pills and down to 155 pounds when he crawled into a cave along the Tennessee River north of Chattanooga to "let God take me from this Earth and put me wherever he puts people like me."

When Cash eventually crawled out, June Carter and his mother were waiting at the mouth of the cave with a basket of food. He married June a year later.

They fought the pills for a dozen years or so after that.

Cash's friend Kris Kristofferson likes to say, "You have to kill your own snakes." Cash had plenty to kill.

A part of me thinks he sang some of them away.

In the liner notes for his masterpiece *Unchained* CD, he wrote, "I love songs about horses, railroads, land, Judgment Day, family, hard times, whiskey, courtship, marriage, adultery, separation, murder, war, prison, rambling, damnation, home, salvation, death, pride, humor, piety, rebellion, patriotism, larceny, determination, tragedy, rowdiness, heartbreak and love. And mother."

He probably is one of the few artists who could get away with putting *Kneeling Drunkard's Plea* and *Memories Are Made of This* on the same CD.

Cash has conceded, "Sometimes at night, when I hear the wind, I wish I was crazy again."

When he was 4, he said brimstone sermons from the Pentecostal pulpit in Dyess frightened him mightily.

"I'd peep out the window of our farmhouse at night," he wrote, "and if, in the distance, I saw a grass fire or a forest fire, I knew hell was almost here."

Hell, in one guise or another, always has seemed to be at Johnny Cash's heels.

Thank God he can still sing about it.

A Case of Slander

July 20, 1997

Libel, someone once said, is what compels newspapers to always use the word *alleged* before Mafioso and never before congressman.

Doubtless there exists an analogous wry quip applicable to slander. Actor Carroll O'Connor undoubtedly thought of borrowing it for the trial in which he finds himself a defendant.

The actor stands accused of calling the man who dealt cocaine to son Hugh O'Connor "a sleazeball."

After battling drug addiction, Hugh O'Connor killed himself two years ago.

Harry Perzigian, who is suing the elder O'Connor, supplied the actor's son with cocaine and even went to prison for a brief stretch for doing so.

Yet Perzigian doesn't like having his standing within the community besmirched by being called "a sleazeball" or, as he also contends, "a partner in murder."

Had he not done young O'Connor the professional courtesy of letting him have the cocaine at cost?

Perzigian says Hugh was his friend.

O'Connor says Perzigian preyed on his son, and kept him from getting the help he needed by ensuring that Hugh never wanted for nose candy.

Regrettably -- though certainly not in defense of the plaintiff -- it should be noted that had Perzigian cut off the supply, Hugh simply would have found another source.

Trials such as this one only confirm the appraisal that America is going to hell on a sled whose skids are greased daily by lawyers.

Has O'Connor's "sleazeball" comment damaged the man's chances for professional advancement?

I think not. Indeed, Perzigian's incarceration probably allowed him to do a bit of postgraduate work in his area of expertise.

What intrigues me most about this case is the incredible irony of it all.

In 1971, CBS premiered a situation comedy of which Norman Lear was chief architect and Carroll O'Connor the showcased star.

Who can forget the irrepressible Archie Bunker? Certainly not African-Americans, women, gays, Jews, Poles, Italians, Hispanics, Chinese, the Irish and other groups for whom Bunker never had to search for a back-alley slur.

Archie's wife (Edith) and daughter (Gloria) were, respectively, "dingbat" and "little girl."

Here is Archie watching a football game: "Look at that colored guy run. . . .. It's in his blood!"

Bunker often was able to piggyback slurs by referring to his "dumb polack" son-in-law as "the laziest white man I ever seen."

Norman Lear's off-the-wall defense of this tack: By exposing society to its prejudices, we would all learn to be more sensitive.

Sure.

All it did, in many cases, was provide closet racists with a champion to rally around. (Remember the "Archie Bunker for President" bumper stickers?)

Now, in the oddest and most ironic of real-life scripts, the man behind the man who never met a demeaning epithet he didn't like is being taken to task for calling a cocaine dealer a "sleazeball."

Lear once defended himself by saying, "My critics don't seem to understand that great humor always comes out of great pain."

Not always.

For all the disparaging names that Archie hung on those who were different, Bill Cosby said he found the show to be a little like watching a junkie shoot up. It was neither funny nor fun to watch.

Today, O'Connor might wince at that analogy.

Having suffered the greatest pain a parent can know, he might beg to differ with Lear.

"Somehow, You Struggle Up"

Sept. 5, 1994

He has a chin that juts like the prow of an icebreaker, but it is the gaps in his grin that give him the look of a failed middleweight too long in the ring without a mouthpiece.

His eyes, a pair of mahogany discs floating in pools of sepia, are hooded by lids he closes to the crush and bustle of lunch-hour pedestrians when he sings. From the spot where he parked his wheelchair on the west side of High Street, he had a commanding view of the Statehouse entrance and of the activity at the nearby intersection of Broad Street.

His left foot tapped the rhythm against the sun-washed sidewalk as he crooned. His right leg had recently been pruned at midcalf, just above the encroaching gangrene. What is left of it -- covered by worn, gray sweat pants -- hung out past the seat of the wheelchair like cigarette ash that needs to be tapped. In his right hand he held a small cup into which strangers had poured a half-inch of pocket change.

A smoky voice, long on earnestness but short of wind, picked its way through *Misty*:

"Walk my way, and a thousand violins begin to play."

A small knot of pedestrians, eyes schooled in the fine, urban discipline of ignoring panhandlers, moved briskly past without averting a straightforward, catatonic gaze.

Samuel Franklin Gilbert, baritone, didn't seem to mind.

He was buoyed by the prospects of a sun-spangled day that emptied offices of workers as if by a mass fire drill.

"On a day like today," he confided from the side of his mouth, "people get away from whatever's the problem, whatever has been dominating or humiliating or bothering them.

"Meet a person on a day like today; fall in love."

He was born in Miami to Bahamian parents, he said. He once made a decent living with his voice and an alto sax.

"I've run into the worst, baddest, most evil times," he said, "but somehow you struggle up."

Diabetic ulcerations cost him part of his leg. A small brown bottle of nitroglycerin tablets was tucked in a pocket next to his cigarettes.

He and a landlord he knew only as "Big Mama" recently had a falling-out about the room he had rented by the week.

"I'm sleeping behind the Revco," he said, nodding toward a drugstore a block away.

"Over there they want spirituals," he observed of those who frequent the sidewalks north of Broad and High streets. "Over here they want Frank Sinatra and the big-band sounds."

For a little spare change, he would sing anything except hard rock.

He related a musical experiment that someone told him about: "When they played hard rock to trees, the trees died; it ran all the birds away. When they played jazz to the tree -- Coltrane -- the tree grew taller than the roof." He was singing *I Left My Heart in San Francisco* when a squat woman with a toddler in tow stopped at his wheelchair and fished $5 from her purse.

She tucked the bill into the cup and sternly cautioned, "I'm giving you this and it had better be for a good cause, you hear me?"

He smiled, warbling in reply: "When I come home to you, San Francisco, your golden sun will shine for me."

He slipped the $5 into the pocket of a jacket lining the seat of the wheelchair and began singing *Misty* again.

He might have been singing for dinner or maybe just for cocktails.

"Look at me, I'm as helpless as a kitten up a tree."

The Bone Hunter

Aug. 7, 1995

TOKYO - Yoshio Nakajima stood before the entrance to Japan's Yasakuni Shrine ("shrine of the warrior") and bowed deeply from the waist, his arms rigid at his sides.

Nakajima is a small, well-muscled man. Though 80, he still arises each morning to perform the military calisthenics with which he kept fit more than 50 years ago on Iwo Jima while waiting for the attack he was certain would come from the Americans.

At the shrine, where he comes often now that he has retired from his small plumbing business outside Tokyo, he claps his hands to attract the attention of the spirits who once were his brothers in arms.

Nakajima, clad in the blue trousers and shirt whose pocket embroidery identify him as a member of the Iwo Jima Association, is a bone-hunter.

Ten times he has returned to the island where more than 21,000 of his comrades died in February 1945. He prowls the dense jungle vegetation, probes the lava sand the Japanese call sahuku, and crawls through the caves and tunnels he once defended.

Eight thousand sets of cremains have been returned to Japan since the bone-hunting was begun in 1952 by Nakajima's commanding officer, the former Capt. Tsunezo Wachi.

Wachi had commanded the Navy garrison on Iwo, supervised the construction of its bunkers, pillboxes, gun emplacements and 15 miles of interlacing tunnels. He was ready for the Americans.

Just before the invasion, however, he was ordered to return to Japan to oversee construction and training for a fleet of one-man, kamikaze torpedo boats whose chief mission was to defend the home islands.

Wachi could do nothing but listen to the grim reports from Iwo Jima as all but 1,083 of its defenders were lost.

More than 6,800 Americans died taking Iwo, more than 5,000 of them

Marines of the 3rd, 4th and 5th divisions. Their gallantry is best recalled in what is said to be the most reproduced photograph of World War II, the picture of Marines raising the American flag on Mount Suribachi.

By the time Mount Suribachi was taken, Nakajima's artillery emplacement had been silenced, most of those around him had been killed, and he had retreated with two comrades into a cave.

"For two weeks we had no food or water," he said. "I tried to drink my own urine, but my throat was too dry to swallow.

"We had three grenades left and had decided to kill ourselves."

His companions succeeded, but Nakajima's grenade was a dud. He tried to detonate it by beating it against his helmet, but it would not go off.

When a dog led by American troops sniffed out Nakajima, he said, "I decided that I would die a brave death. If I was a true samurai, I should die fighting.

"I pulled out my short knife and stumbled out of the cave. The light blinded me."

Half-starved and weakened from loss of blood from wounds he received when hit by fragments of his companions' grenades, he was easily disarmed.

He was taken aboard a Navy hospital ship, and eventually was transferred to a POW camp in Texas.

Capt. Wachi, haunted that he had not been on Iwo Jima when his men were dying, became a Buddhist priest after the war ended.

From 1945 until his death five years ago, Wachi made 150 expeditions to the island to search for remains, pray over them, then cremate them in a portable crematorium he had set up.

He also established the Iwo Jima Association for veterans of the battle, though fewer than 300 of more than 1,000 eligible to join did so. Many of the others, shamed that they had not died in battle or killed themselves, became recluses.

Nakajima took up the work of gathering bones when his commander's health began to flag.

In February, he traveled to Iwo Jima to meet with the U.S. veterans who took the island 50 years ago.

There, he was introduced to Joe Dewhirst, who lives near Cincinnati.

"He didn't speak English, and I didn't speak Japanese," said Dewhirst, whose Army unit had rounded up prisoners on the island. "But I think he may have been one of the ones we captured."

If so, Nakajima is grateful. For he was not shot, as he had been taught to believe he would be if captured.

He went home to Japan to raise a family, to install plumbing, to pray for the dead.

Now, he hunts for the remains of old soldiers.

On Iwo Jima, 12,466 remain to be found.

A Brithday Party in a Cemetery

Sept. 19, 1997

MOORELAND, Ind. -- We saw the balloons first. Silver and shiny, they bobbed beneath the midday sun.

Now and then, one of the children would let one go -- trailing a ribbon with an attached note: "Happy Birthday, Kaleb."

Released from the small fists that held their tethers, the burnished orbs caught the lift of the Indiana breeze and rose until they could no longer be seen.

Lori Jester wanted her son Kaleb's sixth birthday party to be special.

She hadn't planned on having it in a cemetery, but there were all of Kaleb's cousins, running among the headstones and playing with the toy animals on his grave.

Although Kaleb's party did not begin until 3 p.m., Lori arrived several hours early with her daughter, Taylor, in tow.

"She's having a real hard time with this," Lori said of her 2-year-old. "She won't let him go. She pretends he's still here. She holds him in her hand and makes me read stories to him."

Before the guests arrived, Lori and Taylor spread a blanket upon the grass beside the grave. Lori read from a children's book titled *Just in Case You Wondered.*

And God wants me to make sure you know about heaven.

It's a wonderful place. There are no tears. There are no monsters. No mean people.

You never have to say "Goodbye" or "Good night" or "I'm hungry."

You never get old or sick or afraid.

The doctors had diagnosed Kaleb's heart condition, called Wolfe-Parkinson-White syndrome, when he was an infant.

A short in the electrical circuitry of the heart could send his pulse racing to almost 300 beats a minute.

It had happened when he was 3 months old, again during routine surgery when he was 3 years old.

Lori and her husband, Greg, had been warned that the same aberrant impulse that sent the heart racing could also still it without warning.

Kaleb was riding his bicycle with a friend in April when suddenly he announced, `I felt something."

That quickly, he was gone.

"Kaleb lived life at 90 miles an hour," said his grandmother, Sue Jester.

An aunt remarked, "He said he wanted to know everything that God knew."

His grandmother read a tribute to the boy as the wind played with three wooden stars that hung suspended above his grave.

Kaleb's grandmother relighted the votive candle encased in a blue glass holder next to the grave.

It had been extinguished earlier in the day when Kaleb's sister insisted that her mother sing Happy Birthday to Kaleb and that someone blow out the candle for him.

When the party was over, the guests straggled to their cars -- children in tow -- and made ready to drive to Muncie to attend Mass in Kaleb's honor.

Someone once said, "Children hold our hands for a while but our hearts forever."

Travelers exploring America along the 40th parallel get to see a lot of the heartland: Midwest farmers making the season's final hay cutting, high school marching bands practicing in the waning afternoon sun.

We never expected to see a birthday party in a cemetery.

John Macynski, Carver

May 5, 2000

John Macynski studied the form of an open-armed Jesus. He had carved the figure on his old Army mess kit while he was a World War II prisoner of war in Japan.

"There were times when I thought I could see him," the North Columbus veteran said of apparitions of Christ that came to him in the camp. "I had a hard time trying to talk myself out of the fact that he wasn't there."

In rare moments of solace from forced labor in the Osaka shipyards and the Akenobe copper mines, Macynski would reach for a fingernail file that he kept in his shoe. Then he would etch as he prayed.

Macynski had survived the Bataan death march in the spring of 1942. He watched as weak and straggling captives were stabbed with bayonets or shot when they lagged behind.

During the trek, which he estimates claimed the lives of 8,000 U.S. and Philippine soldiers (official estimates range from 3,000 to 10,000), Macynski tried to help along a struggling comrade.

"When I stopped to get a better hold on the guy," he remembered, "the guards ran over and bayoneted him in the side. I could still hear him crying for as far as I could walk."

When Macynski completed the march, he was weakened by starvation and dysentery and contracted malaria. His captors dumped him in a barracks overcrowded with dead and dying. He credits an Australian soldier with nursing him through the most harrowing days of his infirmity.

As soon as his captors determined that he might, indeed, survive, they put Macynski to work in Osaka on the rivet gang. The men worked inside the hull of a warship under construction.

"I was called a thrower," he recalled. His job was to fetch a glowing rivet with a pair of tongs and heave it up to workers who waited with catch buckets on a scaffold. "You learn to do it. It was like fly-casting almost."

Each morning he arose with the other prisoners and they marched to a streetcar. He recalls riding silently and standing while insolent women passengers would spit at the captives and poke them with sewing needles.

The war dragged on and his weight dropped to 67 pounds. Bombing runs by U.S. warplanes kept him from total despair.

"I still dream about them to this day," he said. "Sometimes, they couldn't have been more than 100 yards above my head. Then the whole city would light up. We would pray, 'Come get us. Come get us.' "

In the war's waning months, he was transferred to a prison camp adjacent to a copper mine. He and other POWs did the work of mules. The prisoners moved the filled ore cars out of the dark maw for unloading.

One morning, Macynski awakened and prepared for 6 a.m. roll call only to discover that his captors had fled the camp. He and other prisoners fashioned an SOS sign from scrap cloth, hoping that U.S. pilots would see it. Not long afterward, Red Cross food packages were parachuted to them.

Before he left the camp, one former guard returned and asked Macynski to come to his home in a nearby village for dinner. There he feasted on chicken and rice and was given family photographs by the man who had held him captive.

"He seemed different to me from the other guards. He might have been a Christian. I don't know," Macynski said.

Not long afterward, Macynski and fellow prisoners marched to the railway station and forced their way onto a train whose destination was a mystery to them. Later they arrived at Yokohama. The first American they saw there was a Red Cross worker.

"Where you from soldier?" she asked Macynski.

"Youngstown," he told her.

"I'm from Warren," she said.

Macynski faced a long recuperation at Letterman Army Hospital in San Francisco before he was permitted to return to Ohio. In college, he studied design at Ohio University and later, Ohio State University, where he graduated in 1952 with a bachelor's degree in architecture.

He spoke to no one about his captivity. He married his wife, Faye, in 1949. Even their three children, a son and two daughters, knew nothing of their father's ordeal until they were young adults. When memories overwhelmed him, he turned again to the carving that had occupied his mind during those years in Japan.

"It settles me down," he said. "I'm a different person when I do this work."

He has carved clipper ships and schooners and Depression-era automobiles. His craft has taught him the various personalities of wood. He likes pecan for its hue and utility as an accent wood. Walnut has no blisters; its subtle grain is more forgiving of the carver. Cherry is pleasing to his hands.

During Lent each year, Macynski gives up carving wood to begin painting eggs the way his Ukranian aunt taught him. The work is painstakingly delicate, yet his 80-year-old fingers still can maneuver the fine brushes as deftly as good surgeons make scalpels dance.

Parts of his story and thoughts of absent friends make Macynski's eyes brim. He does not apologize for the tears.

He studied his old aluminum canteen cup, not a space larger than a fingerprint unadorned by etchings.

"I was killing time. I didn't know what was going to happen to me. In case I died, somebody might find it and they'd say, "I remember him.""

The Sweat Lodge

May 3, 2000

CRITTENDEN, Ky. -- In the kiln of the sweat lodge, the lava rocks -- glowing maraschino in the dark -- framed Dennis Banks' brooding face. Freshets of perspiration coursed down the arroyos and flumes that have redrawn the landscape of his countenance.

At 68, the face no longer is the one of the young Chippewa firebrand who helped found the American Indian Movement more than three decades ago.

The muscles of his jaw once set so firmly in defiance at Custer and Pine Ridge, S.D., have slackened. Now they preside over the scallop of a dewlap beneath which great-grandchildren sit.

"Bring 15 more rocks," Banks commanded of the firekeeper who stood outside the squat dome framed by a lattice of bowed willow.

When the pitchfork tines had piled the last porous loaf of stone into the fire pit, Banks' tenor voice snatched the fringe of a chant. His voice lifted it as a gust might ripple the trailing end of a scarf up red cedar crowns flanking the lodge.

Before fires for the evening "sweat" were lighted, Banks indulged a question about the sometimes-fragmented and frequently contentious leadership of the group christened in 1968 as Concerned Indian Americans. The name hastily was changed when it was noted that the initials hardly befit a group that the John Birch Society had labeled as ex-con commies.

"If there were only two people left in this world saying that they are AIM, I would be one of them," Banks said. "I don't know who the other one would be."

Banks was born near Leech Lake, Minn., in the lean years of the early Depression. He was taken from his parents at age 5 and consigned to Bureau of Indian Affairs boarding schools.

His stint in the Air Force was followed by a stint in prison for burglary. After serving time, he connected with Clyde Bellecourt, an Ojibwa. They would found AIM.

The fledgling group threw its weight behind the 1969 seizure and occupation of Alcatraz Island by American Indians. Three years later, AIM organized the Trail of Broken Treaties caravan across the nation to Washington.

Banks was chief negotiator during the 1973 siege on Pine Ridge Indian Reservation in South Dakota. A later confrontation at Custer led to his conviction for riot and assault. He fled to California before he could be sent to prison.

More than a decade later, Banks surrendered to South Dakota authorities and spent 18 months behind bars. Since then, he has championed issues confronting American Indians while running a drug and alcohol rehabilitation camp in the north woods of Minnesota.

Philosophically, Banks sees himself as something of a lightning rod. His presence at disputes often is sufficient to focus media attention on problems. Such was the case in recent months, after eight unsolved killings of American Indians near Rapid City, S.D.

Yet it is not a rally for justice or a protest that brought Banks to the northern Kentucky hills on the last days of April. There were no microphones or cameras. He had come simply to visit old friends and to preside over a "sweat."

Glistening with perspiration in the hot, dim lodge, Banks called to his Chippewa ancestors. He asked them to guide the steps of his brothers and sisters; he pleaded for peace.

In a fat and prosperous United States, unemployment on reservations exceeds 70 percent in some areas. Not surprisingly (and some contend as a consequence of joblessness), American Indians account for 30 percent of prison inmates in states where their total number among the general population is a mere 6 percent.

Darkness had fallen outside the sweat lodge by the time Banks recalled for ceremony participants a story passed down to him. The tale instructed tribal members on the proper way to greet a stranger arriving at their village.

"Take an eagle feather and dust the stranger's ears that he might better hear. Dust his eyes so he might see clearly. Give him fresh, clean water so that his words can be understood."

Banks gave the instructions in a voice unedged by cynicism. This, despite the fact that his people's history is punctuated by incidents of deceit and mayhem authored by white strangers whose ears never heard, whose eyes never saw, whose words no water could make pure.

Felix Cohen, a scholar of Indian law, once observed of the treatment of American Indians, "Like the miner's canary, the Indian marks the shift from fresh air to poison air in our political atmosphere. Our treatment of Indians . . . reflects the rise and fall of our democratic faith."

When the "sweat" had ended, Banks crawled from the mouth of the lodge and rose to speak with each of those who exited the scalding enclosure.

In that moment, he was not Dennis Banks the activist or Dennis Banks, leader of AIM.

He simply was Dennis Banks, great-grandfather, singer of the old songs, keeper of the old ways, a Chippewa come to chant home the shy stars freckling a cloudless Kentucky night sky.

Educational TV

Nov. 7, 1993

Maybe you heard about me on the news. My name is Thelmalou Wandalene Snopes.

That's my husband, Vernal -- Vern, honey, don't scratch your athlete's foot with the schnauzer; it makes him all swimmy-headed -- over there in the La-Z-Boy.

We're just good country people -- me, Vern, Charlotte (we call her "Pookie"), J.R. (he was born when Dallas was all the rage) and Cale.

Charlotte's big into garage sales. J.R. works in London; he may get paroled come March. Caleb -- we call him Cale -- is the one we're worried about.

You maybe heard about the lawsuit. We're the ones that's suing them TV producers.

Didn't have much choice. The way me and Vern see it, they ruined our boy's life. Cale was just a normal kid before all this happened.

He was 16, I believe, 'cause his daddy had took him out in the back yard to get him his first car. There was four of them out there, all '79 Camaros.

Vern said: "Look 'em over. Check 'em out. Kick the cement blocks."

But Cale, he seemed really distant, like he was off in some other world.

"Daddy, I don't want no Camaro. What I'd really like to get my hands on is a Volvo."

Kind of embarrassed Vern, him not knowin' that Volvo is a car and not something that has to do with sex.

Right then, we knew that something was wrong with Cale.

You got to be careful what your kids watch on TV, 'cause it's just like the French say: Monkey see, monkey do. They see some TV movie about kids bungee-jumpin' off the town water tower or playing chicken, and they just got to try it themselves.

He started acting strange. He'd come home from school and lock himself in his room. He stopped listening to Metallica. His friends would stop by and want to do something -- drop some ludes, sniff some thinner -- and he'd make up some excuse. Soon enough, he was studying.

He made the honor roll; ain't nobody in this family ever done that. Dropped wood shop and signed up for French. French!

I guess it was right about that time we found out he'd been watchin' *In the Know*. That's that TV show with all them smarty-smarts on it that wants to be rocket scientists and stuff.

I called up the station and gave them a piece of my mind.

I said: "Y'all done created a monster. We don't know our own boy. All he does is study. And he was OK till he watched that program. Now what do you think we ought to do?"

Man said, "If the boy is that impressionable, you'd better hide *Oedipus Rex*."

I said, "Who's that?" He never did tell me.

Well, that's when me and Vern -- honey, don't feed that groundhog table scraps; he'll want them all the time -- we decided that we was going to get a lawyer and sue.

You just can't put whatever you like on TV. Kids is impressionable. That's what our lawyer said: "impressionable."

'Cause, see, now the boy is so messed up in the head, he don't even want to take up body-and-fender work anymore when he's done with high school.

He wants to go to college. College! And he don't want just any college. He wants to go to one of them ivy schools. Do you know what that costs?

Well, them TV people's gonna pay. Our boy ain't even like kin anymore.

He stopped datin' Earline 'cause he said all she wants to do is get married, have a bunch of crumb snatchers and live in a double-wide. I ask you now: Is there something wrong with that?

It just breaks a mother's heart. You try to raise your kids to be just like you, and someone puts some half-brained show on TV, and off they go.

I feel like I don't have a son no more. And Vern -- honey, don't stack your empties on your belly like that -- he feels just the same.

I just don't know what to do. Maybe when his brother gets out of London he can talk some sense into his head.

A Circle of Snowflowers

May 31, 1994

CAEN, France - The dark secret of the Abbey d'Ardenne on the outskirts of Caen did not keep for long.

When the first flowers of the spring of 1945 began nosing through the soil in the garden by the west wall, the Vico family, owners of the old abbey, noticed that the snowdrops no longer sprouted and bloomed in the circle in which they were first planted.

"They were completely disorganized," farmer Michel Huard explained.

Now 60, Huard was 10 at the time of the Normandy invasion. For generations, his family had tilled the land around the walled cathedral.

After the Allies landed and British and Canadian troops began marching toward Caen, the German 12th SS Panzer Division seized the abbey, using the cathedral tower as an observation post.

In a skirmish shortly after the landing, the Germans captured a large group of Canadian tank troops and infantrymen and brought them to the abbey.

Huard, motioning with a sweep of his arm across the sprawling abbey court, said, "I saw 200 men come through the yard. Their hands were on their heads.

"The Germans took everything from the prisoners: money, identification papers, rings, personal belongings. They burned the identification papers, but kept the money."

The POWs were interrogated, and most put to work as litter bearers for a nearby German field hospital.

Huard and his father returned to their farmhouse.

Later that day, "My father heard several shots. But we heard that all the time. He did not think it could be the Germans killing the prisoners."

Later testimony, from German soldiers who had guarded the prisoners and from one of the Canadians who escaped, argued otherwise.

"A group of the prisoners were brought into the courtyard," Huard continued his story, standing at the point where 19 Canadians were assembled not far from a small archway leading to an out-of-the-way garden tucked between the rear of the stables and the abbey wall.

Sensing what was about to happen, the Canadian soldiers began saying their goodbyes to one another.

"It was a day like this," Huard said. "The sun was brighter, but the wind was blowing as it is now.

"One at a time, the prisoners were marched through the archway," he said, leading the way as he spoke. "Here, they turned left. But there on the right, two meters away, was a firing platoon of German soldiers.

"One of the soldiers escaped," he added, "and informed the Canadian officers that they were massacring prisoners."

But it would be days before the abbey was seized by advancing Allies. And even then, looking for graves simply was not a priority.

When the snowdrops bloomed in a random hodgepodge the following spring, the owner of the abbey estate, who had been away when the killings took place, dispatched workers to dig up the site.

Seven bodies were found beneath the flowers, the remainder not far away. Most of the soldiers had been shot in the back of the head.

Autopsies would reveal that one was probably buried alive.

Two more Canadian bodies were found later and are believed to have been killed 10 days after the first group.

The general in charge of the troops at the abbey -- Kurt Meyer -- was later tried and sentenced to seven years in prison.

Curiously, Huard said, Meyer returned to the abbey in 1957. When asked why, Huard said Meyer defended himself by saying: "A true soldier always comes back to where he fought."

And Meyer contended that he had done his duty because, after learning that one of his adjutants had ordered the executions, he sent that man to the front lines that night. The guilty officer, so Meyer said, was killed there within days.

The exhumed bodies of the murdered Canadians were eventually buried in a military cemetery, though their family members have visited the abbey garden and its small shrine erected in their honor.

Huard, having shown yet another group of visitors the site several days ago, walked them back out into the courtyard, amidst several signs of fresh construction.

He said that Jacques Vico, one of the surviving members of the family that owns the abbey and a former fighter in the French resistance, had given over the place to be used as an international institute for peace studies at which foreign scholars can serve internships.

As for Huard, he continues to farm around the high gray walls, taking time out, when tourists implore, to retrace the Canadians' steps through the darkened garden archway where a neatly lettered message on a tiny white sign requests, "Respect this place."

Just past the sign, each spring, the snowdrops again bloom in a circle.

Marian Anderson's Ghost

May 17, 2000

WASHINGTON -- The ghost of Marian Anderson hovered over the nation's capital on Sunday.

A gliding wraith, smiling serenely, she moved above the treetops that canopied flanks of the throng that stretched along the National Mall for blocks.

Those who saw her said nothing. To have avowed the incredible in the midst of scattered cynics would have only invited censure. "Too long in the sun," the solicitous would have murmured to the curious before pressing toward the first-aid tent with a dazed witness. Together they would whisper the name as though Marian Anderson comprised the first two words of an oft-repeated prayer.

"Who was Marian Anderson?" children, who are curious about such things, would have demanded. Surely, many would not have heard of the courageous young black woman with the stunning contralto.

Parents would feel compelled to explain that, threescore years ago, Anderson had stood on the Lincoln Memorial steps on an Easter Sunday. She had lifted her magnificent voice in a paean to a nation whose heel was at her people's throat.

Anderson, the story would be told, had been refused a chance to perform in Constitution Hall. The reason: The controlling Daughters of the American Revolution did not want a black woman singing the line "My Country 'tis of thee" from a stage built to hallow freedom.

Yet those whose memory still carries the taste of sweet, forbidden fruit would quietly recall, "Oh, she sang, all right."

Above the chants and tears and implorings of the thousands at Sunday's Million Mom March, she sang again.

She always does when skeptics sneer "You can't" in a country where children are taught "You can."

Scoffers wink and elbow one another when those who hear her try to describe the sound. Not everyone's songs are heard after they are gone. It is a dispensation given only to caged birds.

No one will come, organizers of the Million Mom March were told when they began planning the event less than a year ago.

"Yes, they will," mothers replied.

"No one will listen," was the retort.

"We'll make them," the moms said.

Susan Chema traveled from Dayton to take her place on the swale of green that stretches like a taut hammock from the Washington Monument to Capitol Hill.

It wasn't Chema's first rodeo. When she was 10 years old, her mother, Marj Russell, had hauled her to Washington to protest the killing in a far-off nation. The country's name -- Vietnam -- sometimes tangled the Texas tongue of the president who sent the prime of American youth into insanity's yawning maw.

Now Chema was back in the nation's capital. She rode to Washington on a bus with her 16-year-old daughter, Alexis, in the seat to her right. Across the aisle to her left sat her 69-year-old mother, smiling benignly at the closing of a circle.

The girl Sue Chema had grown to a woman who served 10 years in the U.S.Navy. She rose to the rank of lieutenant commander before resigning her commission to raise a family and work in civilian life.

Chema said armed civilians ought to be held as accountable to their government and its laws as the armed services to which she gave a decade of her life.

Her thoughts seemed sane and responsible. If sane and responsible prevailed in America, however, Chema would not have been in Washington with her mother and daughter. Sane and responsible had to be cobbled on the nation's front yard Sunday from a mass of humanity. They kept chanting "Enough is enough" in the manner one might chasten a child who refuses to listen.

I don't know what's going to happen with the moms and their crusade. Only a complete fool could have come away from Sunday's gathering unaware of the lighting of a fire. Those coals yet glowed in the windows of Greyhound buses that snaked through the gathering dusk to return to Iowa, Minnesota and Ohio.

If Chema heard Marian Anderson singing Sunday, she didn't tell me.

But then she would not have. People don't share such sweet solace with just anyone.

If the cynics -- just for a moment -- thought they might have heard a note catch in the boughs of the big oaks, they kept quiet.

Such phenomena make jaded doubters look at their shoes, sense a chill of lost innocence no sun can warm and feel terribly small among believers.

Columbine: One Year Later

April 20, 2000

When the unthinkable becomes a headline, something within us yearns for the pat explanation that distills understanding from mayhem, as if violence were a cryptic tongue that we might better comprehend with the help of an interpreter.

In the fresh aftermath of the shootings a year ago today at Columbine High School, we divined every facet of our culture, seeking the toxic aquifer that could have sustained such madness.

We were only too willing to blame the 15 deaths on everything from shock-rocker Marilyn Manson to the Duke Nukem video game, whose anti-hero drop-kicks the heads of his victims through the gridiron uprights.

We wanted to know the why of horror visited upon children by children and, in this age of instant gratification, we wanted to hear a tidy summation from "a leading expert" before the end of the 11 o'clock news.

"I think it is human nature that we try to do this," Robin Ortiz, a math teacher at Columbine, said less than a week before the solemn commemoration today of the deadly rampage near Littleton, Colo.

"We try to understand things. There is less fear in the known than in the unknown. We try to affix some blame, if you will, and it gives us some understanding."

On a spring Tuesday last April, something caught Ortiz's ear as he taught a geometry class. He stepped into the hall to investigate, only to hear a student scream, "He's got a gun!"

"At that time, a couple of students turned the corner, and I grabbed them and threw them into a classroom," he recalled. "Then I thought that might not be such a good idea, so I started opening doors and yelling, 'Get out of the room! Get out of the building!' "

While Ortiz shepherded students to safety, his good friend and fellow teacher Dave Sanders attempted to do the same.

Sanders, a father of four, was shot twice, asking a student as he slowly bled to death, "Tell my girls I love them."

Sanders was the school's softball coach. Ortiz coaches the baseball team.

The morning of the massacre, Ortiz was preparing for an afternoon game between the Columbine Rebels and Arvada High.

The game, of course, was never played. The balance of the league schedule was replaced by a benefit tournament for Columbine.

Last week, Ortiz's team finally took the field against Arvada, but lost 8-7.

Despite the defeat, baseball provided a momentary diversion for students and teachers dreading the anniversary of the shootings.

"We knew it was going to come," Ortiz said. "We were to a point where we were settling in, back to our routines. Our minds weren't focusing on it on a daily basis. Then suddenly, here we are. I think there are a lot of faculty, students and parents who are nervous about the day. There are several who have made the decision that they don't want to be here on the 20th."

At the high school, the library that became a death chamber has been walled off. There are new tables and chairs in the cafeteria, where students who had converged for "Free Cookie Day" last April found themselves slithering across broken glass to escape the shooters.

At Clement Park, where students grieved and made prayer circles around small mountains of roses and columbine, a candlelight vigil is planned tonight.

Artists' sketches for a memorial to the teacher and 12 students slain by two fellow students who then killed themselves have been reviewed by a committee, and by the second anniversary of the shootings, a permanent tribute should be dedicated.

For the rest of us, despite our gropings to uncover the impulses and incitements that wrought such carnage, we arrive at the first anniversary with empty hands.

"The only blame there is lies with the two young men who perpetrated this crime," Ortiz mused. "I think, in all honesty, it is as simple as that."

Thus are we denied the quick-fix explanation, the epiphanic discovery that reveals the malignant force responsible for so much bloodshed.

Thus, too, are we cheated out of the sort of resolution we love to see at the end of movies made from true-life stories -- movies in which the, tangled threads of evil come to fitting closure as we learn who goes to prison and who rises triumphant from cataclysm.

Columbine, a year later, gives us no such opportunity to "process" our grief or salvage from it "acceptance."

It is the movie whose end is rather like the final scene from *All Quiet on the Western Front*.

A soldier, spying a butterfly in the midst of combat's fever dream, reaches -- as the young ever will -- to touch its disconsonant gentleness. We see the hand moving toward the gossamer wings shudder at the bullet's impact, then stiffen and droop.

There is no closure.

There is only the flinching of the heart, the soul's whispered, supplications for forgiveness for the unspeakable violence of which we are capable.

The News in Amish Country

May 16,1999

SUGARCREEK, Ohio -- The 400-plus correspondents who write for George Smith don't care much about Belgrade bombing runs or business on Wall Street.

A late April dispatch from one of the Sugarcreek editor's far-flung scribes summed up the important news of the day as follows:

"Beautiful spring weather has returned after a few frosty mornings. The cherry trees are starting to blossom. I caught enough catfish in our pond that it was worthwhile heating up the frying pan. They were delicious."

"It's just like getting a letter from home," said Smith, who, at 92, has helped put out the town's weekly newspaper since he was 12.

"It was 80 years ago that I stood right here and set my first type for *The Budget*," he observed last week.

The Budget is two newspapers rolled into one. The outer section is much like any other small-town weekly. The inside, called the national edition, serves the old order Amish and Mennonite settlements across the United States.

Page after page is filled with dispatches with datelines such as Haven, Kan.; Shipshewana, Ind.; Fair Play, S.C.; Montezuma, Ga.

The news reports are written by hand. Until *The Budget* began supplying its Amish scribes with lined paper, Smith would sometimes receive stories written on grocery sacks or the backs of calendar pages.

The missives tell of marryings and buryings and the state of the crops. Almost invariably, though, they begin with the weather:

Feb. 11. Our spring weather has changed and the first rhubarb shoots and spring flowers are deeply covered by a 5-inch blanket of pure, white snow. This is, of course, the children's delight.

"The weather is important," Smith observed. "It is their livelihood."

When an older member of an Amish settlement dies, Smith will receive a report that usually includes a proud notation regarding the ponderous number of surviving kin.

When 97-year-old Bessie Hostetler of Buffalo, Mo., died in 1998, she apparently clinched the record with 10 children, 118 grandchildren, 492 great-grandchildren and 331 great-great grandchildren.

The Budget does not pay its correspondents. They apparently are content simply to have the news from their small corner of the world -- news of a spectacular sunset or the birth of a goat -- reported in a paper.

And they are fiercely loyal.

"She's been writing for *The Budget* for 73 years," Smith noted of Sarah Mae Miller, his reporter from Goshen, Ind. Trying to recall how old she was when she began, he calculated, "She would have been in the eighth grade."

Eighth grade is typically the point at which schooling ends for the Amish.

The abbreviated formal education, Smith said, coupled with the use of Pennsylvania Dutch as their primary language, sometimes produces unintentional, although amusing, glitches in the stories.

One of Smith's Wayne County correspondents reported that a certain fellow "was in a Wooster hospital. He had oral surgery for a twisted bowel."

Another scribe submitted an item informing that a man "had a chimney fire Saturday evening. With the aid of the fire department it was soon out of control."

A Florida reporter, discoursing on strawberries, wrote, "I thought they were called strawberries because they are covered with straw during the winter. One farmer said he put horse manure on his strawberries but another farmer said he put sugar and cream on his."

Smith frets over what the future holds for his Amish friends.

"The sun is setting on the typical Amish settlement," he said. "The land is so expensive, they can't afford to farm it."

The younger generation is being forced to launch new settlements in obscure locations far away from the traditional Amish strongholds in Pennsylvania, Ohio and Iowa.

Smith and *The Budget* help keep them connected, if only in print.

They know whose soybeans are looking good, who held a corn husking or an apple snitzing, who couldn't make church because of illness:

Mrs. Susan Yoder was missing due to a sickness and Mrs. Anna Mae Todd, she has sciatic nerve problems which makes it hard to get around.

South Toward Home

Aug. 6, 1999

Willie Morris greeted me at his home as though I were a cherished friend from the boyhood he spent growing up on the edge of the Mississippi Delta.

In reality, we had never met.

I had wheedled his Jackson phone number from Atlanta columnist Rheta Johnson. Her generosity was based partly on her conviction that author Morris' voice would be indispensable for my 1998 series on the South 30 years after Dr. Martin Luther King Jr.'s assassination.

Johnson, aware that I would be trekking over country where black activists had been clubbed and firehosed, where civil rights workers had been slain, wanted me to know another side of Mississippi. She wanted me to know something that can't be glimpsed through a car's windshield. She knew Morris would be courtly and gracious -- even to an interloping Yankee toting a carpetbag full of stereotypes about the Deep South.

He was.

Morris had a broad face, slightly jowly, pensive in repose, impish when playful. When I arrived, he was haggling long-distance with film producers over the movie adaptation of his book *My Dog Skip*.

He knew a thing or two about how Hollywood worked. He gum-shoed filmmaker Rob Reiner during the shooting of *Ghosts of Mississippi*, then chronicled that odyssey in *The Ghosts of Medgar Evers*, his 16th book.

We chatted about *Ghosts*, a book in which he pointedly quoted a 1997 demographics report confirming that large numbers of blacks were returning to the Deep South, particularly its small towns. They watched as the northern cities in which they had once sought sanctuary became shooting galleries. Finally, they had had enough of it.

Morris was proud of his native Mississippi. Even when his career took him to Texas, then on to New York for his heady days as editor in chief of *Harper's* magazine, it was clear that his heart never was far from the Delta's fringes.

At *Harper's*, he groomed rising stars such as David Halberstam, Marshall Frady and Larry L. King, while wooing as contributing writers the likes of William Styron and Norman Mailer. He transformed the magazine from a dreary literary rag to a feisty and outspoken periodical keenly attuned to the cultural and political riptides of the 1960s.

Through it all, he remained a good ol' boy, looking sufficiently out of place at Manhattan cocktail parties that Ted Kennedy once mistook him for the bartender and ordered a scotch and soda.

Morris spent a good part of his days trying to make outsiders understand Mississippi, even during its darkest hours.

"The obsession with what outsiders think of the place," he said, "is the principal aspect of the Mississippi psyche.

"We have been America's Ireland, a violent, pessimistic land of wonderful writers and poets; a brooding landscape. It's the way people talk and drink and tell stories -- also the sense of defeat."

To have known Morris is to understand that being truly Southern is not simply a geographic claim -- any more than being truly Buddhist could be a mere religious preference. It is in the marrow, the viscera, every drawn breath.

He returned to his beloved state in 1980 to write and to teach other writers.

Now and again, he felt stirred to drive to Yazoo, where, from infancy, he was reared.

He would go to the cemetery where his parents are buried, writing of those visits, "I return here whenever I can, for there is a lot of sky here, and quiet, and its familiar stones and its last sloping hills before the coming of the Delta envelop me with stability, and help me reflect on my own life and where its mysteries have taken me. . . . William Faulkner said that perhaps after death we become 'radio waves,' and I can stand here in some preternatural stillness amid the elms and junipers and magnolias and absorb everything of these people I once knew."

When I visited Morris last year, he confided smiling, "Whether I go to heaven or hell, I'm going from Jackson."

Monday, at 64, he died of a heart attack.

That great fraternity of Southern writers has been diminished by one. Though I barely knew him, I liked him much and am saddened by his death.

Sadness, though, was not my instantaneous reaction to the news of his passing. It was more a frisson -- the sort of shudder one might feel if radio waves were palpable.

A Town in Normandy

May 24, 1994

SAINTE-MERE-EGLISE, France - With the 50th anniversary of D-Day still two weeks away, the first French town liberated by the Allied invasion of Normandy seems steadfastly determined not to be caught -- as it was a half-century ago -- running about in nightshirts in gape-mouthed surprise when the Americans drop in again.

With unhidden urgency, street workers pushing wheelbarrows of steaming road patch repair streets pocked by the winter. Painters and masonry workers add cosmetic touches to shops near the heart of the village.

From the base of the spire of the town's Catholic church, a mannequin in paratrooper garb dangles from a chute harness, the wind kicking billows in the khaki silk above. The curious display recalls the plight of the airborne trooper who had a perilous view of the predawn liberation of the town, thanks to a snared parachute.

By playing dead, the trooper not only lived to tell his story but to see a village cafe renamed for him.

Less fortunate were five men who leaped into the fog-shrouded moonlight over Normandy with Bill Dunfee, a north Columbus veteran of the 82nd Airborne Division's arrival at SainteMere-Eglise. "They were shot while in the air," Dunfee recalled. "Five of our guys were shot and killed and were hanging in the trees."

Ironically, when Dunfee jumped, his chief fear was not of being killed by the German gunners spitting tracers into the night sky but by the American C-47 pilots heading back to England after dropping their "sticks" of paratroopers.

"Hell, I look down, and there were C-47s under us," he remembered. "I was cussing and praying at the same time."

He had seen it happen before, during maneuvers two years earlier in South Carolina. Three men died when the C-47s hit them as they descended.

Dunfee landed safely, a half-mile northwest of this little town 4 miles inland. It was his third combat jump, the earlier two occurring in Italy.

Jim Bashore, a Worthington veteran of the 101st Airborne Division, was making his first jump that night.

"It was pandemonium," Bashore said. "The plane got hit just as we approached. We were losing altitude fast."

Bashore's chute barely opened before he landed in an apple orchard not far from Sainte-Mere-Eglise. It was miles from the intended landing area.

"I heard heavy footsteps," Bashore said. "I was still in my harness. I thought, boy, that's the German army. I'm going to get a bayonet in my belly any minute."

But the vigorous footfalls that he thought spelled his doom were the hoofbeats of horses startled by the sudden fracas. They were running panic-stricken through the apple trees.

Bashore and the 10 motor pool mechanics with whom he jumped had a long day ahead of them trying to fulfill their assignment of commandeering vehicles to be used by the troops soon to arrive on the beaches.

Back in Sainte-Mere-Eglise, Dunfee learned that the main concentration of German troops occupying the town was a flak unit in a park not far from the church. After a skirmish and a shooting withdrawal by the Germans, the town essentially was in American hands, Dunfee said.

"We had the town outposted by 4:30 a.m.," he said.

As dawn approached, members of the 82nd prepared to cut down their dead buddies, still hanging in the trees.

According to one account, two paratroopers had landed in the inferno of a burning building on the town square. Dunfee believes -- nay, prays -- that the two had been killed in the air before they crashed through the burning roof with grenades and other ammunition strapped to their bodies.

The volunteer bucket brigade of Sainte-Mere-Eglise citizens fighting the fire watched it all helplessly.

But Dunfee had made it in unscathed. His 22nd birthday was 10 days away.

He recalled, "My feeling was if I lived until my 22nd birthday, I'd live forever."

Before noon on D-Day, hundreds of his comrades would already have had their bitter reckoning, their bodies gently rocked at tidemark by the ebb and flow of the Atlantic.

Their names grace signposts on the roads leading into Sainte-Mere-Eglise where the tolling church bell -- once an insignificant keeper of the passing hours in an unknown town -- now resonates with the terrible weight of history.

Quoth the Ravens...

Sept. 25, 1996

Of the many curiosities that caught my eye in the 36-page catalog published for yesterday's auction of the trappings and contents of Cleveland Municipal Stadium, few intrigued me as much as Lot No. 274.

The description alongside the color photograph advertised:

Who would want this item? Plenty of people. This brown, luxury toilet comes out of the private restroom in Art Modell's office.

Someone, I am certain, is now the proud owner of the chestnut throne upon which Modell sat in his moments of deep reflection.

Seats and turnstiles, even urinals, have a price.

Accordingly, I have decided to auction off the poem which I discovered last winter at the stadium on the floor of the private restroom of the former owner.

The handwriting appears to be Modell's, and it was penned on "Go

Browns" souvenir toilet paper.

The Browns' former chief apparently intended to call his poem *The Ravens*.

Let me know if you are interested in bidding on it.

Once upon my throne a-setting, filled with woe, I squatted fretting,
As the autumn sun was setting, on Lake Erie's western shore.
Indisposed and nearly napping, suddenly I heard a tapping,
As if fate might be a-rapping, rapping on my throne-room door.
'Tis the wind and nothing more.

Ah, how clearly I remember, once again that bleak September.
Title dreams like dying embers twinkled on the bathroom floor.
"Woe is me," I cursed, boo-hooing,
"Cleveland will be my undoing Lest another town comes wooing, grovel-
ing at my bathroom door.
I'm cursed to stay forevermore."

Again resumed the beaky clamor, on my stall door like a hammer,
Pale with fright I dared to stammer,
"Who is at my chamber door?"
Weakened knees with fear were knocking, while my jellied paunch was
rocking.
"Be done with this ungodly mocking!
Tell me what you've come here for."
Quoth the raven, "Baltimore."

"Speak on," I beckoned. "You may enter.
Stand before me front and center. What business makes you my tor-
mentor?
And would you kindly close the door?"
The raven said, "The Browns are done.
You're tired of this. The town's no fun. Forget the fans.
Just cut and run.
If money's what you're living for
You need to be in Baltimore."

"How much and when?" I dared inquire.
"For money is my chief desire.
I may incur the whole town's ire, when Cleveland's Browns are never-
more."
Laughing did the bird reply, "The fans will rant and rave and cry.
Your effigy will swing from high,"
But you'll be gone forevermore
And making tons in Baltimore."

I said, "The press is sure to whine, and Dawg Pound hounds I know will
pine.

The league may censure, even fine.
`Too late,' I'll laugh. `I'm out the door.'"
"Just one request," the bird exclaimed. "The new team's sure to need a name.
To rally them to certain fame. Grant me this and nothing more."
Quoth Modell, "Forevermore."

"Tough as a Boot"

Sept. 26, 1997

BRUSH, Colo. -- "Look at his eyes," Charlie Eckhardt complained of the dog in the bed of his pickup truck.

The Queensland heeler sheepishly opened his lids to reveal a pair of orbs red-rimmed from blown dust and grit he had accumulated on the range road while hanging his head out the side of the truck.

"I've tried Visine. Everything," Eckhardt continued. "Everybody looks at his eyes and says, `Man, you got to get him off that dope.' "

A cowboy who makes his home in Estes Park when he is not on the range, Eckhardt was in northeastern Colorado herding cattle off the summer grazing lands and into the feedlots for fattening.

He works the cattle with several other hands and the help of a string of Queensland heelers.

"I've seen cattle hook those dogs and throw them in the air," Eckhardt said, nodding toward red-eyed Blue. "They're tough as a boot. They can go 10 hours on a 100- degree day without taking a drink."

As he chatted about his dog in the parking lot of the Empire Motel, another cattle truck rattled by on Rt. 34, doubtless headed for one of several feedlots.

Cattle made the town of Brush in the late 19th century. The place sits smack in the middle of the Texas-Montana cattle trail. Herds were driven north through Brush to a ford in the South Platte River on their way to the grasslands of Wyoming and Montana.

Once fattened and ready for slaughter, the herds returned to Brush to be shipped by rail to packing houses in the East.

A half-a-million head might come through a year, driven straight through the middle of town.

When the big herds were in town, the cowboys would hoist schoolchildren onto their horses, providing safe passage through the cattle to the schoolhouse and then back to their homes.

At the nearby Pinneo Feedlot, manager Joel Chisum watched a truckload of English crossbreeds debark from the back of a cattle hauler and move uneasily down a long metal chute toward a scale.

"We get cattle from as far west as California and as far north as Saskatchewan," he said, looking out over the lot where 40,000 head nosed about the feed boxes.

"Some of these cattle have traveled 1,200 miles by the time they get here," he continued, using his sorting crop to point out a gimpy steer in the isolation pen. "That one broke a leg on the trip."

Moving about through the cattle at Pinneo, pen riders sorted the steer by weight, checked for ailments and injuries, all the while whistling and hooting to move the tentative, sloe-eyed beasts along.

Sixty miles east and west of Brush are a pair of feedlots that will each soon be holding 120,000 head now that summer grazing has ended.

This is the Colorado that is a million miles removed from Boulder, Denver and Vail.

"Don't go to Boulder," Eckhardt urged his Midwest visitors. "It is the flower-sniffin', hippie (expletive) capital of the universe."

Said Chisum of the other Colorado, "When we go to Denver, I just can't imagine what all of those people in all of those buildings do to earn their feed."

In Brush, the tables of office reception areas are strewn with magazines titled *Calf News* and *Feedlot.*

When the weather is dry and the wind is blowing, the wafted dust of Brush carries the mingled pungence of cattle feed and practical fertilizer.

If anyone in Brush is looking for a town motto, it would be tough to find one more apt than, "Your Big Mac will be right up."

Back at the Empire Motel, Eckhardt was talking about the herding lifespan of dogs such as Blue.

"They'll go strong till about 11," he explained.

He had to put one down a week earlier, a heeler named Rocky who had been working cattle for 14 years.

"No one would shoot him. I had to do it. Then I cried for about an hour. We buried him on the ranch, made a little cross that said, `Rocky, the best dog that ever lived.' "

He took a long pull from his beer, looked over at Blue, and said he had to be up by 5 a.m.

Then, almost by way of apology to listeners unfamiliar with range life in the West, he frowned and said, "They get to where they can't get up and you've got to shoot them."

Wow, Mrs. Cleaver

April 19, 2000

News item: Ohio corporate titans Procter & Gamble, Nationwide and Wendy's International helped create a $700,000 fund to encourage the development of TV scripts in harmony with their collective sensibilities and tastes.

In Episode 1 of the new *Leave It to Beaver,* we find Eddie Haskell (now

21 but still obnoxious) leaning on the doorbell of the Cleaver family home. June answers the door.

June: Hi, Eddie. Come on in. Wally and the Beav will be home in a little while.

Eddie Haskell (cloyingly): Thank you, Mrs. Cleaver.

June: I've just baked some chocolate chip cookies, Eddie. Would you like one?

Eddie: Thank you, Mrs. Cleaver, but I just had a Wendy's triple with cheese, Biggie fries and a Frosty.

June: That sounds just yummy, Eddie.

Eddie: Yes, ma'am, and a bargain at twice the price. Say, Mrs. Cleaver, where is Mr. Cleaver?

June (catching her breath and steadying herself against a Swiffer dri-mop from Procter & Gamble): Wally didn't tell you, Eddie? Ward died last month.

Eddie: Wow. Bummer for you, Mrs. Cleaver.

June: It was, Eddie, until I looked in his sock drawer and found the Nationwide Best of America flexible decreasing-term life-insurance policy for $250,000. Say what you will about Ward, but he wanted his family to have that comfortable blanket of coverage for all their needs just in case he kissed the floor early.

Eddie: Gee, Mrs. Cleaver, I feel just terrible that I didn't get to the funeral to see Mr. Cleaver one last time.

June (placing a hand on Eddie's shoulder): Eddie, don't feel bad. You can still see Ward. We had him embalmed and put down in his workshop in the basement. He so loved it down there. C'mon, I'll show you.

Together they descend the steps to a dim corner where a stiff and shadowy specter rests propped against the workbench.

Eddie: Wow, Mrs. Cleaver, I thought dead people were, like, supposed to turn all green and stuff like that.

June: Oh, Eddie. How silly. Once a week, we scrub Ward down with Mr. Clean, then stick a new bar of Safeguard under each arm and sprinkle a half-bottle of Old Spice on him. A little Crest for that smile, and voila.

Eddie: Do you mean the Crest that has been proved to be an effective decay-preventive dentifrice when used in a conscientiously applied program of regular oral hygiene and professional dental care?

June: That's the one, Eddie. And with Fixodent, that smile will stay just where it is forever.

Eddie: I'll bet you still miss him, though, Mrs. Cleaver.

June (slipping an arm around Eddie's waist): Sure, Eddie, there are some things I miss.

Eddie: Probably like those times when you'd always say, "Ward, I'm worried about the Beav," huh, Mrs. Cleaver?

June (raking her fingernails across Eddie's stomach): Cut the crap, Eddie. You think I didn't get the message all those times you said, "Gee, Mrs. Cleaver, what a nice dress"? You think I liked wearing that cocktail dress to make tuna-noodle casseroles? Do you know how hot all that crinoline can be? Did you think Ward was some kind of Prince Charming? Eddie, look at me! Ward never took those sock garters off. Never.

Eddie, it's you I've been waiting for all these years. There's a place for us, Eddie -- you, me. Life's short, Eddie, and the world's cruel, but there's a place where people don't stare or talk and they're always happy to see you.

Eddie: You mean, like, Wendy's, Mrs. Cleaver.

June: Whatever, Eddie. Kiss me -- now, Eddie. I've been lonely so long.

Eddie: Wow, Mrs. Cleaver, I'd like to, but I've got a cold, and Mom says.

June: Shut up, Eddie. I know what that cold needs. Here, this is Vicks VapoRub, from Procter & Gamble's fine family of products. Unbutton your shirt.

Eddie (obliging her request): Gee, Mrs. Cleaver, that kind of tickles.

June: Oh, God, Eddie.

The two hear footsteps on the stairs.

Wally (from upstairs): See if Mom's down there, Beav. I'll get us some cookies.

Beav: Gee, Wally, I think you better come down here.

Wally: What's goin' on, Beav?

Beav: I don't know, Wally, but it looks pretty creepy.

June (smoothing her dress as Eddie buttons his shirt): Hi, boys. What a surprise. I was just helping Eddie with his, uh, cold. Isn't that right, Eddie?

Eddie: Yes, Mrs. Cleaver. That sure was some nice VapoRub, Mrs. Cleaver.

June (whispering): Midnight tonight. Next to the drive-through at Wendy's.

Eddie (swallowing hard): Sure, Mrs. Cleaver. I'll be there.

On Fathers

June 20, 1999

I didn't need a rocket scientist to explain fatherhood to me, though recently one did so.

It was when I was in West Virginia to interview former NASA engineer Homer Hickam Jr. The story of his youth and his relationship with his father are told in his autobiography, *Rocket Boys*, and portrayed in the film adaptation *October Sky*.

Early in the interview, Hickam asked what most had intrigued me about his story. I brushed aside the question with a lame answer about the familial common denominator of coal mining.

Although it wasn't a lie, neither was it the whole truth. I wanted to know about his father.

Hickam's late father and mine were alike in many ways. Stern and distant, they could be stingy with both approval and affection. They didn't mean to be. Men whose early lives were tempered by the Great Depression or World War II or both often turned out that way.

They weren't huggers; they were providers. Fathering wasn't an art; it was a job.

Life at home was not a democracy. It was a dictatorship -- a benevolent one when the fates smiled, tyrannical when they did not.

Fathers of the baby boom were laughably misrepresented by the popular culture of the era. As a child, I studied the warm, wise and avuncular Robert Anderson of *Father Knows Best* with as much bafflement as envy. The bumblingly, good-natured Ozzie Nelson was amusing, though nothing like any of the fathers I knew.

"We weren't big friends," Hickam said of his father.

In *October Sky*, Chris Cooper portrays Hickam's dad. An intense and gifted actor, Cooper asked to borrow something that had once belonged to Hickam's father to help him feel the part. The actor was loaned a watch, a masonic ring and the elder Hickam's lucky silver dollar.

Fathers of Hickam's generation and mine didn't leave diaries or journals to help their offspring understand who they were and why.

They left things.

Hickam got a watch, a ring, a coin. I got a battered old banjo and a tie clip.

We hung onto these things, these talismen. We treated them with a certain reverence and awe, perhaps because they were special to our fathers in a way we weren't always certain we were.

Throughout the *Rocket Boys* narrative one thing is clear: While Hickam is drawn toward rocketry by curiosity, he also is determined to master the field to win his father's elusive approval.

In a scene in the book's last chapter, his father finally shows up at the slag dump where his son and the other rocket boys have been launching their inventions. Young Homer offers his father the chance to throw the switch that will send skyward their last and best effort.

Of that moment, Hickam wrote:

"As AukXXXI raced across the sunlit sky on that glorious day, I instead watched my dad, and waited patiently, and with hope, for him to put his arm around my shoulder and tell me, at last, that I had done something good."

Instead, his father, seized by a coughing fit (the tribute exacted by a life in the mines) was doubled over gasping for breath.

"I went to him and put my arm around his shoulder, supporting him while he fought for air," Hickam wrote. "'You did good, Dad,' I told him as a spasm of deep, oily coughs racked his body."

Black lung disease claimed Hickam's father in 1989. My father had died 11 years earlier.

"The Gypsies say you have to dig a deep grave to bury your daddy," I ventured to Hickam, drawing on a proverb I've worn smooth from handling.

"Dad and I made our peace," he responded.

I suppose I have made mine, too.

Sometimes, though, I wonder -- when Father's Day rolls around -- why there had to be a war.

Hank Williams Last Stop

June 14, 1999

OAK HILL, W.Va. -- The woman behind the counter at the town library said she couldn't recall precisely when the small memorial to Hank Williams was erected just outside her front door. Could have been five years, maybe seven.

From the shelf over her shoulder, she fetched a box of clippings about Williams and a pair of histories of Oak Hill.

The box yielded slim pickings on Williams' life.

The Oak Hill histories chronicled murders and robberies, a locomotive explosion, an attempt by the jilted lover of the widow Basham to blow her to kingdom come by planting dynamite on the sill of her bedroom window. But neither of the volumes mentioned that country music's greatest legend died in the little town the librarian calls home.

Maybe you know the story.

Williams was on his way to Canton to play a concert New Year's Day 1953.

He had left Knoxville, Tenn., the night before in a cloud of vodka, morphine and chloral hydrate, his 17-year-old chauffeur winding through West Virginia at the wheel of the country star's Cadillac convertible.

They had stopped at Bluefield, W.Va., for beer and sandwiches in the predawn, then Williams had fallen asleep in the back seat.

It was 5:30 a.m., New Year's Day, when Charles Carr, Williams' driver, pulled the Cadillac to a halt across from the Pure Oil sign in Oak Hill. He reached around to let the singer know he was stopping for directions, but Williams' hand was cold.

Chet Flippo, the singer's biographer, said Pete Burdette, who ran the Pure Oil station, summoned police who removed from Williams' fist a note that read, "We met, we lived and dear we loved, then comes that fatal day, the love that felt so dear fades far away. Tonight love hathe one alone and lonesome, all that I could sing, I you . . . still and always will, but that's the poison we have to pay."

Was the note to Audrey, the wife who had finally had enough of Williams and filed for divorce? Was it for Billie Jean, the woman he had recently married, friends said, to spite Audrey? Cryptic and disjointed, it might have been the fumblings for a lyric that would never be finished.

Just before he left on his final ride, Williams told Billie Jean, "Every time I close my eyes I see God coming down the road after me. Jesus has told me that I'm gonna die."

He was 29.

Longtime Oak Hill funeral director Joe Tyree recalled the hours after Williams' death: "The pathologist over at Beckley came over and did the autopsy at our funeral home."

The name Hank Williams hardly registered with Tyree when he picked up the body.

"Country music didn't mean anything to me," he conceded, allowing that he might have heard Williams sing a time or two on the radio when he was out on a midnight call in the funeral home ambulance.

Williams' mother flew in from Montgomery, Ala.

"She wanted a silver casket," Tyree said. She selected, from the stage clothes packed in the Cadillac, a suit for her son to be buried in.

Tyree and an assistant loaded the silver casket into the hearse and began the long drive south.

"It rained all night," he said.

When they stopped for gas, locals spotting the hearse and the West Virginia tags were immediately curious.

"They'd ask if we were taking Hank back," Tyree recalled.

Over the years, Williams' fans have trickled through Oak Hill. They snap photos of the former Pure Oil station, now a car lot.

A few years ago, when Hank's daughter Jett Williams was performing at the county fair, she asked to see Tyree.

"We visited about an hour," he said. She just wanted to know about the end. Her father had seen God coming for him, and she wanted to know something about the place on the darkened winter road where the premonition came true.

The Man Who Knew Ernie Pyle

April 23, 1995

DANA, Ind. - The doctors back in Texas gave Riley "Mack" Tidwell the bad news about his cancer less than two weeks after he promised to make the 1,500-mile trek to western Indiana to pay tribute to Ernie Pyle on the 50th anniversary of the Hoosier journalist's death.

The rangy, rawboned Texan, unbowed by a lifetime of wrestling an 18-wheeler cross-country, swallowed the ugly prognosis, pulled himself up to his full 6 feet 5 inches and calmly demanded, "Y'all fix me up so I can go to Indiana."

He later explained, "Whatever I could say or do to help Ernie, I wanted to do it."

Tidwell was a private first class with Texas' 36th Infantry Division in the mountains of Italy on the December day in 1943 when he first laid eyes on Pyle.

It was one of the most anguished days that Tidwell would face, a day whose aftermath would be chronicled by Ernie Pyle and recalled by home-front newspaper readers as stirring the saddest combat dispatch filed during the conflict.

Tidwell had just lost his company commander, a captain named Henry T. Waskow.

If men in combat could know the minute of their death, they might approach it with brave utterances that ring with the resonance of immortality.

Waskow was talking about pop-up toasters when the shells began exploding. He thought he might get one when the war ended, having wearied of burning bread slices skewered on a straightened coat hanger atop a Coleman stove.

"We were being shelled pretty heavy," Tidwell said. "The captain yelled, 'Get down!' He pushed me and the first sergeant to the ground. He pushed us down, and that probably saved our lives. He got hit and killed just like that.

"It was like taking my daddy away from me."

A radioman and runner for his company, Tidwell was ordered to take the news to the battalion commander.

The senior officer acknowledged the grim dispatch, then ordered Tidwell, whose painful feet were swaddled in gauze from an advanced case of trench foot, to go down the mountain to a medical aid station.

Pyle was there when Tidwell gingerly entered.

"He was a little fella with a satchel over his shoulder," Tidwell recalled. "I didn't know Ernie from anyone."

The Hoosier columnist tried to comfort the lanky, 19-year-old Texan as they sat in the cowshed-turned-triage.

"I kept talking," Tidwell said. "He asked me when they would be bringing the captain down."

Two days passed; the fighting remained too intense to remove the dead from the side of the mountain.

On the third night, Tidwell took matters into his own hands, stealing a mule tied up in a nearby olive grove and -- walking on his heels to stave off the pain -- heading up the mountain.

He found the body in the darkness, draped it over the mule's back and headed back down. He had made it only a little way when a German shell exploded nearby, peppering him with shrapnel; bleeding from the temple and from his arm and back, he trudged on.

"Somebody said, 'Here comes Riley,' " he remembered. "They laid the captain down, and everybody from that cowshed spoke to him. I knelt down and straightened up his shirt collar and uniform."

Tidwell did not know how far and wide the story of those final, tender mercies would spread until he returned to the States in late 1944.

"I'm no hero," he tried to tell people, but folks from Ed Sullivan's radio show were calling.

He was asked to appear at a war-bond drive in the nation's capital with Dinah Shore and Burgess Meredith, the actor who portrayed Ernie Pyle in the film The Story of G.I. Joe.

He obliged a request to travel across Texas with Robert Mitchum, the actor who played Waskow.

After a while, Tidwell's life quieted down: He put away his Bronze Star medal and Purple Heart, and reared a family, drove a truck. Now and then, a journalist would show up to poke around scars visible and otherwise.

In Dana, on the 50th anniversary of the April day in 1945 when a

Japanese sniper killed Ernie Pyle, Riley Tidwell took a seat on a platform reserved for friends and associates of the journalist.

There, among the likes of actor William Windom (who portrays Pyle in a one-man stage production) and Andy Rooney (who served as a fellow war correspondent), Tidwell looked out on the faces of scores of his former brothers in arms, veterans who had traveled to Indiana from around the United States.

Rooney recalled sharing a tent with Pyle, remembered his bartering rations with French farmers to obtain enough butter and eggs to cook breakfast for his fellow scribes.

One by one, the honored guests summoned up anecdotes as a rambunctious prairie wind snapped at the flaps of a tent spread in front of Ernie's modest birthplace and the adjoining visitors center.

The listeners that morning had jammed the two-lane road leading into Dana, swelling the town of 600 to 10 times that number, according to more than one crowd estimate.

A Cleveland veteran named Louis Pastor had traveled to Dana to recall the man he had seen die on the island of le Shima on April 18, 1945.

Through his binoculars on that fateful day, he had watched a jeep in which Pyle was riding approach along a jungle trail and seen the driver and war correspondent bail out when a sniper opened fire.

Pyle might have lived if he had not raised his head to look around.

Near the end of the ceremonies beneath the tent, Windom read the column about the death of Waskow, then introduced the Texan who had carried the captain from the mountain.

Tidwell had heard the column read dozens of times before.

"He was my father, my best friend," he had said of Waskow a day earlier. "He would not ask you to go anywhere or do anything he wouldn't do himself."

At the commemoration, having already listened to the echo of taps, Tidwell was being crowded tight in the turns by intimations of his mortality.

"This may be the last one," he conceded only hours before the events honoring Pyle. "It's in my liver. They're feeding me through my stomach."

"Six months," said Tidwell's son, Mark, echoing the doctor's prognosis.

"I came here to talk of Ernie Pyle," Tidwell managed to say before his voice caught. "I can't."

He asked God to bless the old soldiers who had gathered in Pyle's memory, reached for a hankie to staunch memories too heavy to contain and quietly returned to his seat.

Afterward, the news crews from distant cities piled into their trucks and headed off; the veterans sat down to a dinner of chicken and noodles at the Dana firehouse or browsed at an antiques sale that didn't seem to have much to do with Ernie Pyle Day.

Tidwell, eventually taking his leave of the day's commemoration in strides the length of a yardstick, prepared for his return to the inn where he and his son were staying.

A bronze plaque outside the Ernie Pyle Visitors Center embraces a quotation from the columnist on the random cruelty of war: "They died and others lived and nobody knows why it is so."

Not far away, a flag, lowered to half-staff, snapped and popped in the cold, unrelenting wind.

The chill in the air, though, had nothing to do with the chill against which Riley Tidwell was bracing himself.

Homage to a Knave

April 24, 1995

Old soldiers never die; they just fade away.

Old defense secretaries? Well, they write books.

Robert Strange McNamara, JFK's and LBJ's secretary of defense, has penned a ponderous apology for the Vietnam War that Random House is selling at $13.75 a pound (for 2 pounds).

You remember McNamara: horn-rimmed glasses, hair slicked back with automatic transmission fluid.

A quarter-century ago in Da Nang, we were certain he had sent us to Vietnam because we had made fun of him while he was president of the high-school science club.

These days, he admits that the course he helped Presidents Johnson and Kennedy chart for the Vietnam War was simply "wrong, terribly wrong."

There's something about an aging Harvard MBA in a hair shirt with a vinyl penholder that looks a little ridiculous.

The title of the book is *In Retrospect*.

Because titles aren't protected by copyrights, though, McNamara could have recycled *Dumb and Dumber*, thus employing a more apt title and borrowing a bit of the limelight from a more thought-provoking work.

His list of the "11 major causes of the disaster in Vietnam" is laughably pedantic, if only because it proves that even his ghostwriter couldn't stop him from making parts of the book read like a science-fair outline.

McNamara insists on telling us that enemy strength was miscalculated, South Vietnam's will overestimated and foreign policy flawed.

Guess what? We already knew.

We were the ones who wrote the graffiti on the outhouse walls: "Would the last Marine to leave Vietnam please turn out the light at the end of the tunnel?"

We were the ones who made self-mocking gallows humor of the "Saigon Follies" -- the press briefings -- by mimicking their unintended similarity to TV weather reports: "Casualties were light to moderate, with some gusting in outlying areas."

McNamara comes off looking like a guy who, on the 20th anniversary of his divorce, finally decides to tell his ex-wife (who already knew) that for most of their last years together he was having an affair with a topless dancer. Only McNamara decides to come clean by writing a $27.50 hardback, selling excerpts to *Newsweek*, cadging interviews from anyone who will listen and -- who knows? -- maybe even landing on *The Oprah Winfrey Show*.

So why didn't McNamara go public with the guilt besetting him when he resigned in February 1968 at the moment when the North was revealing, with its Tet Offensive, just how wrong Washington's best and brightest had been at estimating enemy strength?

"I believe that would have been a violation of my responsibility to the president and my oath to uphold the Constitution," McNamara says in defense.

That doesn't wash.

A half-million Americans were in Vietnam fighting for their lives in that awful early spring of 1968 and also feeling duty-bound to their commander in chief, having sworn an oath to uphold the Constitution. If they had refused to continue with their part in the dreadful fiasco, they would have invited courts-martial.

McNamara risked only estrangement from a circle of policy makers who had already proved themselves a "confederacy of dunces." Indeed, by speaking out today, he might even be remembered as a man of conviction.

He is simply telling America -- and for a price -- that he was one of the architects of foreign-policy decisions who knew early on that grievous miscalculations had sealed the fate of tens of thousands of innocent hod carriers. Worse, he kept silent.

He is extorting money for a literary act of contrition that Arthur Schlesinger Jr. describes in a book-jacket blurb as "brave, honest, honorable."

Shame on you, Arthur: Robert Strange McNamara's name is not among the Vietnam conflict's 58,191 participants who earned -- the hard way -- the words of homage you pay a knave.

Lipstick on a Headstone

Oct. 30, 1996

FAIRMOUNT, Ind. -- "I take it you saw the lipstick on the headstone," Brad Sweat ventured, spading the last few clods of dirt onto a fresh mound 20 yards from James Dean's grave.

"They kiss the headstone, leave him cigarettes, beer," Sweat's gravedigging partner, Phil Seward, said of the visitors to Park Cemetery, where Fairmount's most famous son lies.

The noon sun had cut through a light morning haze. The day was cool and dry. Along the road to Fairmount, farmers were out on combines finishing their work among parchment-like stalks of corn.

It had been a day not unlike this when Dean was buried. The mourners and the press spilled out of the small sanctuary at Friends Church.

The Fairmount News, front page edged in black, ran a photo of Dean in his Fairmount Quakers high school basketball uniform. The accompanying story recalled that during the sectional tournament in 1949, the senior guard had lofted a last-second basket to beat Gas City, 39-37.

When Dean was 12, he had written a ponderous essay titled, "My Career as a Farmer." An unabashed paean to the agrarian life, it outlined his plans to work the billiard-table plain of central Indiana, just as his Uncle Marcus had.

This world's James Deans are always outgrowing places such as Fairmount.

Dean won a few medals in speaking contests sponsored by the local Women's Christian Temperance Union, played the monster in a Fairmount High production of *Frankenstein*.

From then on, it was clear that he would never be content to watch the world go by from atop a John Deere.

"It's a boring drive any way you cut it," the desk clerk at a West Lafayette hotel had warned me when I told her I was heading over to see Dean's grave.

She was right.

Sprawling brown fields run to the horizon, broken but occasionally by a farmhouse, a grain elevator, a windbreak of trees.

The central irony of such vastness has always been its capacity to make one feel confined.

I passed a hamlet so tiny the funeral home doubles as a furniture store. I passed up a chance to swing through Kokomo and gaze upon "the world's largest tree stump." A hand-lettered sign flanking the two-lane road beckoned me to try ostrich meat: "Looks and tastes just like beef."

So this is what Dean left behind when he outgrew the essay he wrote at 12.

Page 2 of *The Fairmount News* memorial edition offers the reader all he needs to know of the life that awaited Dean had he stayed on his uncle's farm.

There is an ad for a 1-cent sale at Rexall, a photo of auctioneer and real-estate broker Everett E. Corn, a recommendation to try Purina Pig Startena, "a partner to help you make more money from hogs."

In the gossip column, titled "U and I," I learn that Hude Dyson and his wife were back in town from Steubenville, Ohio. Bethel Friends Church had acquired a new bench and four folding chairs for the choir.

"U and I" columnist Mary Ward observed, "While talking on the phone taking news, a little brown bird with a yellow breast kept hopping up and down in the maple tree. Guess he was having a buggy lunch."

Such stuff tends to have a mitigating effect on long-held and unflattering appraisals of Charles Starkweather.

Rural central Indiana could be a dangerous place in the dead of a January night if the cable ever went out.

I was wondering whether anything exciting had happened in Fairmount since James Dean when the woman who runs the historical museum hauled out photographs documenting the theft of the actor's headstone a dozen years ago.

Pranksters made off with the marker, then deposited it out in the far reaches of the county on a tree stump.

It wasn't the world's largest tree stump, but it was impressive.

The Other Columbus

July 7, 1997

COLUMBUS, N.M. -- This town may not be the end of the world, but you can see it from here.

A withering sun blanches a hodgepodge assemblage of manufactured housing and whitewashed cinder-block abodes. The only sign of life is an occasional passing car or a dust devil meandering across the flats outside town.

Blame it on Pancho Villa.

His name is invoked by locals as mitigating testimony among the "ifs" and "buts" that pepper the story of why a wildly thriving, turn-of-the-century border town never became the bustling metropolis promise and fortune once suggested.

The local museum, dominated by artifacts and photos of the town's singular national distinction, is housed in a former railway depot given to the people of Columbus by Southern Pacific in 1963 when it pulled up its tracks on the way out of town.

Its keeper, 69-year-old Angel Borunda, was born in a long-vanished house once situated halfway between the two water tanks near Columbus' main crossroads.

Borunda's father worked for the village's most thriving merchant, a fellow named Sam Ravel.

"My father used to go across the border and bring back coyote and bobcat pelts," he said. "They were very much in demand. Ravel shipped them all the way to St. Louis."

As was typical of merchants on the West's outer fringes, Ravel sold a little bit of everything. His best customer for weapons and cartridges was the Mexican revolutionary Villa.

In the autumn of 1915, Villa had been on the brink of a stunning victory over the troops of the Mexican Carranza government at Agua Priete when he was submarined by President Woodrow Wilson.

Not only did Wilson deal a blow to Villa by recognizing the Carranza government, he permitted Carranza to reinforce his embattled soldiers by allowing the shipment of troops and artillery across U.S. territory.

The move saved the day for Carranza at Agua Priete. An angry Villa led the remnants of his guerrillas up into the Chihuahua Mountains to regroup.

Low on arms and ammunition in the early spring of 1916, Villa sent one of his generals to Columbus to gather supplies. Villa had several hundred dollars credit at Ravel's store, though when Gen. Candelario Cervantes showed up to redeem that credit for rifles and cartridges, he was unceremoniously shown the door.

"Villa had already paid for the weapons," Borunda explained, "but Wilson had put a stop to selling guns and ammunition to Villa."

Smarting from this affront, Villa ordered 500 men to their mounts and began a trek out of the Chihuahuas, aiming to settle the score in Columbus.

He knew that 500 men of the U.S. Army's 13th Cavalry were posted at Columbus, but he believed that if he crossed the border at midnight he could take them and the town by surprise.

One of the first to fall was a private named Fred Griffin, whose bad fortune it was to have pulled guard duty that night.

"Who goes there?" he demanded, giving a voice and target to Villa's horsemen, who quickly shot him dead to cries of "Viva Mexico!"

The Villistas looted Sam Ravel's store and likely would have killed the owner had he not been out of town.

Villa's raiders stormed the Commercial Hotel and torched it, killing one of its guests and sparing a second only after he produced a checkbook and nervously began writing personal checks to several Villistas.

Rousted by the sound of gunfire, the 13th Cavalry stormed out of its garrison and opened fire.

"In all," said Borunda, "from the U.S. side, 19 soldiers and civilians died. Villa lost about 100 men."

The main commercial block of Columbus was burned to the ground.

Villa's dead raiders (and at least one who, though wounded, was still living) were thrown in a pile and cremated.

Villa retreated, having lost most of the booty he had captured from Ravel's store in the confusion of the 13th's counterattack.

The last raid on continental U.S. soil by a foreign military force had ended.

Within a week, Gen. "Black Jack" Pershing would lead 10,000 U.S. troops into Mexico in pursuit of Villa.

A $5,000 bounty on his head, the elusive Villa would escape Pershing's men only to die at the hands of his own people seven years after his attack on Columbus.

A dying Villa, his dreams of ruling Mexico thwarted, is said to have uttered, "Don't let it end like this. Tell them I said something."

Columbus was never the same. A population of 700 gradually dwindled to a third that number.

The same year the Southern Pacific closed the rail line, a new state park opened in the center of town.

A forgiving New Mexico state legislature christened it Pancho Villa State Park, and the aging widow of the former revolutionary came to Columbus from Mexico to cut the ribbon.

Borunda, whose Uncle Faustino had ridden with Villa, remembers it well.

By then, the raid was more than a half-century behind Columbus, and the only thing more distantly feeble and indistinct to the town was the future it once had.

Mass on a Turnpike

Sept. 12, 1997

NEW BALTIMORE, Pa. -- The Catholic church on the Pennsylvania Turnpike pounces into the windshield vista of passing motorists like a divine mirage induced by white-line hypnosis.

A pair of signs on the edge of the east- and westbound berms list Mass times. Concrete stairs lead up from the roadway to St. John's Church.

At first blush, the notion of Mass on the turnpike seems a little bizarre, like seeing John Paul II hunched over the wheel of a Greyhound.

Along the vast expanse of what Pennsylvania boasts is "America's first superhighway" are dozens of exits and service plazas where travelers can fill gas tanks and bellies. St. John's is the only legal pulloff for Mass or confession.

The first Catholic church built in New Baltimore opened to the faithful less than 50 years after the Declaration of Independence was signed.

The present St. John's, in which road-haggard tourists kneel and truckers make confession, is 107 years old.

Though Pennsylvania's highways are littered with scores of markers detailing famous military victories and defeats, the turnpike Mass signs at St. John's are the only indication of who won the Battle of New Baltimore, when the Pennsylvania Turnpike Commission foolishly tried to take on the Catholic Church.

When divine right and eminent domain collided as the turnpike was being built during the Great Depression, former St. John's pastor the Rev. Sebastian Urnauer proved a worthy adversary.

The Rev. Mark Begly, the current pastor, explained, "Father Sebastian made a deal with the state -- he would give them the land if they would create a permanent access to the church from the turnpike."

According to one historical account, that deal made St. John's the only church with private access on any toll road in the United States.

Not only was Father Sebastian able to wrangle a stairway-to-heaven ingress for roadbound Catholics, he also persuaded the state to give over 49 acres of its right of way so cattle belonging to the church could graze it.

At the time, the rural complex that was St. John's included a Carmelite monastery and a working farm.

Brown-robed novices could once be seen hoeing pole beans and herding cattle on the 60-acre farm, while silently contemplating their spiritual readiness to take vows of poverty, chastity and obedience.

The commerce of the secular world roared by only yards away. Yet these men, most only 19 years old, had disconnected their lives from it. They could not receive visitors and were permitted to write only one letter a month.

When the Carmelites closed the monastery in 1968, they left a pair of priests to continue serving turnpike travelers as well as the 250 area families who belong to St. John's parish.

A placid retreat from a roadway annually traversed by 123 million vehicles, the sanctuary of St. John's is never locked.

East of the church, the land rises slightly where cedars look down on 19th-century headstones. Time and the elements have done their best to obliterate the old epitaphs, though a few choice ones remain:

Dear friends who live to mourn and weep,
Behold the tomb wherein I sleep.
Prepare to come for you must die.
And be entombed as well as I.

The greatest number of worshipers climb the roadside stairs to Mass in the summer.

Some of those who stop are merely curious, Begly said.

They peek into the church, nose around the cemetery, lounge on a park bench near a small outdoor shrine enclosing a statue of the Blessed Virgin and a pair of praying children.

The place is a monument to the insight of Father Sebastian, a man who knew that with a pair of well-placed signs and stairs he could accomplish as much as the lights on the road to Damascus.

The Man Who Loved O. Henry

May 15, 1998

The man who loved O. Henry was almost 40 before he discovered the American short-story writer.

He had come from a country with a strong oral tradition, where the keepers of stories were the griots, roving troubadours who had memorized epic poems about the gallant deeds of warriors past.

It might have been difficult for him to have found a collection of O. Henry's works anywhere in his native land on Africa's northwest coast. For decades, only one adult in 10 there could read and write, and more than half of the children old enough did not attend elementary school.

His people had languished under the thumb of one European ruler or another for centuries: the Portuguese, the Dutch, finally the French. Traders robbed the country of its ivory and gold and took its people as slaves.

Today, the economy is based precariously upon agricultural production -- millet, peanuts and cotton. Not uncommonly, drought wipes out much of that.

So the man came to the United States to make something of his life and -- though he was unaware when he arrived -- to fall in love with O. Henry.

Sister Rebecca Costello, a teacher at the Dominican Learning Center, introduced the man to the short-story master who had perfected his narrative skills behind the walls of the Ohio Penitentiary while serving a stretch for embezzlement.

"He was trying to get a GED," Costello said of her student. "I tutored him one-on-one."

She quickly discovered that he was conversant in French, Arabic and English.

What he needed were the reading comprehension and math skills to take the high-school equivalency test.

Making the trip two days a week to the learning center, he sailed through the math portion of his curriculum.

"I was able to take him from a third-grade level clear up to algebra and geometry," Costello marveled.

But those odd and enchanting little vignettes by William Sydney Porter -- stories such as "The Last Leaf" and "The Gift of the Magi" -- were what spellbound him.

"He loved the O. Henry stories with surprise endings," his teacher noted. "He would roll his eyes and say, `Ohhhhhhhhh!' and he would understand."

Though the stories were set in another era, he could identify with the lives of everyday folk in New York City trying to get by. He had been one of them when he first came to the United States.

"In New York, he was a vendor for a while," Costello said.

He moved to Columbus five years ago to get away from the crime.

In the reading assignments at the learning center, O. Henry shared the stage with Aesop.

"These fables," the sister told the man, "when you are married and have children, you can read these stories to your children, because they have a moral."

In a small way, he worshipped Sister Costello.

"He gave me a gold vase," she said. "A candelabra. When my brother died, he brought me a beautiful bouquet of flowers. He said, `Oh, Sister, I am so sorry you lost your brother. This is just a little gift to make you feel better.' "

He was a Muslim, his teacher a Catholic, but he made it a point to know the holidays and holy days of her faith so he could call and wish her well on each of them.

Not long ago, during a tutoring session, he told Costello, "I have a beautiful wife. I am going to bring her here in July."

"He showed me her picture," Costello said. "Beautiful.

"His last assignment, I gave Monday, was to write me a couple paragraphs describing his wife to me."

A day later, he was dead, murdered by a man who, it appears, had summoned a taxi solely for the purpose of robbing its driver.

Mamadou Ndiath -- the man who fled New York's crime looking for peace and quiet in Columbus, the man who loved O. Henry -- will go home now, to the red-sand plains of his native Senegal.

Irony's cruel twists engage us only in fiction. In life, they make us sick at heart.

Orphan No. EE18: Parents Unknown

Oct. 11, 1998

HIEP BINH, Vietnam - Mrs. Chau, who runs the grocery in the heart of the town's old quarter, studied the letter and the picture for several seconds, saying nothing.

Slowly, the perplexity wrought on her broad, smooth-featured face gave way to a look of congenial sympathy the kind one might extend to a lost motorist or an ugly suitor.

"There were many soldiers here then," she began, her eyes beseeching our guide and interpreter, Mr. Tu, for his assistance in negotiating propriety's tricky shoals.

"Many," the guide picked up. He said the sprawling Song Than army base of the South Vietnamese pressed against the western outskirts of Hiep Binh. Soldiers and women from town fell in love. Babies were born.

"Some of the parents were poor, very poor," he continued. "They could not afford to raise these children."

So, perhaps, it was with Annie.

Annie was born five months before North Vietnamese tanks rolled unimpeded through her native Hiep Binh on their way to nearby Saigon. Her mother named her Thanh Tuyen.

She was taken to the Catholic orphanage at Vinh Long the day after Christmas 1974. A month before, in the Columbus offices of Catholic Social Services, my former wife, Suzanne, and I had begun the paperwork to adopt a South Vietnamese orphan. We had no idea who our child might be. It was pure coincidence that we filed our application the week Thanh Tuyen was born.

The caseworker cautioned that the process would take at least two years.

We nodded our understanding. Our oldest biological son was 4, our youngest, 2 months.

It would not take two years. Oddly, the move that changed everything was made not by U.S. adoption agencies, but by the high military command in Hanoi.

In late 1974, orders went out to the jungle base camps of the Viet Cong and the North Vietnamese army. They were told to launch a final offensive to rout the South Vietnamese army and topple the precarious government in Saigon.

"Mr. Tu," I ventured, "is it possible that there are elders or local officials from before the fall who might remember something?"

Mrs. Chau shook her head. When the end was in sight, most of those with ties to the old government fled. Some went to the United States. Some were sent to re-education camps or were resettled in rural areas to work the rice fields as the communists implemented collectivization of agricultural lands.

Mrs. Chau agreed to take a handful of the photocopied letters seeking information on my adopted daughter, perhaps more as a gesture to placate a blank-faced American stranger than because she thought townsfolk might know anything.

At a small outdoor cafe down the road, proprietor Nguyen Van Chac, 46, read the letter.

He was 23 when my daughter was born. The town has changed. Refugees seeking a better life closer to Ho Chi Minh City have swelled the population to 50,000.

"It will be very difficult these days," he said. Still, he promised to show the letter to patrons of his cafe. "Maybe her father was an American soldier?"

Possible, but not likely. Only a skeletal U.S. military presence existed when Thanh Tuyen was conceived.

Mr. Tu and I handed the letter to anyone who would take a copy; a stooped and elderly woman, her face half-hidden beneath the ubiquitous, conical *non la*; a lottery vendor, who refused to accept it until we purchased a ticket for the day's $1,800 drawing.

We had learned, before traveling to Hiep Binh, that the orphanage closed shortly after the new government assumed power. The Catholic sisters, who operated many of the orphanages in the South, either were expelled or forced to return to their motherhouse.

The nuns had processed the court paperwork on Thanh Tuyen and photographed her in the first few months of 1975.

The situation was desperate then. The orphanage was brimming with children.

World Airways president Ed Daly, who had volunteered his commercial jetliners to assist with evacuation, hatched a plan to shuttle orphans out of the country to waiting families in the United States.

Daly was viewed by some as a grandstanding publicity hound, though the White House quickly realized that his plan offered a compelling humanitarian diversion to counter public bitterness at home surrounding the imminent collapse of South Vietnam.

Stealing Daly's thunder, the U.S. government launched Operation Babylift.

Adoption agencies quickly alerted families that the anticipated two-year wait had been compressed to two weeks.

Thanh Tuyen was scheduled to be on one of the first planes out.

On April 4, 1975, an Air Force C-5A Galaxy was loaded with 243 children at Tan Son Nhut airport in Saigon. Many of the five dozen caregivers who accompanied the children were women employees of the U.S. Defense Attache's Office. The office had been attempting to evacuate the employees as the situation deteriorated around the capital.

The plane scarcely was airborne before the pilot radioed the tower that he was in trouble.

A pressurized door in the aft section had exploded. As the pilot made a, beeline for Tan Son Nhut, many of the orphans strapped into seats in the craft's suddenly depressurized lower level died of lack of oxygen. Others were sucked out the open rear hatch.

Unable to keep the plane aloft, the pilot tried to bring it in on its belly in a rice field.

Two reports of the crash agree that as the wreckage settled in the rice paddy, water rushing into the fuselage drowned dozens of orphans.

Two witnesses to the rescue efforts recalled that infants were so covered with mud that nurses were passing them under a shower near a triage unit, announcing simply, "This one's alive" or "This one's dead."

Only 43 children and one of the Defense Attache's Office evacuees survived.

In Columbus, the telephone rang.

"I don't want to alarm you," adoption caseworker Dorothy Benning said, "but there has been a plane crash near Saigon and we don't know whether your child was on the flight manifest."

For 36 hours, we waited, watching the heartbreaking news footage of the crash, hearing nothing.

A South Vietnamese official, quoted later in *The Fall of the South*, reportedly remarked only hours after the crash, "It's good that the American people are taking the children. They are good souvenirs, like the ceramic elephants you like so much. It is too bad that some of them broke today, but don't worry, we have many more."

In the end, we would hear two different stories of why our Thanh Tuyen hadn't made it aboard the ill-fated flight.

One suggested that a handful of high-ranking South Vietnamese government officials had bumped a number of orphans from the flight so they could evacuate their own children. Another indicated that Thanh Tuyen had developed a middle-ear infection, and a decision had been made to keep her at the orphanage for treatment.

Whatever the case, she was flown out of Vietnam on April 8. By the time she reached San Francisco, a few days later, she had spinal meningitis.

"She's a very sick little girl," we were told by a doctor at the bay area's Letterman Army Hospital. Her condition was listed as critical.

Outside the cafe in Hiep Binh, a street vendor selling baguettes studied snapshots of the child born in her hometown and designated "Orphan No. EE18."

She promised to ask older family members whether they could recall anything, and took my address in Ohio.

Mr. Tu, sensing my gloom, was momentarily silent as we stood on the berm of the city's main thoroughfare and pondered our next move.

Vinh Long Orphanage was gone. Files on adoption cases from the old South Vietnamese district and provincial courts had vanished. The site I had long envisioned as a tidy, rural hamlet was a sprawling suburban city where roadside signs touted Tide detergent and Doublemint gum and vendors hawked everything from Marlboros to Moon Pies.

Orphan No. EE18 arrived at Port Columbus amid televised reports of the last helicopter lifting off the U.S. Embassy in Saigon. The accompanying paperwork listed only her Vietnamese name, her adoption designation number and the notation "Born on 18 November 1974 in Hiep Binh Village,

Thu Duc District, Gia Dinh Province, to unknown parents."

Like most adopted children, as she grew Annie became absorbed from time to time in thoughts about her roots.

"I've wondered why you left me to be adopted?" she posed in a letter she wrote, at 13, to the mother she never knew. It seemed less important that she had no one to send it to than that she was able to get a few things off her chest.

"I have sat up many nights and cried thinking about you. . . . I wish I could have been in your arms at least once.

"Even though I have never known you or seen you, I will always love you with all my heart. And there will be an empty place in my heart until I find you."

A decade after she wrote that letter, as I was preparing to return to Vietnam in August, I asked, "What do you want me to say if I find your birth mother?"

"Just tell her I love her," Annie answered. "Tell her thanks for giving me a better life than she had."

In Hiep Binh, we had almost exhausted our supply of the photocopied letters that inquired about Annie's family.

We had worked our way down the road to yet one more outdoor cafe, one more round of shrugs and sympathetic smiles.

"We go now?" ventured Mr. Tu.

"We go," I said.

The Violin

Oct. 7, 1998

Robert Kahn's last violin recital was a serenade to a mob of vigilantes and Nazi SS officers as they burned his family's possessions in a bonfire outside his apartment.

He played from the balcony, hands trembling, a storm trooper at his back commanding him to continue each time he finished a song or faltered.

He hasn't played since that fever-dream spectacle in 1938 that the world would come to remember as *Kristallnacht* ("the night of the broken glass").

In a 24-hour rampage, tens of thousands of Jewish homes and businesses in Germany were attacked; 191 Jews were murdered. Thirty thousand Jews were arrested and sent to concentration camps. Almost 200 synagogues were torched. Jewish children were expelled from orphanages; elderly Jews were evicted from nursing homes.

"It was the beginning of what we know now to be the Holocaust," Kahn, now 75, recalled from his home in Dayton.

"I was playing and crying at the same time."

Early in the day of his forced performance, he had ridden his bicycle to vocational school on the outskirts of his native Mannheim only to find the building in flames.

He headed home.

Even from a distance, he could see the smoke rising from the courtyard of the apartment complex.

"As I approached I could hear my mother and father shouting and crying."

An SS officer led him through the angry throng.

As he entered the building, he stole a glance over his shoulder just in time to see his bicycle being flung atop the bonfire.

"My father was on the floor being beaten up. One SS man had his boot on his back, and the others were beating his head."

He could hear his mother wailing from the bedroom in which she had been locked.

"Is that your violin?" demanded an SS officer.

When he acknowledged that it was, he was dragged out to the balcony by his ear and ordered, "Play!"

"When I see a violinist today, I see myself again and again."

When he was finished, after ducking several burning sticks of furniture hurled at him, he and his father were hauled to the police station.

Boys were dispatched to one holding pen, their fathers to another.

He could not help but notice that, as those around him were ordered to state their ages, anyone 15 or older was sent out a back door and onto a waiting truck.

He said he was 13 and was instructed, "Go home."

His father was sent to Dachau along with the boys.

Several weeks passed before a German woman arrived at the Kahn's apartment one morning. She said her husband was a guard at Dachau and informed Robert's mother, "Your husband has turned over his business to my husband."

The family textile business was gone.

Each night, in the immediate aftermath of *Kristallnacht*, Robert and several of his friends would sneak to the railroad station in defiance of the curfew on Jews and watch the trains come and go.

Clutching pencils and scraps of paper, they approached the tracks as the cattle cars, crammed with human cargo, slowed to a crawl.

The boys collected as many names and addresses as they could, sending postcards to distraught families. Kahn said the messages were simple, terse:

"We saw your husband coming through Mannheim on a train going south."

On a brittle winter night in early 1939, Robert was at the station, taking names and addresses, when he saw a shadowy figure approaching from alongside a stopped train.

It was his father.

"Josef," an SS guard had told the elder Kahn at Dachau, "if you want to get out of here alive, you have to sign your business over to me."

Surprisingly, the SS officer kept his word.

The Kahns fled to Luxembourg and, eventually, to the United States.

Robert's sister had been sent to France to live with family before *Kristallnacht*. Her life was spared thanks to a Catholic priest who risked his own neck to hide the girl in the parish house and a nearby hospital until France was liberated.

In the United States, Kahn enlisted in the Army and was sent to the South Pacific. He saw action in New Guinea and the Philippines.

When the war was over, he penned a letter to the janitor of his family's old apartment building. Was it possible, he asked, that a violin might still be hidden in the attic?

The janitor sent the instrument to Kahn, in Dayton.

He could never bring himself to play again, though.

"The umbilical cord between the violin and the events (of *Kristallnacht*) were just too enormous to ignore."

When Kahn's Dayton friend, Renate Frydaman, began assembling items for a mobile Holocaust exhibit a few years ago, Kahn donated the violin, along with the German Iron Cross his father had been awarded for gallantry in World War I.

Kahn is pleased that the instrument is helping to tell the story.

"A violin is a beautiful instrument," he said. "It makes a beautiful sound, but it has a lot of memories, too."

Where the War Lived

Nov. 1, 1998

DAI LOC, Vietnam - Reminiscence is the flaming hoop through which we compel past truths to leap that they might conform to present sentiment.

Standing on the brow of Hill 55, I had expected to hear the echo of voices, and heard only the soughing of the wind in the eucalyptus trees.

Trudging through Dai Loc, I had presupposed the certainty of ghosts, yet beheld only an achingly beautiful field of lotus.

It didn't take long to realize that I little knew this country.

The Vietnam that had been baying at the moon off in some fog-shrouded reaches of my psyche was merely the tattoo of the American military presence, the long-vanished props and backdrops of a massive and wickedly macabre outdoor drama that was part Dante's *Inferno* and part *Catch-22*.

Without the booming howitzers, the hollow whomp of the mortar tubes; without the stench of cordite and spent diesel fuel; without the staccato metronome of Huey rotors ferrying the wounded to triage and the body bags to graves registration, I had to grope for my bearings.

Where memory's map suggested I would find the wasted terrain of the aptly nicknamed free-fire zones of "Dodge City" and "Arizona Territory," I confronted instead a boy with a penny whistle. He was lounging on the back of a water buffalo in a rice paddy where his parents gathered the last crop of the growing season.

Our second guide, Mr. Tru, had taken considerable pains to ensure that I would miss none of the haunts where, 30 years earlier, I had endured far more boredom than terror, marked off my days on a short-timer's calendar and in the long monsoon nights proposed a truly imaginative variety of plea bargains to God in exchange for a safe return home.

At the crest of Hill 55, a site once rued by its temporary occupants with signs that proclaimed it "The Golden Buckle of the Rocket Belt," the only trace of American presence is the crumbled asphalt that was once a chopper pad.

A local farm girl had commandeered the spot to dry chopped cassava root to feed her family's hogs.

"When the famine came, this is what we ate," Tru recalled of the lean days that followed reunification. He laughed. "We told ourselves it was ginseng."

To feed their children after the North triumphed, many rural families throughout Vietnam took to scavenging scrap metal in areas that had been carpet-bombed. There was a good market for it thanks to eager buyers from the more industrialized nations of the Pacific Rim. But in the first three years after reunification, an estimated 3,000 Vietnamese were killed digging up unexploded bombs and artillery rounds.

Even today, leftover ordnance from the American war still claims a number of casualties every year. Last summer, when an extended heat wave drove the temperature to 104 degrees for several days, three bombs detonated spontaneously near Dong Ha. A fourth, a napalm device, exploded in Quang Tri province, igniting a fire that wiped out 75 acres of forest.

The legacy of a conflict that ended for the United States more than two decades ago is yet everywhere apparent in Vietnam.

Birthing hospitals preserve deformed stillborns, the issue of mothers who live in areas heavily defoliated during the war. These sad specimens, photographed for display in war museums, are labeled simply "victims of the orange poisonous chemical."

Our guide, Tru, was 10 years old when I arrived in the Da Nang area in 1968, yet his family already had been scarred by war.

His uncle, who fought with the Vietminh, had been decapitated by the French. To give the man a proper burial, his family had been compelled to beg his executioners to retrieve the head they had half-skewered onto a bamboo stake, fixing a cigarette in the corner of the lifeless mouth.

Of Tru's siblings, one would die for the South in the American war, another would lose both legs. Tru would come to manhood only to be conscripted by the victorious North to fight the Chinese and Cambodians.

He is only too familiar with the scars war has left upon his people and his land, and is genuinely perplexed by U.S. policy toward Vietnam since 1975.

"We need U.S. know-how," he said. "Your embargo, your policies hurt us. We just want to be treated the way you treated Japan, Germany, even South Korea after your wars there."

"But we defeated Japan," my photographer-partner protested to Tru. "We defeated Germany."

"I tell you," Tru replied evenly, "you did not win the war with bombs and guns, but Americans finally won Vietnam. The American way is penetrating Vietnam."

We won it, he suggested, with our culture, our ways, the trappings of our success after which young Vietnamese lust.

Tru was only half-right.

After the war, we did not try to inflict our culture and our ways on the Vietnamese people. We didn't have to.

They courted it. They learned all they needed to know through the Viet Kieu, the "overseas Vietnamese" who had fled the South in the war's last days. They learned it from the boat people who made it to the United States. The money those new U.S. citizens sent back to Vietnam helped spread the word.

Moreover, once the communist government gave up on its draconian economic policies and began to flirt with capitalism in the late '80s, there was no way the people could be expected to swallow the propaganda about the importance of the struggle to build a noble socialist order.

The inequity of the socialist order already was everywhere apparent.

"There are a lot of new millionaires in Vietnam," we had been told by professor Phan Hoang Quy in Ho Chi Minh City.

"The problem is controlling the money," Tru allowed. "It goes into the pockets of the high-ranking generals. We call them the new rich of 1975."

The cadres, the party apparatchik, got theirs.

Why shouldn't the rest of the population want a share?

"They're schizophrenic," a U.S. State Department official lamented of the leadership in Hanoi. "Vietnam has taken on many aspects of the modern capitalist world, but the political system hasn't changed. They have a one-party communist state hellbent on not relinquishing power at all costs. They're very much in the command mode.

"They don't understand the free market; they don't trust it. They talk the talk, but they don't want to walk the walk.

"Right now, there is an exodus of foreign investors, a flight of capital, a flight of people tired of their monkeying around. They need to get rid of the dinosaurs."

"So who is in charge?" we asked this U.S. official, who had agreed to meet with us in Hanoi under the condition of anonymity.

"No one," he said.

The stratification of class that was the dominant feature of life during feudalism and colonialism is once again a disturbing reality of Vietnam. Only the political ideology of the mandarins has changed.

Professor Quy observed of his nation's leadership since 1975, "At first they said, `We can do everything.' Now they have to tell the truth. They can't do it for the poor."

The prospects for the future are hardly auspicious.

Some believe that nothing short of a massive humanitarian aid effort on the scale of a Marshall Plan will reverse the frightening levels of infant mortality, disease and famine.

Tru hopes that aid will come from us.

He is unable to grasp that, in the United States, the mere mention of Vietnam is still capable of conjuring up bad memories, bitter divisiveness, the aftertaste of tragedy and loss, the stirring of ghosts.

He cannot understand that, among the U.S. people, there yet could be a reservoir of hostility toward the idea of coming to Vietnam's aid.

"We used to wonder where the war lived," Albert Camus wrote, "what it was that made it so vile. And now we realize that we know where it lives, that it is inside ourselves."

Here Comes That Rainbow Again

Dec. 2, 1998

Eve Yearwood climbed behind the wheel of her car and put her head in her hands.

She was hurting, and only part of her misery could be attributed to the flu.

"I have given 200 percent of myself to teaching for 17 years," she heard herself say.

Yet she couldn't see anything in front of her but the yawning abyss of burnout. Ten toes were hugging the lip of that chasm. Nothing would have been easier than to spread her arms, take one step forward and let it consume her.

It was October, 1995. The high school where she taught was a ticking bomb.

"The school was out of control," she said. "The day before, I couldn't even get in my office because it was full of policemen. They had to be called in to break up a fight.

"I can't remember a time when I felt such despair."

Yearwood switched on the car's CD player and hit the random-play button.

The gravel of Kris Kristofferson's voice rumbled over a set of lyrics the singer-songwriter had penned to capture a defining moment in John Steinbeck's *The Grapes of Wrath*.

The Joad family, rolling across the Southwest in a wheezing Nash, has stopped at a roadside cafe. Pa is trying to buy a half a loaf of bread from the waitress. Two of the Joad children are staring hungrily at a jar of peppermint sticks. They have a penny between them.

Sounding like the oldest alligator in the Everglades, Kristofferson sings of the exchange between the children and the waitress:

"How much are them candies?" they asked her.
"How much have you got?" she replied.
"We've only a penny between us."
"Them's two for a penny," she lied.

And the daylight grew heavy with thunder
And the smell of the rain on the wind.
Ain't it just like a human
Here comes that rainbow again.

A devotee of Steinbeck's work, Yearwood. immediately recognized the shadow it had cut across Kristofferson's creativity.

In that scene, Steinbeck transcended literature to remind the world that only compassion replenishes humankind's reservoirs of hope and faith, and that hope and faith are sometimes the only armor we have to steel ourselves against unremitting brutality.

Ball had never thought of hope as a coping skill until that morning when she almost quit teaching.

"I needed a coping skill that morning," she conceded.

But how do you teach hope to students, some of whom come to school with a bellyful of squalor from their home lives?

Yearwood explained of the at-risk students she counsels, "I had a 16-year-old sleeping with a knife under her pillow because her aunt's boyfriend had raped her, yet she couldn't flee the house because she was responsible for the care of a 3-year-old sibling."

How do you sell hope to such a person? Yearwood had to ask herself.

You begin, she decided, by using the most elemental of examples, by reminding youngsters beaten down by life that compassion is not a myth, that hope can become a coping skill.

She had that in Steinbeck's passage and Kristofferson's lyrics. To enliven it more, she turned to artist and art teacher Robin Cook.

This was no small project the two undertook. They wanted to produce a comprehensive resource document that would allow middle- and high-school teachers to use Steinbeck and Kristofferson across a broad range of teaching disciplines, from geography and history to home economics and math.

While Yearwood worked on the text for *Here Comes That Rainbow Again* Cook, who teaches at Columbus Alternative School 2000, labored at the art. Neither could entertain the luxury of quitting her day job to plunge full time into the project. It took three years for Cook to produce 14 mural-size oil paintings that captured the moment in the cafe.

"I was trying to make it appealing to kids," Cook said. "I wanted a certain feeling, so I watched *The Wizard of Oz*."

The black-and-white scenes gave her a sense of the fabric of the era. Yearwood had asked Cook only that light and radiance be a link among the oversize paintings that she would incorporate in her teaching guide.

The project had its "gut check" when it was time to go to the printer. If Yearwood truly believed that Steinbeck and Kristofferson had a lesson for us all, she was going to have to put up or shut up.

She borrowed the money to finish printing the 52-page book. Several days from now it should be in her hands. It will not shake the publishing industry to its eyeteeth.

But then that was never Eve Yearwood's goal.

All she wants to do is bring literature and lyric to life, proving that it is possible to employ them to teach the most fragile and elusive of subjects: human hope.

British Correspondents

March 4, 1998

Give me the dateline and I'll tell you the accent -- from Kabul to Peshawar, from Buulo Berde to Batangas.

If it is some godforsaken pass in Sudan's Nuba Mountains, where the locals are cooking goat heads on dung fires, I'll lay 3-to-1 that the journalist whose radio report reaches you first is British.

The era has long passed when England -- with its typically fatuous chauvinism -- could boast that the sun never set on the British Empire. However, one still could make a fairly compelling case that the sun never sets on British journalists.

I listened for years to radio reports on the Soviet-Afghanistan war and never once heard a voice that wasn't British.

Oh, sure, "Gunga Dan" Rather put in a cameo to plant the flag of American journalism somewhere along the Khyber Pass. But it was the British who were there to greet the Soviets when they arrived. And when the Red Army pulled out a decade later, it was the Brits waving goodbye while lacing their radio dispatches with appropriately disdainful quotes from Kipling's *The Naulahka*.

When the Soviets were gone and the Afghan mujahedeen began skirmishing with government troops (and later, among themselves), it was some poor fool from Liverpool pinned down in the crossfire:

"Hadley Hopcraft here in Eshkashem, where -- as the warring mujahedeen factions retreat to their hideouts -- the government appears ready to lift the military curfew. (KABOOM!) But then again, that may be premature speculation."

So why is it that in the most obscure malarial jungles or parched deserts, it is always a Brit reporting?

"We see ourselves as terriers," Oliver August responded. August is a Manhattan-based financial correspondent for The Times of London, but he cut his journalistic teeth in Bosnia.

"The British press has a tradition of exposing violent and eccentric behavior," he said. "If you can't find it at home, you must go abroad to find it."

August found it in Bosnia in one of those towns with too many consonants and Serbs.

"The first time I went, it was a particularly stupid venture as an intern for the BBC," he explained. "Today, I'm not sure I would do that again, though it was the most exciting thing I've ever done."

It was quite nearly the last thing he ever did.

"I was standing on one side of an armored personnel carrier when a mortar round hit on the other side of it."

It killed the unlucky fellow who was standing on the other side.

August has a theory about why it is usually a British journalist dodging bullets whenever there is a far-flung rebel uprising or coup.

"A lot of British journalists who go to these places often have been there as soldiers," he noted. "They're basically war junkies."

He said that two of the men on the *Times* foreign desk staff served as officers in the Gulf War. One reports on mayhem from Chechnya to Bosnia; the other covers hostilities in Africa.

August suggested that people like to listen to British reports, from Dowlatabad to the Hukawng Valley, because there is something consoling in the accent.

"It exudes the air of empire, of strength and conviction," he said. "People have grown up with the BBC and instinctively trust it. I think people find it very reassuring."

So it is the British accent that makes people trust the journalist behind it.

"Many American marketing people abuse that trust," he said, "using a British actor for class or cachet." (Jonathan Pryce and Infiniti, for example).

"Look at Sean Connery. The man could sell anything or get any woman into bed, and he's over 70."

And what does that have to do with British journalists slogging through 115-degree heat in the African veldt?

"There is a self-assurance bordering on arrogance, but without being offensive," August said, "a little bit like James Bond."

The Tuskegee Incident

Oct. 10, 1991

NOTASULGA, Ala. -- Ask Charlie Pollard about farming and he will talk cotton until the cows come home.

Bring up the subject of carpentry and he will tell you how he built the house he lives in with his own two hands.

"I helped build Shiloh Church up here, too," Pollard, 93, added for good measure.

Then ask Pollard about his participation in the infamous Tuskegee syphilis study. The little dining room where he spends his afternoons falls uncomfortably silent.

When Pollard himself breaks the silence, talk again will turn to cotton or carpentry.

"I've been farming all my life," he said. "I imagine I was 5 or 6 years old, dragging a cotton sack behind me. My daddy could figure out cotton in his head faster than some could with a pencil."

Macon County, where Pollard was reared, was dirt-poor sharecropping country. Cotton was king, but those who broke and harrowed the land, planted the seed and thinned and weeded, didn't live like royalty. The average wage in 1932 was only $2 a day. Four homes in five did not have electricity or indoor plumbing.

Most of the families who picked and baled cotton and lived perpetually in debt to the company store, received little, if any, medical care. When Pollard heard about a free medical program for African-American men at nearby Tuskegee Institute, he investigated.

He and 600 other rural, black males signed up for the "study." In exchange for their participation, they were promised free meals and medical care, transportation and a stipend to cover burial expenses.

The U.S. Public Health Service administered the study, which was launched in 1932. Of those who signed up on the promise of medical care, 399 were told they had syphilis.

What program administrators did not tell those with the disease was that they had no intention of curing them. The study was to investigate the long-term effects of untreated syphilis. Those who had the disease either went untreated or were given medication at dosage levels insufficient to cure syphilis.

Amazingly, the program continued for 40 years. In 1943, the health service began to use penicillin to treat syphilis patients, but not for the men in the Tuskegee study.

Year after year, Pollard made his way to Tuskegee believing that he was being treated.

"They didn't give me nothing," he said.

In 1972, a public health investigator leaked the story of the Tuskegee study to the press:

"In 1972 it came out in *Ebony* magazine," Pollard said.

A $1.8 billion class-action suit was filed on behalf of the men who were subjects of the study; Congress launched an investigation.

John Heller, a director in the venereal disease unit during the study, was questioned about the ethics of the organization's actions. He responded, "The men's status did not warrant ethical debate. They were subjects, not patients; clinical material, not sick people."

When the suit was settled out of court, Pollard received $32,500 for living 40 years with a disease he was led to believe had been cured.

No one apologized. Not until 1997.

Two years ago, President Clinton invited the eight survivors of the study to the White House. Pollard was among the five men who were able to make the trip.

He listened as Clinton said, "The United States government did something that was wrong -- deeply, profoundly, morally wrong. It was an outrage to our commitment to integrity and equality for all our citizens.

"What was done cannot be undone, but we can end the silence. We can stop turning our heads away. We can look at you, in the eye, and finally say, on behalf of the American people, what the United States government did was shameful, and I am sorry."

The apology came too late for the 391 men who died during or after the study.

In the room where Pollard sits, he keeps a framed photograph taken in the White House East Room and inscribed, "To Charlie Pollard, with appreciation. Bill Clinton."

Behind him, on the living room wall, hangs a faded tapestry depicting the Rev. Martin Luther King Jr. flanked by John F. and Robert F. Kennedy.

"Are you angry?" Pollard was asked.

"No," he replied softly.

Eva Parker, his caretaker and niece, responded on her uncle's behalf. "You know they was wrong. They know they was wrong. I don't like to go to bed with anger on my mind. I like to sleep at night."

Pollard nodded in agreement, turning the conversation to cotton farming, then carpentry once again.

"I built this house for $3,500. It was 1954. Helped build the Shiloh church, too."

Son of the Morning Star

Oct. 24, 1999

LITTLE BIGHORN BATTLEFIELD, Mont. -- From the window of a 737 sloping toward Billings, the approach to the site of Custer's last stand resembles a scalloped and sorrel moonscape.

Closer to the battlefield, cottonwoods bunched like watering ponies hug the banks of the coiled Little Bighorn River. I-90, a meandering scarf of asphalt that rides the lift and fall of hummock and gully, offers a bermside vista of signs beckoning: "Sitting Bull's Camp. Exit now. Clean restrooms."

We are hostages to our legends and our myths. Nowhere is that more apparent than on the browning prairie grass of southeastern Montana. Here, Sitting Bull, Crazy Horse and their warriors struck their last great blow against encroaching whites.

In the fever-dream chaos of a withering June afternoon in 1876, Lt. Col. George Armstrong Custer and five companies of the U.S. 7th Cavalry (approximately 210 men) were wiped out. Fifty-three men under the command of Custer's subordinate officers also died.

Indians rode out to thwart the cavalry chief variously known as "Long Hair" or "Son-of-the-Morning-Star" and made short work of his annihilation.

"It took about as long as it takes a hungry man to eat his dinner," is how Cheyenne chief Two Moon described the duration of the battle at Custer Hill.

"It was the biggest Indian victory in the West," said Neil Mangum, the National Park Service's chief superintendent of Little Bighorn Battlefield. Of the triumphant warriors, largely Sioux and Cheyenne, he said, "I don't think anybody fights any harder than in defense of their home. They had everything to lose -- their women and children, their land."

Until Little Bighorn, Manifest Destiny had been westbound on cruise control. After the battle -- fought while backslapping celebrants of the U.S. Centennial prepared to toast one another in Philadelphia -- an embarrassed Washington redoubled its efforts to subdue Western tribes.

"In less than a year's time, there is no Indian force on the northern Plains to contest the U.S. Army," Mangum said. "All the Indians are either in Canada or back on the reservations."

After the Little Bighorn battle, three days passed before cavalry reinforcements made it to the site of Custer's Last Stand.

Lt. Edward Godfrey found Custer's body near the brow of the hill, along with 41 other soldiers' bodies. Desperate for cover in the thick of the fighting, the men had shot their horses to use as breastworks.

After the battle, Sioux and Cheyenne warriors reported that a group of soldiers encircled not far from Custer Hill were shooting one another and themselves. Before the advancing warriors could kill them, Cheyenne chief Lame White Man would recall, 36 cavalrymen did the job for them.

"There were some suicides," Mangum concurred. "There had to have been. I think it was at the end with the disintegration of command. Was it wholesale? I think not."

Five members of the Custer family were killed at Little Bighorn, including two of the commander's brothers, a brother-in-law and a nephew.

On the afternoon when Custer fell, his body was approached by a Cheyenne woman named Me-o-tzi who was said to once have been the lieutenant colonel's Indian wife. She watched as two other women used sewing awls to puncture Custer's eardrums so that he would hear better in the spirit world. The Cheyenne chiefs had warned Custer that if he tried to attack their villages, he would die. He apparently had not heard them, the Indian women calculated.

Most of what is known about the last minutes in Custer's life has been passed down generation to generation by Sioux and Cheyenne who fought him.

The warriors knew how Custer died, but their stories -- for decades -- were not the stories being told at Little Bighorn Battlefield.

"For many years," Mangum acknowledged, "it was a monocultural story told from the point of view of the 7th Cavalry."

The story told was of Custer's bravery and daring. It was the white man's story, a story in which American Indians were dismissed as "hostiles" or, worse, "savages."

For 112 years, the battle site was called Custer Battlefield. Not until 1991 did Congress see fit to rename it Little Bighorn National Monument and authorize building an Indian memorial adjacent to the monument for Custer and his men. Congress authorized the Indian memorial, yet it did not appropriate funds to construct it. The National Park Foundation Indian Memorial Fund is trying to secure the money through public contributions.

"It's going to be a circle memorial," Mangum explained, noting that a "spirit gate" will open toward the 7th Cavalry's monument. It will create a figurative path to encourage intermingling of the spirits of former enemies. The memorial also will depict a trio of Indian warriors atop striding horses to represent the 40-60 warriors believed to have fallen in the fighting.

"We are going to have a ground-breaking on the 11th of November," Mangum said. "I thought it was appropriate, that being Veteran's Day.

"We want to see it built," he said, "so we can tell a more balanced story."

Doing so will please Sioux and Cheyenne descendants of those who fought and died protecting their homes and families from attacking white soldiers.

That also will please Joseph Medicine Crow, the octogenarian grandson of White Man Runs Him, one of Custer's Crow Indian scouts.

Joseph Medicine Crow, who lives near the battlefield in Lodge Grass, recalled of his grandfather and the other Crow scouts. "Six were selected to help Custer. They were with Custer on the day he died.

"Some tribes felt that the Crows shouldn't help the white man, but for our people it was a matter of survival. The Sioux wanted us to fight with them, but they had forgotten the fact that they had tried to take our land away from us, to wipe us out."

Only minutes before Custer began his fateful engagement with the Sioux and Cheyenne, he released his Crow scouts, telling one, "If we win this battle, you will be one of the noted men of the Crow Nation. If I die today, you'll get this land back from the Sioux and stay on it, happy and contented."

Today, the land around Little Bighorn Battlefield is Crow land.

The land where the memorial is planned is Crow land, though once the memorial is built, it will belong to all tribal nations.

Mangum, kneeling among the prairie grass and yucca at the site of the planned memorial, scooped a handful of dirt, then watched as the wind lifted the fine powder from his palm.

He observed, "The Cheyenne say, 'This is the dust and blood of our ancestry.' "

Funny How Time Slips Away

Nov. 20, 1998

"This is the only bad part," the doctor told me, easing a needle under my skin near the sternum.

Within a minute, the area was numb. I felt the pressure of a scalpel, nothing else.

Eight hundred miles away, near Pawleys Island, S.C., my friend Bill Miller was getting into his car in the parking lot of the hospital where he works.

He didn't know anything about me having a bit of outpatient surgery. Nor would he have reason to.

Although Bill and I have been friends since our Navy days, we saw less of each other after he and his wife moved to Virginia and then went their separate ways.

Now and again, he would drop by when he came to Ohio to visit family in Elyria. Eventually, Bill remarried and settled near Pawleys Island.

Ours was never a friendship that needed constant attention and nurturing. It mattered little whether it was three weeks or three years since our last visit. Camaraderie and spontaneity never flagged.

But at 3:30 Monday afternoon, I wasn't thinking about him.

I was too busy feeling sorry for myself.

The doctor who called me at home one night a few weeks ago asked whether I had ever worked with toxic chemicals and hazardous materials.

"Agent Orange," I told him, recalling the defoliated hills and passes of Vietnam from 1968 to 1969.

"The good news," he said, "is that it is not a melanoma."

Instead, it was a low-risk, slow-spreading cancer that had announced itself with an odd little skin eruption.

It wouldn't hurt anything, he suggested, to have a plastic surgeon cut out the surrounding area to be sure the cancer had been contained.

So there I lay on the treatment-room table, antiseptically scrubbed and draped, waiting for the good doctor to begin.

As close as I can calculate, that must have been the approximate moment when Bill Miller turned onto the road on which he would die.

If I know Bill, he had a stack of tapes on the seat beside him and was probably listening to soulful oldies - Al Green doing *Take Me to the River, I Stand Accused, Funny How Time Slips Away*.

"We're just about finished," the surgeon advised me.

I could feel the tug of the sutures: one, two, five.

When we were done, I dressed, shook the surgeon's hand, then made an appointment to have the sutures removed.

"You were very fortunate to have done something about this early," he commented.

I tried to be upbeat, yet for some reason my mood was inexplicably glum. Maybe I wanted to hang onto pity a little longer. He essentially had removed all reason for concern with his scalpel.

Monday evening, I moped around the house. When the phone rang shortly after midnight, I was sound asleep. It was "Charlie," Bill's ex-wife, Charlotte.

The accident was a head-on collision. Bill was gone.

She asked whether I would call a few of our old and mutual friends to break the news. At 2 a.m., I was still on the phone to the West Coast.

Sleep brought only a nightmare. A car was crumpled on a South Carolina back road. A tow truck driver had hitched a hook to it without ever checking inside. Bill was still in it, still alive, trying to muster enough strength to scream for help. The dreamscape changed to a vast junkyard. It was night. I was making my way through the wrecks trying to find the one from which I could hear a low moaning.

Startled awake, I slipped out to the kitchen table, where I broke down.

Bill would never grow old listening to Aretha and Al and the Temptations. He would never get to walk daughter Emmy down the aisle.

On Tuesday evening, I called his wife, Vikki. A small and cowardly part of me was grateful when there was no answer. I would have one more day to bolster my courage.

I turned on the CD.

I felt terribly fortunate and selfish and sad.

A small scar will remind me of the day Lady Luck smiled on me when she should have been on a South Carolina road taking care of Bill.

Al Green was singing, "Time, time, time, time. . . . Ain't it funny how time slips away."

Flight to Freedom

March 17, 1997

Cheryl, the flight attendant on Delta's Miami-to-Atlanta hop, knew Friday would be a long day.

The morning started with a "gate hold" of Flight 844 after a fast-moving wall of thunderstorms and a few funnel-cloud spottings muddied the skies over greater Atlanta.

The control tower at Miami International instructed the crew to stay put until a window opened in the weather. Cheryl could almost feel the blood pressure rising on the 767 full of passengers already fretting about the likelihood of missed connections in Atlanta.

"Thirty minutes," Cheryl guessed the big plane sat at the gate. "Then, when we were released to go, we had a mechanical. It wasn't anything serious or life-threatening."

Back to the gate the 767 rolled.

Behavior researchers say humans are only nine or 10 missed meals from cannibalism. Flight attendants will tell you that it takes only one missed connection to begin the disintegration of common civility among commercial travelers.

"Everybody was stressed out," Cheryl said. "They had connecting flights out of Atlanta. Some were getting irate. We have to be very diplomatic."

Some stalked down the jetway, cellular phones glued to their ears, glowering at the skies and barking commands to subordinates in Boston and Los Angeles.

Cheryl could spot only one passenger who seemed to be taking the delays in stride.

"He was a small man," she said. "Maybe five-three, five-four. My height. He had on a Big Bird yellow shirt. He was well-tanned. At first, I thought he was just a tourist on vacation."

There was something odd about his shape. Both shoulders were contorted at odd angles, as though twisted freakishly beneath some invisible burden.

The flight crew got the bad news immediately after the good. Mechanics had cleared the plane for takeoff, but the control tower was putting it back on gate hold because of more storms over Atlanta.

Scheduled departure had been 11 a.m. It was after 2.

"Could you help this man, please?" a passenger asked Cheryl, nodding toward the man in the yellow shirt. "I think he is supposed to connect in Atlanta with a flight to Wilkes-Barre, but he doesn't speak English."

All around Cheryl, passengers were fuming and fussing, frowning at airline tickets they had already looked at a dozen times.

Cheryl quickly located a Spanish-speaking passenger and brought her to the little man.

"I need you to help me translate," Cheryl told the woman. "Tell him when we get to Atlanta I will walk him off the plane and find an agent who will take him to his next gate."

The passenger translated this.

Cheryl continued, amazed that the man seemed so patient, so unruffled by the long delay. "Tell him that his luggage will probably arrive on a later flight."

The passenger relayed this, listened to the reply, then turned to Cheryl: "He has no luggage. He has what he is wearing."

Hesitantly, in the manner of a man conditioned to keeping his mouth shut, the fellow continued.

He had been a political prisoner in Cuba. He had just been released. The National Catholic Conference had helped secure his freedom. The smoothing of relations between the Vatican and Castro may have had something to do with it. Catholic Social Services in Miami had located a parish in eastern Pennsylvania willing to adopt him.

He was no longer a young man. He had been held captive many years.

Eavesdropping passengers began leaning toward the exchange, forgetting their grousing.

The translator's curiosity got the better of her. She asked the man what had happened to his shoulders.

His captors had broken both of them -- blows with either the butt of a rifle or the flat of its bayonet, it wasn't clear; either during interrogation or because of some infraction in prison. Maybe because a guard woke up in a bad mood.

The man said it was all OK, though. He was free now.

The woman in the next seat fumbled for a Kleenex. Other passengers looked away. The center section of the 767 fell silent as a tomb.

Once off the ground, Cheryl loaded a bag with snacks and fruit from the galley and took them to the man. He hadn't eaten for hours. He had stayed in his seat while fellow passengers left the plane to posture and fume as though the next rotation of the globe could not successfully be effected until they arrived in Los Angeles carrying the proper instructions.

At Atlanta, Cheryl walked the man off the plane. She looked at his short-sleeved shirt. It would be cold in Wilkes-Barre.

"I gave him a hug," she said, "I told him, `Welcome to America. I hope it will be OK. Maybe it will be OK. It will be better than Cuba.' "

He hadn't comprehended, but he said goodbye and, with an airline escort guiding him, headed for Gate B-17.

Cheryl was crying.

Not infrequently on her Florida-to-Atlanta flights she glimpses small reminders of life's cruelties, frailties, occasional miraculous deliverances. "You see children on their way home from their last-wish trip to Disney World." Stocking caps hide heads made bare by chemotherapy.

She isn't sure why she decided to walk down to Gate B-17.

When she got there, the little man was buying a pack of gum from a shop adjacent to the gate. Unseen, she watched as he handed the clerk $1, then-studied, with perplexed disappointment, the 15 cents that had been placed in his palm.

"America," Cheryl told him.

Maybe he understood.

Exit Mike Royko

May 2, 1997

Try not to get too misty over Mike Royko. If he's up there looking down, you don't want him confusing you with the tubeheads on Chicago's WGN-TV.

On Tuesday, the day he died, the same blow-dried TV clones who had chased Royko through the Tribune Tower parking garage (using their mini-cam microphones like cattle prods to get a quote on the columnist's drunk-en-driving bust) were suddenly acting crestfallen by Chicago's loss.

TV types do "crestfallen" almost as well as they do "outraged." In unctu-ous mock grief, they furrowed their brows and contorted their mouths into something that looked like torn pockets.

They were sure sorry, they said, about journalism's great loss.

Royko probably was rolling his eyes and grunting something unprintable.

To find as much sorrow as the TV types were demonstrating over Royko's passing, you'd need a very big shovel and a well-used barn stall.

Slats Grobnik would have punched one of them in his cosmetically altered nose.

"In a robotesque time, he is daringly flesh and blood," Studs Terkel once said of Royko.

He was a two-fisted journalist who unclenched his paws only long enough to toss back a draft or reach for another Pall Mall.

At 64, he was too young to die and too young to have become an anachronism, yet his last years were witness to changes in the profession that he could have regarded only as depressing (take a second look at *The Dweebs on the Bus*).

The last time I saw Royko, he was jawing with a small knot of ink-stained wretches at the Carter Presidential Center in Atlanta.

It was 1988.

Jimmy Carter was standing 20 feet away from Royko, a wallflower at his own party, watching guests "ooh" and "ahh" and try to get close enough to

Royko to tell him how much they liked his column.

I should know. I was one of them.

I'm glad now that I didn't get close enough to drool on his sleeve. He loathed being regarded as a "celebrity."

He knew he swung with clout, but he still viewed himself as a "flat-above-the-tavern" son of a Chicago bartender.

Royko had an ear for the all-defining laconic remark, a marvelous built-in BS detector and an uncanny eye for the irony hidden under the rumps of the pontificating self-righteous.

Never was this better revealed than in a column he wrote after sports commentator and oddsmaker Jimmy "The Greek" Snyder was fired by CBS for his stunningly stupid comments comparing the development of black athletes to the breeding of thoroughbred horses.

Few quibbled with CBS' decision.

Royko certainly didn't, but he was brassy enough to inquire in print whether there might be a double standard on matters of racial and ethnic sensitivity.

At the time, presidential hopeful Jesse Jackson had just referred to New York as "Hymietown," an epithet that shocked and stunned New York Jews.

In his column, Royko suggested what Jimmy "The Greek" would have had to call Detroit in order to sink to the level of insensitivity Jackson had demonstrated about New York.

But then, Royko mused, perhaps we have different expectations of our presidential candidates and of our bookies: "We expect better of our bookies."

Royko had taken irony's razor to the gonfalon banner of the political correctness movement, cutting its double standard to ribbons before its bearers knew what had hit them.

I'll miss his voice. The world needs it just now.

I'm glad Mark Twain finally has someone to talk to.

But it cost us dearly.

Hibakusha

Aug. 6, 1995

HIROSHIMA, Japan - Her scarred fingers laced before her atop the long conference table, Miyoko Matsubara drew a deep breath and squared her slight frame as though telegraphing the gravity of the words she was about to utter.

The recounting of her oft-told, A-bomb survivor's odyssey--a blizzard of anguished, graphic images--was delivered in urgent bursts, impressing her listener with the sensation of having heard the plaintive summons of an abandoned nestling.

The ordeal made her tired. She said so. Yet there was one thing she wanted to make clear, she interjected, raising for emphasis an index finger crooked slightly by contracture.

"You can understand why I hated America when I was a child," she ventured.

Had she wished to dramatize the comment, she would have needed only to nod toward the small clutches of schoolchildren out beyond the high windows of Hiroshima's International Conference Center, paying their respects at the eternal flame in Peace Memorial Park.

"But the enemy is not America," she observed. "Had we possessed the bomb, we would have used it.

"The enemy is war. The enemy is nuclear arms."

Within a week of the summer day on which she spoke, the leading story in Hiroshima's chief daily newspaper would detail France's announced intentions to resume nuclear testing.

The news caused a sudden and collective lurch on the emotional Richter scale of a city attuned to the slightest vibrations on nuclear proliferation issues.

Half-a-city away from Peace Memorial Park and the site of the first A-bomb drop, Akihiro Takahashi wearily contended, "We have to overcome."

Like Matsubara, the 64-year-old Takahashi was a Hiroshima middle-school student on the day the bomb was dropped. And, like her, he has spent the prime of his life pleading for a halt to the spread of nuclear weapons.

"You are a living witness," he said he was told during an audience with the Pope several years ago.

Takahashi was standing with classmates outside Hiroshima Municipal Middle School 50 years ago today, when the *Enola Gay* released Little Boy.

"I heard a growing noise and it became dark," he said. "I thought Hiroshima had vanished. The school building had been flattened."

He had been blown several yards from where he had been standing. The right side of his body and his back, turned toward the flash, were hideously burned.

"My friend and I fled to the river," he said. "He was crying. I said, 'Don't cry. Crying doesn't help.'

"On the way to the river I saw terrible things. I saw a middle-aged man still managing to walk although the skin of the upper half of his body had been completely burned away . . . a man with slivers of glass embedded in his chest; a woman with an eyeball dangling on her cheek; a baby wailing beside its mother, who had burned to a charred lump."

Matsubara, like Takahashi, was about 1 mile from the target used by the bomber crew.

A 12-year-old in 1945, Matsubara shared with Takahashi the common distinction of being one of 8,600 Hiroshima middle-school students mobilized by the Japanese government to assist the military with war-related tasks, such as clearing fire lanes. Most of those students were working outside and were heavily exposed to the heat, shock wave and radiation when the bomb hit.

"When I saw the blast, I lay flat on the ground," Matsubara remembered.

"Both arms were completely burned."

Knocked unconscious, she awakened to a smoky pall over the city and began making her way to a bridge crossing one of Hiroshima's seven rivers.

"I felt unbearably hot," she explained. "I jumped into the water and found myself among bodies being carried by the river. Some were sinking. Some were floating."

Takahashi, immersing himself in the cool waters of the Yamate River, also discovered himself amid a logjam of the dead.

Scores of victims were begging for water, crying, "Mizu! Mizu!" to rescuers who, in many instances, denied the requests in the mistaken belief that drinking water would mean certain death to burn victims.

A man in the river next to Takahashi plunged his face into the water to slake his thirst. His head never rose from the surface and the stunned youth watched as the river carried him off.

Reports from the city on the day of the bomb noted how strange it seemed that, even amid such epic carnage, the formal politeness so much associated with the Japanese was still present.

Victims trapped in the rubble that lay before fast-encroaching fires often screamed not "Help!" but "Help, if you please."

Fifteen-year-old Michiko Yamaoka, mobilized as a telephone operator in the waning months of the war, was on her way to work when she saw the fireball that she, at first, thought strangely beautiful.

Burned from head to toe and peppered with flying shards of glass, she was thrown by the explosion against a heavy fence only seconds before it toppled upon her, trapping her.

Believing herself to be dying, she remembered whispering, "Goodbye, mother," just before she lost consciousness. When she awakened, still trapped, one of the first voices she heard was that of her mother calling, "Michiko."

Pulled from the debris, she discovered that an entire layer of skin had peeled from the front of her body. Her work pants hung in tatters.

At nightfall, she was transported by river ferry to a temporary hospital at a nearby island in the inland sea.

Takahashi, Matsubara and Yamaoka were all extremely fortunate to receive medical treatment in a city where a reported 65 of 150 physicians had been killed and most of the remainder were too severely injured to assist bomb victims. Of almost 1,800 nurses in Hiroshima, more than 1,600 had perished or were among those seeking medical attention.

Carried to his family's home on the outskirts of the city, Takahashi was treated by a physician friend of his grandfather's.

He lay unconscious for three weeks and for another six months was unable to rise from his bed to take a step.

At the island hospital, Yamaoka's hair began falling out and she began to evacuate blood.

In constant pain from her burns, she told her mother, "I want to go home and die."

But her mother told her, "We have no home to go back to."

Of the estimated 76,000 commercial and residential structures in

Hiroshima, only 6,000 remained standing after the bomb.

Recuperating in a mountainside shelter on the outskirts of the city, Matsubara said that eight weeks after the bomb was dropped she still could smell the smoke-borne stench of Hiroshima's cremation fires.

As the years passed, Yamaoka and Matsubara began the long process of reconstructive surgery.

Matsubara had a dozen surgeries in Osaka. Yamaoka was one of the 25 "Hiroshima Maidens" brought to the United States for surgery in 1955.

Neither of the two married. Both acknowledged that as "hibakusha", as the Japanese called A-bomb survivors, they were considered undesirable. In addition to their disfigurement, it was feared they would bear deformed children.

Many of the "hibakusha" became social outcasts. Yamaoka and Takahashi both recalled being turned down for jobs because they had been damaged by the bomb.

"Children threw rocks at me," Yamaoka remembered.

In time, Matsubara, Yamaoka and Takahashi began telling their stories. All have traveled abroad to speak out against nuclear arms.

At a restaurant across the street from Peace Memorial Park, Yamaoke removed a small cache of snapshots from her bag. In one, she is smiling into the camera along with Chelsea Clinton at the Quaker school near Washington, D.C., attended by the president's daughter.

Takahashi eventually became director of the Hiroshima Peace Memorial Museum.

He has suffered chronic liver problems attributed to his radiation exposure.

Yamaoka has battled breast cancer.

"We survivors are dying," she acknowledged, "but the children of the 21st century will be the new victims if we repeat the past."

Cradling with his good left hand a right arm that appears almost vestigial for the withering damage to it, Takahashi embraced the thoughts of both Matsubara and Yamaoka when he noted, "I have heard that the brain has a mechanism to suppress traumatic memories. I have not let that happen. I have disciplined myself not to forget, however painful it may be to remember, for that day was the turning point of my life."

To a Hero Unsung

May 25, 1995

BOUCHEVILLIERS, France--The grave of Charles Saint is tucked among three dozen others in a small Normandy churchyard adjacent to the manor house and estate that once belonged to his father.

Only 57 when he died 30 years ago, his passing drew scant attention outside the small rural village of which he was mayor during the last few years of his life.

In the years preceding World War II, Saint had been a rising star in the French diplomatic corps, serving as first assistant to the French ambassador to the United States from 1936 to 1939.

He returned to Paris not long before Germany invaded Poland and, as France mobilized for war, accepted a commission in the French Air Force. When France fell to the Germans, he took a position with the Vichy government of Field Marshal Henri Philippe Petain.

There were those among the French who considered him a collaborator for not joining Charles de Gaulle's government in exile in London or becoming involved in the French Resistance. But the position he created for himself during the occupation, an attache to the Vichy government's delegation to Paris, provided him an opportunity to play a role similar to that of Oskar Schindler.

"He had fantastic powers of persuasion," Saint's brother, Guillamme, recalled. "He created a bureau titled the Delegation for Special Administration in order to intervene on behalf of men and women in the French Resistance who had been sentenced to death, life imprisonment or deportation for their activities."

Guillamme Saint knew the role his brother was playing but did not begin documenting it through research at the French National Archives until Charles had been dead for a decade.

Archive files produced hundreds of appeals Charles had prepared and presented before the German high military command arguing for mercy and the commutations of death sentences of arrested members of the French Resistance.

He was quite imaginative in their defense, grasping any shred of mitigating evidence he could find. In the case of one 20-year-old French Resistance member convicted of cutting German telephone lines and sentenced to death, he argued that the man had been a mental incompetent all his life and had been duped into committing the deed.

For a French priest accused of hiding downed U.S. and French pilots in his church, he argued that the unfortunate cleric already had suffered a terrible life after being gassed during World War I. The plea spared the priest being shot.

As the allied invasion of Normandy drew nearer, there was a predictable increase in French Resistance activities and, correspondingly, a groundswell in the number of cases in which Charles Saint found himself arguing for the lives of defendants.

The records in the archives indicate his efforts spared the lives of 595 men and women scheduled to be executed and won the release of 7,371 of those sentenced to prison or German forced-labor camps.

When a triumphant de Gaulle returned to Paris following the liberation of France, Guillamme Saint explained, "All the people who worked for the Vichy government had to explain why."

Charles Saint was considered *persona non grata* in the new regime, ousted from government, forbidden to pursue a career in the diplomatic corps in which he had hoped to earn his livelihood once the war was over.

"France was divided," Guillamme contended. "We knew my brother had saved a lot of people." But the taint of having dealt with the despised occupiers of France haunted him.

For a while, he returned to his native Bouchevilliers to work in the factory his grandfather had founded in the mid-19th century.

The government refused to compensate him for the years he had served without pay, begging for the lives of those condemned to death by the Germans, despite the stacks of letters in the French National Archives expressing the gratitude of families he had spared terrible grief.

He dabbled a bit in local politics in Bouchevilliers, was elected mayor of the town, then died suddenly of a heart attack while on a trip from the Normandy countryside to Paris in 1964.

Now, throughout the region where he was born and grew to manhood, an epic commemoration is about to honor not only those allies who fought to liberate France but, as well, the courageous members of the Resistance who aided them.

How sad that so many of the latter will recall how boldly they courted execution or imprisonment yet forget the French Schindler who saved them and whose simple grave will go undecorated June 6.

Moving Day Blues

May 7, 1997

I am moving at the end of this month. I would rather bungee-jump into the settling tank at a sewage treatment facility, but I have little choice and less Valium.

My father so loathed moving that, the few times our family did, he insisted it be done while he was at work.

"Just call the shop with the address when you get settled," he would instruct my mother.

The act of moving is enchanting only to the hopelessly deranged. The reason California boasts the highest per-capita rate of certifiable lunatics is that most of them are spawn of the toxic gene pool of "movers" who settled that state.

Those who ended up in California so loved moving that they spent months at it on the trail West. Some got typhoid or tomahawked and left their bones to bleach in Death Valley. Their idea of fun was to become snowbound in a mountain pass with all their belongings on a wagon, and then to survive till spring by cannibalizing the frozen bodies of in-laws.

My chief beef with the process of relocating can be summed up with an oxymoron: professional movers.

I have never seen a "professional mover."

I usually get three guys named Snake, Cooter and Mongo, along with their probation officer.

These are guys with pierced eyebrows and Metallica tattoos who first bonded during group therapy at Lucasville and have stayed together to network toward mutual long-term goals.

If I were casting them in a movie, I'd get Nicolas Cage, Steve Buscemi and Michael J. Pollard.

Of course, I never get the real Cage, Buscemi and Pollard. The three I usually get have appeared on film only in bank security cameras.

They arrive an hour late, driving a truck emblazoned with the logo for Walleye Sam's Seafood. They explain that they picked up the vehicle for a song a week earlier after its refrigeration unit failed while carrying 15,000 pounds of perch down from Lake Erie.

It smells like the kitchen exhaust fan at Long John Silver's.

It is folly to expect that men who have been eating off metal trays for the past 2 to 5 (longer if there was a gun specification) would have much respect for the china of total strangers. Remember the apes in the Samsonite commercial?

I try to accommodate the movers with small talk, though it often takes unsettling turns:

"Nice place. You folks got a security system?"

"No. Not yet."

"Ought to. Someone could come out of those woods and strip this place clean in, oh, maybe, nine minutes. Nearest police substation is 10 minutes away."

"You think so?"

"Sure. See these window locks on this side of your house that's hidden by the bushes from the road? Pop these babies in two seconds."

I try to keep things vague when it comes to professional movers. It helps little that I'm married to an obsessive-compulsive.

I label boxes: "Dining room stuff."

She labels them: "Waterford crystal" and "Coin collection: 19th-century $20 gold pieces."

Another problem with movers is that no matter how thoroughly you try to prepare for their arrival, they always manage to find something from Frederick's that fell behind the dryer.

This you discover after Mongo bellows, "Hey, Snake! Cooter! Check this out. Looks like a swimming cap for a guy with a mohawk."

I'd just as soon burn down the house and all the packed boxes in it and start fresh.

Yet I know that, several days from now, I will be seated at my dining room table at sunset of a very long day looking at Snake, Cooter and Mongo, hearing:

"It's, uh, $1,100, dude. That don't include no tip or nothing, which is up to you."

I will tip, wave goodbye, call the home-security sales rep.

Bad, Bad Country

April 1, 1996

It's April again.

Shy daffodils are nodding their tiny heads. Spring is in the air, and I'm singing *I'd Rather Pass a Kidney Stone Than Another Night With You.*

Time again for my annual list of Worst Country Song Titles of All Time Until the Next Time.

Thanks to Colleen and Gus Sariotis, of Colleen's Collectables, for letting me peruse everything from CDs to 78s (large disks with little holes that Mom used to listen to).

This year's expanded list represents my 100 worst (just in case I get run over by a beer truck before next April). Say, that would make a pretty good country song: "I never saw the Bud Light sign when I stepped off the curb/I was thinkin' little sweet thing just of you/Well the bumper caught me first/But the back tires hurt the worst . . ." Ah, never mind.

Here's the list:

1. *Let's Do Something Cheap and Superficial*
2. *I Don't Mind Goin' Under (If It'll Get Me Over You)*
3. *Has Your Lawyer Talked to Jesus?*
4. *High Cost of Leaving*
5. *I Guess I Had Too Much To Dream Last Night*
6. *How Can I Miss You (If You Won't Even Leave)*
7. *Shut Up and Talk to Me*
8. *I'm Left, You're Right, She's Gone*
9. *I'm the Only Thing I'll Hold Against You*
10. *May Old Acquaintance Be Forgot (Before I Lose My Mind)*
11. *Who's Been Sleeping in My Bed?*
12. *Hurt Her Once for Me*
13. *I Can Still Hear the Music in the Restroom*
14. *The Jukebox Never Plays 'Home Sweet Home'*
15. *Kiss It and Make It Better*
16. *Lock, Stock and Teardrop*
17. *Here's a Quarter (Call Someone Who Cares)*
18. *Bridge Washed Out (I Can't Swim and My Baby's on the Other Side)*
19. *I Cried All the Way to the Bank*
20. *Honky Tonk Amnesia*
21. *I Bought the Shoes that Just Walked Out on Me*
22. *Don't Hand Me No Hand-Me-Down Love*
23. *I Just Started Hatin' Cheatin' Songs Today*
24. *I Married Her Just Because She Looks Like You*
25. *We Used To Kiss on the Lips (But Now It's All Over)*
26. *If Whiskey Were a Woman I'd Be Married for Sure*
27. *Somebody Must Have Loved You Right Last Night*
28. *I Wish I Could Hurt That Way Again*

29. *Your Alibi Called Today*
30. *This Ain't Tennessee and He Ain't You*
31. *All-Day Sucker*
32. *I Forgot That I Don't Live Here Anymore*
33. *Hank Drank*
34. *I Gotta Mind To Go Crazy*
35. *I May Be Used (But Baby I Ain't Used Up)*
36. *Touch Me With More Than Your Hands*
37. *Walk Out Backwards Slowly (So I'll Think You're Walkin' In)*
38. *Defrost Your Heart*
39. *I Wish You Could Have Turned My Head (And Left My Heart Alone)*
40. *Get Your Biscuits in the Oven and Your Buns in the Bed*
41. *I'd Rather Be Picked Up Here (Than Put Down at Home)*
42. *I'm Drinkin' Canada Dry*
43. *Bad Girls Don't Have Suntans*
44. *I'm Throwing Rice (At the Girl I Love)*
45. *You Make My Heart Want a Dip of Snuff*
46. *How Come Your Dog Don't Bite Nobody But Me?*
47. *Normally, Norma Loves Me*
48. *Flushed From the Bathroom of Your Heart*
49. *Did I Shave My Legs for This?*
50. *If I Ain't Got It (You Don't Need It)*
51. *Her Body Couldn't Keep You Off My Mind*
52. *Why Don't We Get Drunk and (expletive)*
53. *I'm All He's Got (But He's Got All of Me)*
54. *I've Enjoyed as Much of This as I Can Stand*
55. *Lay Something on My Bed Besides a Blanket*
56. *I've Fallen in Love (And I Can't Get Up)*
57. *It's Hell To Know She's Heaven*
58. *It Don't Feel Like Sinnin' to Me*
59. *If I Say I Love You (Consider Me Drunk)*
60. *You're the Hangnail in My Life*
61. *If I Said You Have a Beautiful Body (Would You Hold It Against Me)*
62. *Don't Come Home a-Drinkin' With Lovin' on Your Mind*
63. *Loving Here and Living There and Lying in Between*
64. *Lord If I Make It to Heaven (Can I Bring My Own Angel Along)?*
65. *Walkin', Talkin', Cryin', Barely Beatin' Broken Heart*
66. *The Pint of No Return*
67. *I've Done Enough Dyin' Today*
68. *I'm Ashamed To Be Here (But Not Ashamed Enough To Leave)*
69. *She Feels Like a New Man Tonight*
70. *He's a Heartache (Lookin' for a Place To Happen)*
71. *All My Exs Live in Texas*
72. *I Gotta Get Drunk (And I Shore Do Dread It)*
73. *You Done Stomped on My Heart (And Smashed That Sucker Flat)*
74. *I Just Came Back (To Break My Heart Again)*
75. *I Learned All About Cheatin' From You*
76. *You Won't Be Back But George and Jack Will Help Me Make It*

Through the Night
77. *If the Jukebox Took Teardrops (I'd Cry All Night Long)*
78. *I Don't Know Whether To Kill Myself (Or Go Bowling)*
79. *Should I Come Home (Or Should I Go Crazy)*
80. *I'd Rather Have a Bottle in Front of Me (Than a Frontal Lobotomy)*
81. *You're Going To Ruin My Bad Reputation*
82. *She Can't Get My Love off the Bed*
83. *Does Steppin' Out Mean Daddy Took a Walk?*
84. *It Took a Lot of Drinkin' (To Get That Woman Over Me)*
85. *If 10 Percent Is Good Enough for Jesus*
    (It Ought To Be Good Enough for the IRS)
86. *Don't Believe My Heart Can Stand Another You*
87. *Every Day's a Happy Day for Fools*
88. *This Night Ain't Fit for Nothin' But Drinkin'*
89. *I'm Only in It for the Love*
90. *You Can't Have Your Kate (And Edith, Too)*
91. *Hell Stays Open All Night*
92. *I'll Be Your Bridge (Just Lay Me Down)*
93. *That's More About Love (Than I Wanted To Know)*
94. *After 'Sweet Memories' Play 'Born To Lose' Again*
95. *I Got in at 2 with a 10 and Woke Up at 10 with a 2*
96. *It Ain't Love, But It Ain't Bad*
97. *You're the Reason Our Kids Are So Ugly*
98. *I Got You on My Conscience But at Least You're Off My Back*
99. *If Fingerprints Showed Up on Skin (Wonder Whose I'd Find on You)*
100. *Get Your Tongue Out of My Mouth Because I'm Kissing You*
    Goodbye.

Christmas In Prison

Dec. 23, 2000

In the brittle winterscape outside Joe Castorano's van, his fellow deputies trudged across the parking lot for the first shift at the Franklin County jail on Jackson Pike.

Heads bowed against the gusts pushing a minus 20 wind chill yesterday morning, they could see their breath come and go in frosted plumes.

"Gotta get some gas," Castorano reminded himself, waiting in the dark for wipers to clear a rind of frost smudging the windshield.

With Dec. 25 only three days away, Castorano readied his shuttle for the last batch of Franklin County inmates to have learned they're getting two-to-five for Christmas. His job is to trundle the newly convicted from the county lockup to the state prison system.

In this season of good will to all, the least likely beneficiaries of humankind's sympathy may be freshly sentenced felons. Pastor Nehemiah

Chambers, chaplain at the jail, knows that only too well.

"The general public would say: 'It serves them right. They had a chance like everyone else. They're better off going to prison.'

"They finally have to face the reality," Chambers said. "God can't pull any strings anymore."

And it's Christmas.

"Hey, did they throw my cigarettes away, Elvis?" an inmate called to Deputy Sheriff Ken Hahn while being handcuffed for his van ride to the Correctional Reception Center at Orient.

"No," Hahn assured him. "They go with you."

"Can I hit one before I leave?"

"No," Hahn frowned. "Bad for your health."

The morning's first clutch of travelers -- arms laced like promenading square dancers -- shuffled into the van.

"Colder than a sumbitch," one groused.

"Don't put my name in the paper," the fellow behind him warned. "I don't want to see my name in no newspaper." He sighed, then spat, "Assaulting a police officer. They said I assaulted him. He was 6 feet 7, 250 pounds. I'm 140. How am I going to assault him?"

The inmate in the seat beside him mused, "You sure talk a lot for a man who doesn't want to be in the paper."

Through one-way windows latticed with bars, the riders drank in the passing vista -- the light froth of snow on winter-shorn fields, the bluestem and ironweed hugging the guardrail along I-71 south of Columbus.

A few men, wearing nothing on their shoulders but the short-sleeved shirts they were arrested in last summer, stared blankly at Christmas lights and creche kitsch set out for the season.

"Christmas? What's it going to be like?" inmate David Evans said, parroting a question thrown his way. "It's just another day in here."

Tyron Johnson, all too familiar with life on the inside, said of Christmas: "This is when you really get depressed and lay on your bunk with tears in your eyes. You feel like you've let your people down.

"There's a lot of tension at Christmas -- lot of fights."

An inmate in the seat ahead of Evans lamented of his sentencing judge, "She tells me I'm a menace to society and sends me to the penitentiary for seven months."

Evans mocked: "Seven months? That's winehead time. I'm not even going to talk to anyone doing less than five years."

Deputy Sheriff Bob Cox, riding shotgun in the prison-bound van, would later observe of his riders, "The guys that it's their first time, they're the quiet ones."

Eighteen-year-old Prince Hickson, going to prison for the first time for receiving stolen property, initially seemed cocky.

"These two chickenheads stole this car off the airport lot," he explained of the young women he said heisted the car he was caught with.

"Am I going to be in the paper? What day?" he interjected occasionally throughout the false-bravado spiel of a "jitterbug," as old cons call such novitiates.

The closer the bus drew to Orient during the 10-mile drive, the quieter he became, the more introspective -- at one point pressing his palms together in prayer despite a few derisive glances from fellow travelers.

"I got faith in God. He's going to get me through this."

"I left with hope," Johnson said of his brief respite outside the walls to wrangle with prosecutors on another charge. "Now I'm coming back in with hate and anger."

Chambers has counseled those leaving for prison on the cusp of Christmas: "You just have to pray. There are a number of genuine Christian men who have done a lot of Christmases inside the walls. Get with them."

The van slowed to a halt outside a stretch of high fence laced with the garland of razor wire.

The snow spit and sputtered, reminding a guest in the van of a line from John Prine's song, *Christmas in Prison:*

The searchlight in the big yard
Swings 'round with the gun,
Spotlighting the snowflakes
Like dust in the sun.
It's Christmas in prison,
There'll be music tonight.
I know I'll get homesick.
I love you. Goodnight.

"Pie," said one of the passengers who had been down the road before. "Regular chow days, you maybe get fruit cocktail.

"Christmas, you get pie."

Jesse's Place

May 17, 1996

On June 7, as the Olympic flame snakes its way ever southward to Atlanta, it will be borne past the Oakley Avenue home Jesse Owens left to travel to the 1936 games in Berlin threescore summers ago.

As torch and runner pass the lemon-colored foursquare with the squat stone marker in the front yard, throngs lining the sidewalk will cheer the notion of the world's quadrennial effort to momentarily rise above bombings, starvation and ethnic cleansings in the name of athletics.

Earl "Wimpy" Potts and Lois Neff -- vice president and president, respectively, of the Hilltop Historical Society -- have worked hard to make sure the torch passes the house where Owens lived while attending Ohio State University.

Four gold medals once rested on the living room mantel of the home, and the name of the man who earned them by embarrassing Hitler's Aryan "supermen" became synonymous with the triumph of democracy over fascism.

It didn't take long after Berlin for life on Oakley Avenue to settle back into business as usual.

Owens once conceded, "After I came home from the 1936 Olympics with my four medals, it became increasingly apparent that everyone was going to slap me on the back, want to shake my hand or have me up to their suite. But no one was going to offer me a job."

In my youth, my house was only a few blocks from the one Owens lived in during the Depression. South Oakley was on my paper route.

It was a decade after Owens' triumph in Berlin before the runner's Hilltop chums finally were permitted to enter the neighborhood movie theaters nearest Oakley. Even then, for a while, they were restricted to Sunday matinees.

"Blacks were not allowed on the streets south of Sullivant," Potts recalled. "Bankers had a restrictive covenant that kept them from loaning to blacks who wanted to buy in neighborhoods outside this one."

The reason Owens lived on Oakley Avenue in the first place was that black OSU students were not permitted, in 1936, to live on campus.

At the whim of business owners, blacks were barred everywhere from ice cream parlors to barbershops on the Hilltop and elsewhere throughout Columbus.

Potts' mother, Ruth Carter, who worked in the office of the OSU president while she was a student, was forbidden to live on campus.

In 1957, when I was 11, a barber on my paper route offered me a penny apiece to deliver his business cards to West Side residents.

Nodding out his window in the direction of the house where Owens lived, he advised, "Not down there."

Jesse Owens' life was a paradox.

He triumphed over the forces of racial hatred in Berlin but couldn't watch newsreel footage of his feats at the local theater.

He could travel the globe as a goodwill ambassador as long as the trek didn't take him onto streets south of Sullivant Ave.

He gave speeches about the power of athletics to transcend racial injustice at hotels where he couldn't stay and country clubs where he couldn't belong.

God bless Earl Potts and Lois Neff for helping ensure that the torch won't miss Owens' old home.

God help the torch route organizers if -- when the torch goes through the OSU campus -- it bypasses the plaque that reads:

As long as athletes compete in sports, or people strive for success in any undertaking, the life and accomplishments of Jesse Owens will remain an enduring inspiration.

Owens' greatest athletic achievements reminded Germany that greatness is color-blind.

It just took awhile for his native country to get the message.

World's Oldest Columnist

Sept. 20, 1998

"How old are you?" Rose Nix Leo asked, after an amiable phone chat about our mutual calling, the column-writing business.

"Fifty-two," I replied.

"You got a long way to go," she observed, chuckling at the realization that she is twice my age and still churning out a weekly column for *The Elk County Citizen-Advance News* in southeastern Kansas.

She wrote her first column at 17, in 1911, the year Ronald Reagan was born, the year before the Titanic went down.

She remembers well the subject of that maiden effort.

"Dead Man's Gulch," she recounted. "There was a tree there that they used to hang criminals. They hung 'em there and buried 'em there. There were several graves.

"The law wasn't like it is now. People took it in their own hands and did the punishing. No trial. No lawyers."

It was a different Kansas into which Leo was born 104 years ago.

She was only 4 when her father was kicked to death by a horse. Three years later, her mother suffered a heat stroke while picking cotton and died several days later.

Relatives reared the five Nix children.

Rose finished one year of high school, but that was enough to land her a teaching job at a one-room rural school in 1918.

"The first year I taught, I got $35 a month, and I paid $10 for room and board."

She didn't quit the column, though her initial efforts were rewarded only with a sheaf of writing paper, enough postage to mail the next column, and the lofty title "county correspondent."

"I just started writing local news," she said. "Who went where. What they did. I've advanced a lot since then."

She married John Leo in 1920. He farmed, but the drought, dust and Depression made for a precarious existence in the 1920s and '30s.

"In '36," she recalled, "the corn was about 2 feet high, the gardens burned up and the grasshoppers took everything."

She sold her column to any editor who would have it, grateful for the pocket change it provided to help put food on the table for three growing children.

Her oldest son went off to fight in World War II. Seriously wounded in the South Pacific, he did not live long after he was returned to the States.

A daughter and another son remain.

Her husband died in 1967.

At that time, she was writing a column for the *Citizen* titled "Rose's Last Scrap."

"I read in the Bible that after Jesus fed the multitudes, he said, `Pick up every last scrap of food.' I decided that I'd write about every different thing,

130

about the last scraps."

It is about friends, reminiscences, the changing seasons, the transactions of nature in the garden she yet tends.

Some years ago, she wrote about a bag of seeds she discovered near the lumberyard in Howard. She planted them in her garden and used the five-pointed compound leaf the plant produced in her flower arrangements.

"I took some to church," she said. "They looked awful pretty.

"It was marijuana."

She wrote about it, of course. By then, the plants were more than 6 feet tall.

A couple of interlopers sneaked into her garden one night after the column appeared and made off with her crop.

Lately, she has been sticking to sweet potatoes.

When asked how she writes her column, she replied tersely, "I write it with my right hand. I have an easy chair and a 300-watt reading lamp. I've got a pad to write on, and that's it. I send it longhand, and they type it at the paper."

Although no one has actually certified that she is, indeed, the oldest working columnist in the country, she doesn't hesitate when asked about that distinction.

"You don't have to look any farther."

It's a title she plans to keep a little longer.

"As long as my brain will function," she said, "and when it doesn't I don't even care to be here."

Three days from deadline, she was still pondering possible topics for the next "Rose's Last Scrap."

"I don't know. I'll think of something.

"My basket isn't empty."

Bellaire, Ohio. USA

Sept. 14, 1997

BELLAIRE, Ohio -- When a train rumbles across the Bellaire trestle along the Ohio River, you better have a good hold on the steel supports beneath it or the vibrations will shake you right into the water.

Boys of 12 know such things just as they know which expletives make the best adjectives and which girls everyone is whispering about.

"They say we're river rats," said John Fekete, a 12-year-old from Bellaire. "I don't care what they call us. This is what we do every day since the pools closed."

As he spoke, his toes pinched a grip on the edges of a pair of railroad ties almost three stories above the Ohio River.

Full of the heedless bravado that youth wears like a fresh tattoo, he raised his arms above his head, flashed a nothing-to-it smile and leaped.

For a long time, it seemed, he hung suspended in midair above the brown Ohio, limbs outstretched, grinning like a madman, his back to the gritty river town that is his home.

Bellaire is not one town, but two.

The Bellaire of the youths plunging from the trestle and flinging salty taunts at one another is different from the one that invokes a beer-marinated wistfulness at the Sons of Italy Club on Belmont Street.

Men named Gianangeli, Piccin and DeBlasis remember a tough, broad-shouldered town where Italians, Slovenians, Irish and Poles tended the engines that were America's industrial might.

That was before the steel mills grew old and were undercut by foreign competition, before environmental regulators read the death-warrant on high-sulfur coal, before the glass factories shut down.

Some of the men, many now retired, speak of that vibrant time as though it were a waltz they once danced with an achingly beautiful young woman they knew they would never grow old with.

The Sons of Italy Club, though, has been a constant to them. When their fathers came to this country, the club was an institution founded for the purpose, among others, of helping them get acclimated to their adopted home. It encouraged their mastery of the new language, their professional and social assimilation into the mainstream of American life.

Assimilate they did.

But life changed. Economic forces pitched and heaved. The cult of self gave short shrift to previously unquestioned values, and once-hallowed institutions sank in cynicism's mire like the worth of Third World currency amid stampeding inflation.

The fraternity of ethnicity is one of the few things that survived unshaken in Bellaire. It is, as ever, the rock of their solace.

Last Sunday, the Sons of Italy inducted 11 new members. Their membership has nearly doubled in 15 years, a rare phenomenon in an age when many fraternal orders and brotherhoods are faint shadows of what they once were.

"We're one of the few businesses in Bellaire that is expanding," Marshall Piccin wryly observed.

"We just had our 80th anniversary as a club," Ed Gianangeli said.

His younger cousin Vince Gianangeli, president of the Sons, has played an aggressive role in promoting the club and calling the members to their obligation of preserving the culture and heritage of their home country.

Many of the town's Sons of Italy were boys together, growing up in that other Bellaire, the Bellaire of unlimited possibilities.

At least, like an older version of the "river rats" on the trestle, they still have their club.

Young John Fekete shimmied back up the trusswork and steeled himself for another dive.

He said that sometimes, when the weather is right, 20 to 30 youngsters hang out at the trestle.

"It's not as polluted as most people say," he said of the river. "I swallow it sometimes and never get sick."

On a Belmont Street bench not far away, a small knot of old-timers talked and joked about the other Bellaire.

Youth has no patience for nostalgia, nor fear of what economic hardship presages for their future.

When you're 12, everyone you know is unemployed and broke.

"Ready?" John Fekete shouted to no one in particular.

One day he will tell adult contemporaries that, as a youth, he leaped from the trestle in Bellaire.

"Where is that?" they will probably ask.

LeAnn Rimes Tells All

June 15, 1997

I bought the definitive biography of LeAnn Rimes (*LeAnn Rimes: Teen Country Queen*) at the supermarket last week.

It has large letters, lots of white space, and the only real big word in it (except for *superstardom* and *skyrocketed*) is *differentiate*.

It was written by Grace Catalano, who, in modest self-appraisal, reminds us that she is "author of two *New York Times* best sellers: *New Kids on the Block* and *New Kids on the Block Scrapbook.*

If you are looking for those two best sellers, chances are pretty good that you'll find them right next to the Spandau Ballet LP in the everything-for-a-quarter box at finer garage sales everywhere.

Forgive me, but there is something a little strange about a publishing industry that thinks the world needs to know the vast life experiences of a girl who was still being potty-trained when the New Kids' star was plummeting like a spent bottle rocket.

What burning truths can best-selling author Catalano glean for readers from a 14-year-old?

Here are just two tantalizing nuggets:

• "One of LeAnn's favorite things to do when she has some free time is go to the mall. There's no doubt about it: LeAnn loves to shop, especially for clothes, jewelry, makeup and hats."

• "LeAnn also likes catching up on her favorite TV shows, *Beverly Hills, 90210* and *Friends.*"

We also learn from this page-turner that LeAnn's favorite nail polish colors are purple and pink, her favorite midnight snack is Cheez-It crackers, the worst thing she ever tasted was an anchovy, and the best-kept secret about her is that she used to dot the i in Rimes with a circle.

C'mon.

LeAnn Rimes is a great singer, but the way I see it, her life story at this point might be compelling reading only if she had stumbled into a recording studio after having been raised by wolves for the first 13 years of her life.

At 14, your biggest life crisis is the burgeoning zit on the end of your honker that's beginning to look like the taillight on a '59 Coupe de Ville. And, at that age, you don't tend to see much beyond it.

Are you listening, Grace Catalano? Are you listening, Bantam Doubleday Dell?

Here is the sort of insightful dialogue most pubescents produce:

"So then he like goes, `I really don't care what movie we see,' like he's Dylan on *90210*. So I go, `We don't have to go to the movie. We could go to the mall,' 'cause, like, I needed to pick up some Purple Vamp nail polish anyway. And he goes . . ."

I don't mean to diminish LeAnn. She has a set of pipes to rival most any vocalist in country music, and 14 is probably as good an age as any to begin a career in a business that considers you over the hill at 35.

Rimes' handlers have capitalized on comparisons of her to Patsy Cline, even to the point of milking a somewhat tenuous connection to the hit song *Blue*.

True, Patsy Cline had heard the song, written by Dallas-Fort Worth dee-jay Bill Mack in 1958. It stretches truth a bit, however, to imply that Patsy was ready to go into the studio with it when she was killed. She had a demo of the song for three years and never chose to record it.

It doesn't hurt the legend any that Rimes claims in her biography, "Just before I recorded *Blue*, I had a dream about Patsy Cline. I could see her face, and she told me she couldn't record *Blue* and wanted me to do it. It was pretty cool."

And even more convenient.

I hope LeAnn makes music for a good, long time. But I don't think there is much of a biography to write until she ponders "superstardom" at 14 from the vantage point of 50.

When that time comes, if Brenda Lee or Tanya Tucker are still around, I'm sure either will be happy to write a sympathetic introduction.

His Brothers' Keeper

July 24, 1998

CHILLICOTHE, Ohio -- Clarence Dennewitz rested a hand upon the pink granite headstone crowning the graves of his three brothers in Chillicothe's Greenlawn Cemetery.

A lift in the morning breeze ruffled a trio of small American flags arranged around the grave sites of John Paul, William and James Harold Dennewitz and the engraved legend "The three sons of Joseph and May Dennewitz."

Clarence, now 67, was barely a teen-ager when his brothers were killed in World War II.

Yes, he said, he had seen a few short TV clips of the new movie *Saving Private Ryan*.

No, he didn't intend to make a special effort to see the film.

"Every time I go through all of that, it just brings so much back," he said. "I kind of try to shun a lot of it."

He was working on his family's Ross County farm in the summer of 1944 when he learned that his eldest brother, John Paul, had died as a result of an artillery barrage near St.-Lo, France.

"During those days, they sent the telegram out with a taxi driver," he recalled.

John Paul had seen action in north Africa and Italy, helped train U.S. troops in England for D-Day, and made it through the Normandy landing. Then he was killed on July 18.

He was buried at an American cemetery in France.

James Harold was the next to die, killed by machine-gun fire in Germany only three weeks before the end of fighting in Europe.

He was buried in Holland.

Clarence's mother, May, having given two sons to the cause, decided after learning of James Harold's death to appeal to the War Department to have son William, serving with the Navy in the South Pacific, removed from combat.

What she could not have known was that the War Department already had received word that William Dennewitz had been killed.

"He was close to Okinawa on minesweeper duty," Clarence said. "His ship was hit by a suicide plane, a Japanese kamikaze, the day after the one brother was killed in Germany."

William was buried on an island in the South Pacific.

Uneasy at the prospect of her dead sons' graves being so far from home, May Dennewitz requested that the bodies be disinterred and brought back to Ohio.

"They brought them on the N&W railroad to the depot here in Chillicothe," Clarence remembered.

It was March 1949. "They had held them at a receiving depot in Norfolk until they got all three together."

The bodies were transported to the family farm, three flag-draped caskets flanking the walls of the parlor, a framed photo of each son atop each flag.

May and her husband, Joseph, could have had a funeral home handle the visitation, but it was yet the era in which many families preferred to take care of their own.

"There were a lot of visitors," Clarence said. "A lot of friends called."

The funeral was set for the first day of spring.

"They showed those boys the same honor they would show a president. They took them down the streets on caissons.

"Governor Lausche came. He wept at the funeral."

Two years after her sons were brought home, May Dennewitz, 55, was laid to rest next to their graves.

"That loss does something to a person," Clarence mused of his mother's attempts to deal with her grief.

In 1955, when the state of Ohio decided to construct a new bridge across Paint Creek, an appeal was made that the bridge be dedicated to the Dennewitz brothers.

Plaques were erected at each end of the bridge.

"We used to fish down here," Clarence said, nodding toward the creek as traffic on business Rt. 23 roared across the Dennewitz Brothers Memorial Bridge, many of the drivers probably clueless as to the distinction of the span they traversed.

"We'd catch catfish, carp, suckers. My brother Bill made his own boat, a 16-foot rowboat. We ran a trotline across the creek."

Though his brothers have been gone more than half a century, the part of Clarence that mourns what might have been is just beneath the surface.

"These guys have done so much," he said.

"I appreciate . . . " he tried to continue, wincing, then turning his face away. "I appreciate when someone remembers what they did."

He closed a small, worn scrapbook of snapshots and clippings, then climbed into his pickup truck.

He hadn't wanted to pose for a picture near his brothers' headstone. It wasn't stubbornness. It was reverence. He said he didn't want his presence in the photo to distract the beholder from what was truly important.

Death in the Night

April 5, 1998

MONEY, Miss. -- The roof of the old brick grocery has collapsed in the middle, plunging splintered rafters onto dusty shelves and display cases, wedging timbers against a front door that only a brown wasp seems obsessed with entering.

Not far away, a sun-bleached mobile home, once headquarters of the U.S. Post Office, Money, Miss., sits abandoned. On the hamlet's far reaches, a nameless clapboard church squats amid the tangle of myrtle and fescue enveloping five-dozen headstones.

Signposts in nearby Greenwood exalt the name of the latest crowned beauty to reign queen over an area that likes to call itself "the cotton capital of the world."

No plaque or marker certifies Money as the site of the nativity of the civil-rights movement in America, yet this unlettered delta hamlet rivals Rosa Parks' Montgomery bus ride, Brown vs. Board of Education and the ugly discord that attended the integration of Little Rock's schools as the seminal and tragic launch pad of the struggle for equal rights.

With frightening impunity, blacks had been lynched and murdered for decades in the Deep South. But the brutal details of the killing of one 14-year-old Emmett Till in 1955 in Money were like a fire-bell summons to the conscience of the nation.

Till, a Chicago native, was spending summer vacation at the home of his great-uncle, Moses "Preacher" Wright, a delta sharecropper.

Unlike his Mississippi-born cousins, Till did not move about in groveling fear of the local whites.

On a steamy August day, Till traveled into the town of Money with a handful of kin and friends. There, he walked into Bryant's Grocery & Meat Market to buy a piece of bubble gum. Accounts of what happened during that brief exchange between Till and Carolyn Bryant, the 21-year-old wife of the grocery's owner, are widely divergent.

Some say Till whistled at the woman. Others say he propositioned her.

Whatever the case, Carolyn Bryant's husband, Roy, and his half-brother J.W. Milam paid a visit to "Preacher" Wright's home in the dead of night not long after the encounter.

Both Bryant and Milam were armed with .45s. They ordered "Preacher" Wright to produce "that Chicago boy," and ordered Till into their truck.

After pistol-whipping Till throughout the night, Milam decided to kill him, shouting, "I'm tired of 'em sending your kind down here to stir up trouble. Goddamn you -- I'm gonna make an example of you just so everybody can know how me and my folks stand."

Milam and Bryant drove Till to a cotton gin near the town of Boyle, where they picked up a cotton-gin fan.

On the banks of the Tallahatchie River, Milam demanded of the beaten boy, "Nigger, you still as good as I am?"

Stoic and largely silent throughout the all-night ordeal, Till said nothing.

He was ordered to strip. Milam leveled his gun and fired one shot.

He and his half-brother tied the cotton-gin fan to Till's neck and pitched the youth's body into the Tallahatchie.

Three days later, along the river at Pecan Point, a boy fishing spied the body.

Bryant and Milam were arrested and brought to trial for the killing.

"Preacher" Wright, kept in hiding in the days leading up to the trial, was hurried into the courtroom by the prosecution where, in two words, he delivered one of the most courageous indictments in the history of the civil-rights movement.

"Thar he," he pronounced, stabbing a finger at Milam when the prosecution asked if he recognized in the courtroom the man who ordered Emmett Till from his house that night.

For "Preacher," his daring would leave him no choice but to flee the delta. He sold his hunting dog, and left his car at the railroad station that carried him out of town.

Bryant and Milam were acquitted by an all-white jury.

In a glaring episode of checkbook journalism, the two were later paid several thousand dollars to detail the particulars of the murder for an article in *Look* magazine.

"What are we Mississippians so afraid of?" William Faulkner wondered in print after *Look* published its piece on the Till slaying. "Why do we have such a low opinion of our blood and tradition as to fear that as soon as the Negro enters our home by the front door, he will propose marriage to our daughter and she will accept?"

In the aftermath of the trial, a young Hollywood scriptwriter, Rod Serling, was so moved by the injustice of the Till case that he wrote a TV script about the murder for *The U.S. Steel Hour.*

White citizens councils in the South lobbied the show's sponsor, persuading the corporate giant to make changes in the script.

Ultimately, according to writer Stephen Whitfield, Serling's "Noon on Doomsday" was so stunningly transfigured that a TV viewer watching its presentation depicting the murder of a Jewish pawnbroker in New England would have had no idea that the original script dealt with the killing of Till.

In Money, in the chill drizzle of March's last day, there is no one to speak for the youth who put the delta village, now almost vanished, on the map.

Till stares back from photos grown old, his handsome face blind to the unwitting role his death would play in jump-starting the civil-rights movement in the Deep South.

He was simply a boy who blundered inadvertently into the path of racists and became a martyr.

Upon the railroad tracks across from what was once Bryant's Grocery, a passing coal train rumbles toward Greenwood.

A short blast from the engine's whistle signals its fleeting and perfunctory notice of that which much of the rest of the world has forgotten.

The Circle of Life

Oct. 25, 1999

BUSBY, Mont. -- The 26 graves are arranged in a circle on a windswept hill overlooking the hamlet of Busby.

To find many of them, it is necessary to poke through the browning grass, for the graves are designated only with flat aluminum markers no larger than a man's hand.

Clifford Long Sioux, a fifth-generation descendant of Cheyenne chief Dull Knife, is unofficial caretaker of the melancholy little cemetery. A chain-link fence protects the graveyard from grazing stock. Three strands of barbed wire protect it from vandals.

Waving a stick across the sweep of the graves, Long Sioux noted, "Most of these people were women and children who were with Dull Knife when he broke out of Fort Robinson."

Following Lt. Col. George Armstrong Custer's 1876 defeat at Little Bighorn, the Northern Cheyenne had been removed to what was then called Indian Territory (now Oklahoma).

Cheated and ill-used by the whites, discontented with reservation life so far from their traditional hunting lands, 278 Cheyenne set out to return to the Yellowstone River in 1878.

U.S. soldiers pursued and hunted down many of them. Dull Knife and an estimated 150 Cheyenne were captured during a winter storm and imprisoned at Fort Robinson in northwestern Nebraska.

Dull Knife, informed by the fort's commander that he and his people would be returned to Oklahoma, replied, "I will die before I go south."

To force Dull Knife and his people into submission, rations to their prison barracks were cut off -- food and firewood first, then water.

The angry Cheyenne decided to break out on the night of Jan. 9, 1879. By that time, they had not had food for four days nor water for two.

"Some were killed right at the fort when they ran," Long Sioux said. "Some made it to the White River. Some made it to Pine Ridge and hid there for a year."

The 26 whose graves Long Sioux now tends were killed near the fort. A warrior named Sitting Man, weak from starvation and nursing a fractured leg, was barely outside the fort when he realized that he would not be able to keep up with the others.

Cheyenne Autumn author Mari Sandoz wrote, "He sat there against a high drift singing his death song as a soldier put a gun to his head and blew his brains out, splattering them dark against the moonlit snowbank."

When white civilians living near the fort heard the commotion of the escape, they mobbed the fields where dead and wounded Cheyenne lay. According to testimony in a military review later, the civilians finished off the wounded, scalping some. They stripped the bodies and violated the corpses of Cheyenne women.

One soldier, attempting to rescue wounded Cheyenne before civilians could get to them, told a comrade, "There's a small girl not over 6 months old up there with her hip shot to pieces, and so frozen she will surely die, and she doesn't even whimper."

A pair of six-mule death wagons was dispatched from the fort to gather the bodies.

Several years after the Cheyenne were buried, the military disinterred their bodies. Each set of remains was crated and sent to the Smithsonian Institution in Washington.

"We knew museums had remains," Long Sioux explained, "but they would not say if they were Cheyenne or Crow or Arapaho. I was the one who pushed the whole issue to get these back. These are our ancestors."

Six years ago, Long Sioux finally succeeded in his quest. The remains were returned to Montana.

"These were buried in cedar boxes," Long Sioux said. "Along with the bodies, we put in food and water for their last journey back to the spirit world -- cedar chips and sage, too."

Standing amid the ringed graves, Long Sioux said, "We believe in the circle of life."

Not far from where he stood, a sun-bleached, stuffed toy lamb rested near a grave marked "Killed Jan. 1879. Age 3 to 5. Buried 10/16/93."

The bluff upon which Long Sioux and his contemporaries decided to bury the Fort Robinson dead is adjacent to the resting place of Two Moon, the Cheyenne chief who battled Custer at Little Bighorn.

It is high ground that some beholders might describe as "bleak" especially if they are unaware of Long Sioux's story and don't understand that the hill's chief occupants spent 114 years waiting to return to it.

Ruth Ann's Letter

Feb. 16, 1998

I was presented with the most curious of Valentine's Day remembrances this year, eight days early and 30 years too late.

A gift from my high school sweetheart, Ruth Ann Neil, it was a tatter-edged Pangburn's chocolate box, the scarlet bow on top mashed flat from all the years in the bottom of her closet.

Filled with letters I had written after I left West Jefferson full of myself and bold threats to make my mark on the world as a novelist, the box held enough self-centered and conniving prose to reveal to me that love, like youth, is probably wasted on the young.

"I kept them because I thought someday you might write a book about yourself," she said. "Maybe they'll help you remember."

They helped me remember what a jerk I was.

Ruth Ann and I dated for the better part of our high school years.

Her parents ran a restaurant out of the home they owned on Rt. 40 just east of West Jefferson.

There was little need for letters while we were dating, for we were constantly together.

I was poor, something that mattered not one whit to Ruth Ann. Her mother, Lena, was forever trying to stuff a buck or two into my jacket pocket, aware that my job as a bagger at the IGA paid only 65 cents an hour.

It was the tenderest of gestures, but I was ashamed of being poor and I took it the wrong way.

Though Ruth Ann was only 15 and I 16 when we began dating, we both thought that we likely would one day marry. I don't know when that changed, but there came a time when I began to see my parents' lives as an intimation of what lay ahead for me.

I didn't want to be someone living from paycheck to paycheck and nursing the bitterness of what might have been.

When I left West Jefferson a week after high school to take a job as a summer camp counselor in Wisconsin, the Greyhound bus was carrying me outside Ohio for the first time in my life.

I took a beat-up Underwood portable typewriter, a $5 Sears guitar and a stunningly arrogant notion about what destiny held for me.

Looked at now, the letters to West Jefferson and Ruth Ann sound as though I wrote them while preening before a mirror.

The worst mistake I made was to presume that because her aspirations were different from mine, she needed coaching on how to become more cosmopolitan and wise.

I sent her a long list of books I believed she should read, an act whose blunt condescension I would not grasp for years but one she immediately forgave.

The last thing she needed was me, though I hovered around the fringes of her life for two or three years, writing pretentious letters from summer camp, then the Navy -- letters full of mixed signals about our relationship.

When wisely she began dating other guys, I assumed the role of correspondence-school instructor on matters of the heart, inflicting unwanted counsel on how to manage her relationships.

To her credit, she wearied of me and began dating a fellow named Jim whom she eventually would marry.

He was caring, considerate, handsome and intelligent, and he didn't presume to know how she should run her life.

He was the smartest decision she ever made.

Their first and only child was a spina bifida baby, but with immense courage and love they handled each successive challenge -- the hydrocephalus, the paralysis, surgery after surgery for shunts and steel rods in the spine. More than once, young Rachel's heart ceased beating in the operating room, but she lived and was loved and cared for beyond measure.

She and my oldest son are the same age.

I don't know that I could have risen to the daunting charge thrust upon Jim and Ruth Ann only a few years out of high school.

I was too full of me then.

To her immense credit, Ruth Ann probably knew that, and fate took care of the rest.

"I did read *The Good Earth*," she told me when she gave me back my letters, recalling the must-read book list I had issued her.

I started to apologize, but she shook her head.

"It's a pretty good book," she said.

Irish Music

March 23, 1998

I killed sweet Molly Malone last week.

Had to.

St. Patrick's Day and all, you see.

Oh, sure. The song says "She died of the fever."

But I couldn't get the smell of cockles and mussels off my hands, and what jarred me from sleep in the dead of night last week probably was less the rumbling of the corned beef in my belly than a frightening dreamscape in which I saw poor Molly's ghost wheeling a barrel of bivalves through Dublin's back alleys.

Do me a favor. Shoot me if I ever again book my band to play a gig the week of St. Patrick's Day.

Don't get me wrong. I love the Irish. It's half my blood and most of my sensibilities, and I could die a happy man if I went to my grave knowing that Ireland's hostage counties had thrown off the yoke of a meddling England.

That said, I must confess that much of Irish music leaves me in a bleak and melancholy state for days after the parade and pipes have come and gone.

Please don't write to remind me that Ireland paid dearly for the shadow of tragedy in her music, fighting the famine or the black-and-tans or bidding grievous farewells to the heart of her youth seeking a better life elsewhere.

I know all that, but knowing it doesn't make it any less depressing.

This year, I made a point to find an Irish songbook with a counterbalancing collection of happy tunes. Surprisingly, I discovered that many tunes Americans think were carried over from Ireland are actually Tin Pan Alley ditties (George M. Cohan wrote *Harrigan*).

Unwilling to go off on a tangent about hiding the razor blades to get through the week after St. Patrick's Day, I telephoned Pat Mogan, for two decades a member of the celebrated Irish Brigade.

"Isn't a lot of this Irish stuff just bluegrass tragedy with a brogue?" I ventured.

He allowed as much.

"Where you from, Yank?" they ask him in pubs in Ireland.

"Ohio," he responds, his reply smothered in an outburst of praise for *Banks of the Ohio*, a traditional American folk tune about a thwarted suitor who murders his beloved and throws her in the Ohio River. Now there's a tune to charm the green socks off an Irishman.

Anyone who knows bluegrass is aware that the old tragic songs trade heavily on spurned or unrequited love, murder, remorse, the gallows. A lot of that is the Irish influence on Appalachian music.

Mogan agreed that death and grief are common motifs in the music he cherishes.

There is the song he sings about an IRA operative, Sean South.

"Put to the sword by the British," Mogan said.

Then there's the one about Kevin Barry. "He was in the 1916 Easter rebellion. He was hanged in prison, but he wanted to be shot like a soldier." Mogan sings:

Shoot me like an Irish soldier,
Do not hang me like a dog.

And then there's poor Roddy McCorley. Mogan knows that one, too:

Up the narrow street he stepped, smiling and proud and young,
About the hemp-rope on his neck the golden ringlets clung,
There's never a tear in the blue eyes, both glad and bright are they,
As Roddy McCorley goes to die on the bridge of Toome today.

Stop! Please! Isn't there anything whimsical?

Well, there's *The Ballad of William Bloat* Mogan resumes his crooning:

He had a wife, the bane of his life
She always got his goat
Till one day at dawn
With her night dress on

He slit her bloody throat.

That one is supposed to be comical, or at least ironic. For, after Bloat takes a razor to his wife, "He twists the bedsheet off her feet," fashions a noose and hangs himself in the pantry. The wife lives because he used a razor made of cheap British steel, and he dies because the sheet was pure Irish linen.

Ha! Boy, there's hilarity. Woman bleeding all over the place. Husband hanging in the pantry, gurgling and doing a little impromptu death jig in the air. Sure, let's teach that one to the children.

And we can't forget *Danny Boy*. It is the quintessential song of loss and grieving.

"True," Mogan concurred. "That's kind of like the national anthem of the Celtic people."

Here's the rub: The tune may be rooted to the bedrock in Ireland, but the lyrics were penned by a British bard and barrister, Fred Weatherly.

Oh, well. If it will break your heart in a thousand tiny pieces and make you think about what you want sung at your funeral, who can fault the Irish for making it one of their own?

John Wesley Hardin

Nov. 19, 1999

EL PASO, Texas -- Sure, John Wesley Hardin killed a few people -- maybe as many as 50. Nevertheless, El Paso biographer Leon Metz would like us to understand the gunslinger's other side.

"If Hardin were sitting here right now," Metz said, "he would be the life of the party. He might dance a jig, tell a joke, spout a few biblical quotes or spin a story. Before he left, he might very well shoot somebody. You couldn't want for a better guest, although you'd have to search him as he came through the door."

Hardin is buried in El Paso's Concordia Cemetery beneath Texas hardpan so unforgiving that little more than cactus grows between the crosses and headstones.

"This grave wasn't even marked until 1965," Metz said. "Today," the writer-historian added, "it is El Paso's most frequently visited tourist attraction."

Metz should know. He routinely is pestered by out-of-towners (some have called him on Christmas Day) who want to be led to the burial site. Metz long ago ceased to be amazed by what he encounters at Hardin's grave:

"I have found whiskey bottles here, decks of cards, toy six-shooters."

It is strange that people feel compelled to pay their respects to a psychopath more than a century after his death. Then, society didn't call this world's John Wesley Hardins serial killers. We called them gunslingers and shrouded them in myth and lore. We made it tough work for serious writers such as Metz to sift fact from legend and apocrypha.

To his credit, Metz was not easily misled, even when his chief deceiver also was his subject. He explained, "Hardin is the only gunfighter to have written his own autobiography. Actually, he dictated it to his mistress."

Unfortunately, Hardin's recall was selective and his appraisals of his acts totally subjective. He obviously didn't live to tell about the last shooting in which he was involved.

Metz calculated that Hardin killed his first man when he was 15. It wasn't a quick-draw affair on Main Street with all the locals diving for cover. "(That) is a product of Gary Cooper and the *High Noon* walkdown," Metz said. "That isn't the way they did it. You could get killed doing it that way."

Evidence suggests that Hardin stalked his first victim at night and shot him without warning.

"Hardin was totally without mercy when it came to shooting people," Metz said. "There was no such thing as a fast draw or a fair fight."

The gunslinger had a wife and children, although he was so frequently on the lam that he was husband and father only in a nominal sense. Dead at 42, he had spent 15 of the last 16 years of his life in prison. His wife died six months before he was released. By the time of his parole, his children were strangers to him.

Hardin, who became something of a jailhouse expert on Texas law, said he intended to practice as a lawyer in El Paso after his release. He went so far as to print business cards and establish an office in the Wells Fargo building.

Metz recounted, "So far as we are aware, Martin M'Rose was his only client, and he had him murdered."

A sometime cattle rustler and general ne'r-do-well, M'Rose found himself a wanted man in 1895. With a bounty on his head in the United States, he hid out in Juarez, Mexico, and retained Hardin to straighten out matters.

Hardin used his client's wife, Beulah, as a legal go-between and then lover. He knew that Beulah was holding all of her husband's money in El Paso. Metz believes that Hardin helped set up the ambush in which M'Rose was killed. By that time, Hardin and Beulah already had set up housekeeping.

Hardin squandered much of M'Rose's booty by summer 1895. He was earning his drinking money by performing sharpshooter feats for gunslinger groupies in El Paso. He could put three rounds in the center of a playing card from a long five paces, even when he was half-full of cheap whiskey.

If a fellow could foretell the moment of his death, he might spend a few moments crafting the final utterance for which he would be remembered. Yet Hardin died the way he often killed his victims -- by surprise and without warning.

Hardin had his back to the front door of El Paso's Acme Saloon on the August night that Constable John Selman stepped through the door and put a bullet through Hardin's head.

The gunslinger had just rolled dice from a small cup, playing a game called Ship, Captain & Crew, to determine who would buy the next round of drinks.

"Brown, you've got four sixes to beat," he crowed to the grocer drinking next to him. Hardin was dead before he hit the floor.

The $77.50 it cost Beulah M'Rose to bury John Wesley likely was the last of her late husband's cache that Hardin hadn't spent.

When Metz was working on Hardin's biography, his publisher thought the book should be titled *The West's Most Notorious Gunfighter.* Metz had other ideas. He insisted on *John Wesley Hardin: Dark Angel of Texas.*

Metz won, contending that "Hardin's youth had passed silently during the dark night of his prison years. At a little over 42 years of age, Hardin had outlived his era. He was an anachronism, a psychopathic gunman out of the past, a man more or less waiting to be buried.

"John Selman not only killed John Wesley Hardin; more importantly, he did him a favor."

Selman himself would be gunned down within the year.

In Concordia Cemetery, Hardin is buried somewhere in the general vicinity of Selman and only three graves away from the luckless M'Rose.

Hardin's manuscript of his autobiography became his children's property. No doubt it told them more than they cared to learn about the father they never knew.

Forever Hollywood

Nov. 7, 1999

HOLLYWOOD, Calif. -- It was a balmy autumn night in 1932 when 24-year-old Peg Entwhistle walked to the end of Beachwood Drive on the vista overlooking Hollywood. There the stage actress studied the huge and now familiar letters mounted on the hillside.

Entwhistle moved determinedly through scrub brush toward the 50-foot-high "H." In those days, the letters spelled HOLLYWOODLAND and advertised a real-estate development in the hills above the city.

Not much of that mattered to British-born Entwhistle. She had come to Hollywood after appearing in several plays in Boston and New York. She wanted to get into movies but -- after a year in town -- had landed only a bit part in one film, a fleeting cameo made even briefer in the cutting room.

She apologized in the note she left: "I am afraid I am a coward. I am sorry for everything. If I had done this a long time ago, it would have saved a lot of pain."

Had Entwhistle been able to make it through despondency just one day more, she would have received the Beverly Hills Playhouse letter that offered her the lead role in an upcoming production. Ironically, the play was about a woman driven by circumstance to suicide.

Poor Entwhistle -- dead at 24 with an O. Henry twist to her epilogue and nothing to show for the pain but the distinction of being the first to leap from the big sign on the hill.

On a recent afternoon, it was difficult not to think about Entwhistle while waiting for the Oh Heavenly Tours hearse and studying the hillside sign that shimmered through a gossamer scrim of smog.

A youthful Duncan St. James held open the silver-gray door to a vehicle already past its prime when he purchased it several years ago from a Kansas funeral director.

St. James turned the key in the ignition and the '71 Caddy let go with the wake-up cough of a three-pack-a-day smoker.

"It's had its share of problems," St. James said of the death sled as it wheezed down Santa Monica Boulevard.

He acquired the hearse earlier this year from Graveline, a defunct Hollywood death-tour enterprise for which he once worked as driver.

"I started (my) company in June, and I haven't turned a profit yet," he said. "The hearse keeps breaking down."

During his Ohio childhood in Columbus, St. James was better known as Curtis Duncan. He modified his name when he began trying to make his mark in Hollywood. St. James has clawed out a few parts, portraying a prisoner in *Face Off* and a cameraman in *Dante's Peak*.

"I worked on *90210*," he said, "*Friends* and *Buffy, the Vampire Slayer.*"

For now, he is driving a hearse, pointing out the street corner where William Frawley dropped dead, the house where "Bugsy" Siegel bought it, the motel room where Janis Joplin overdosed.

St. James is only too aware that inasmuch as the public is intrigued with lifestyles of the rich and famous, we also are captivated by how they die. We have seen them (many of them time and again) die in cinema. Yet someone always called, "Cut! That's a wrap," and they went home to die again another day on another film set.

On St. James' tour, what is revealed more than anything else is the mortal side of the legend.

Hollywood Forever is the tour's centerpiece. Long known as Hollywood Memorial Cemetery, it is the resting place of many Hollywood greats, including Rudolph Valentino, Tyrone Power, Douglas Fairbanks and Cecil B. DeMille.

Until a few years ago, the grounds, headstones and mausoleums had become disquietingly neglected. Then the cemetery was purchased at auction for $375,000.

New owners have cleaned up the place, rechristened it and vigorously begun marketing available gravesites and crypts.

The Egyptian revival Abbey of the Psalms features a computerized directory of those interred at Hollywood Forever. The directory includes short clips from memorable films of each person.

Tom DeMille, a Hollywood Forever staff person, hit a few computer keys and watched a snippet of Valentino in *The Sheik* play out.

"There were 5,000 people here the day of his funeral," DeMille marveled, "and 40,000 outside the gate trying to get in. He's still popular. Seventy-five years after his death, and no one ever heard him speak. Still popular."

Before leaving the Abbey of the Psalms, St. James pointed out the crypt of director Victor Fleming and noted, "He directed two of the most well-known pictures in the same year: *Gone With the Wind* and *The Wizard of*

Oz."

No tour would be complete without a few Hollywood ghost tales. St. James does not disappoint.

"Here we have Clifton Webb," he said, motioning toward a crypt. "Clifton Webb is known mainly for his hauntings in this area. The maintenance men have claimed to have heard him holler, 'Hey, come back here.' Certain people have claimed to have seen an apparition."

St. James seems untroubled by the ghost stories. What occasionally unsettles him is not the professed supernatural occurrences around Hollywood cemeteries, but the real and frightening ones he himself has experienced.

"Al Jolson's grave," he recounted. "If you walk by his grave, a sensor goes off and he starts singing, 'Mammy! Mammy!' It scares the hell out of you."

Back out on the road, St. James guided the hearse past grim milestones -- the apartment from which Diane Linkletter leaped to her death during a bad acid trip, the nightclub where River Phoenix went down.

At the residence where Jack Webb (TV's Joe Friday) died, St. James punched the button on his tape player: "Here's where Friday died on Thursday," a voice said. "His wife frantically called the paramedics, but Webb had already turned in his badge."

St. James is revising the script he inherited when he bought the hearse from Graveline. Parts of the tape simply represent bad humor (the Jack Webb quips) and some just plain bad taste (he already had excised a sound-effects "splat" that once was played at the Diane Linkletter stop).

When he was learning the route and rehearsing the solo drive at night, St. James typically would pause for a breather at the halfway point along the trek.

"I would take my break at Jimmy Stewart's house," he said. "I'd look up and see a light on in the bedroom." Recalling the awe of that moment, he continued, "I was in the play *It's a Wonderful Life*. I was old man Potter."

St. James had finished his training at Graveline and was escorting a tour on the day when he saw ambulance and police vehicles at Stewart's house.

Had they ever met, Stewart probably would have liked St. James. Here he was -- a young man from Columbus trying to get a leg up in the film business, an actor who temporary inconveniences had placed him behind the wheel of a 28-year-old hearse, delivering a death tour to tourists for $40 a pop.

A slight few of the names recited on such Hollywood tours make it to the status of the late Jimmy Stewart.

Most are remembered for tragic reasons:

Carl "Alfalfa" Switzer, an Our Gang has-been shot dead over a $50 dispute. Or Virginia Rappe, the 25-year-old star whose death after a wild party ended her Hollywood dreams and dashed the career of silent-film comic "Fatty" Arbuckle.

And Peg Entwhistle, who climbed atop the big "H" and made her last act a Hollywood first.

Where Love Lives

Dec. 24, 1994

She introduced herself by her first name, in a room where people guard their last yet reveal the spectacular squalor of lives they once lived in skins they are still shedding.

Listeners huddled with plastic cups of coffee strong enough to strip paint. A few newcomers stared thoughtfully into their steamy cups of joe, perhaps glad, perhaps not, to be drinking something not still wrapped in a bag from the store.

Not far away, a fire sputtered in a flagstone hearth.

The voice of the woman recounting her regretted past had a childlike whimsy. One listener imagined he was hearing the description of a horrific crash as told by Betty Boop.

Still, the story was as compelling as its teller was disarming. The kindred ache that makes the universal personal soon made the room quiet enough to hear a heart drop.

"I come to these rooms because love lives here," the woman said in the measured tones of one who doesn't care whether her listeners forget every sentence she utters but one.

Her words reminded one listener of Lee Remick trying to explain herself to Jack Lemmon in *Days of Wine and Roses:*

I want to come home. I know what you're thinking about me. A lot's happened - lots of detours. There were plenty of 'em, but they were nothing. I never looked at them; they had no identity. I never gave anything out of myself to them. I thought they'd help me from being so lonely, but I was just as lonely because love is the only thing that keeps you from being lonely - and I didn't have that.

When she hit bottom, the woman found herself living in a federal housing project with three children, little postcards from a trio of ex-husbands who were glad she was anywhere but wherever they were.

The only sunlight she saw was refracted through the prism of the empty she had just drained.

She had family in an upscale suburb of the city. Still, she had not only burned her bridges but also wired the approaches to the charred remains with plastique.

When she got sick and tired of being sick and tired, she stumbled into the rooms where love lives.

A woman who had been down the road herself took her under her wing. The new friend made her call each day and recite three things for which she was grateful.

Cynical, she told her new patron she was grateful for coffee filters.

"Coffee filters?" the other woman asked.

"Yeah," came the sharp reply, "because I'm out of money and I don't have any toilet paper."

That was six years ago.

She got herself off welfare a long time ago, moved out of the projects, found a job.

Along the way, she even had lunch with ABC News anchor Peter Jennings.

The network had been doing a series on welfare mothers, and she thought he ought to know about a few of the ones fighting to get off public assistance.

Her note to Jennings got her 15 minutes of fame and a free BLT. The experience also gave her a few ideas about corporations that can be persuaded to help women trade public assistance for paychecks without wrapping the notion in 42 pounds of red tape.

She still preaches that gospel.

Truth is, she still has too much month left at the end of the money, but she makes it work. The "kindness of strangers" sometimes helps.

Her three children's Christmas will be brighter this morning because her gumption and spunk impressed an Orthodox Jewish elf named Bernie Abrams, whom she has not met.

He has never known the rooms where she says love lives.

Life is curious.

Deep in December's heart, in a borrowed Presbyterian church room full of cynics, a woman recounted an ordeal that has infinitely more in common with the story of the prodigal son than the birth of Christ and touched the heart of a stranger.

"Love lives in these rooms," she said.

A listener marveled, "Damnedest Christmas story I ever heard."

Africatown

Oct. 8, 1999

MOBILE, Ala. -- Henry Williams stepped gingerly through the litter-strewn fescue of Plateau Memorial Cemetery. He announced as he went, "In this graveyard you will find most of the Keebys, the Lewises, the Shades.

"Here is one who was the housegirl of President William McKinley at the time he was shot.

"This is Isaiah Whitley, the man who got Alabama to establish salaries for teachers in 1910."

Pausing at the Cudjoe Lewis grave, Williams observed of the rude crypt's occupant, "He was the last living male who was on the Clotilda."

The Clotilda (sometimes spelled Clotilde) is the tie that binds most of those who rest in the old cemetery near Mobile's Africatown. The ship is believed to be the last one that brought Africans from the "slave coast" to the United States. The Clotilda arrived in Mobile Bay in late summer 1859.

Importation of slaves was forbidden in the United States for more than 50 years before the Clotilda's voyage. Federal agents in major U.S. ports scrutinized shipping traffic to assure that the prohibition was not violated.

The presence of agents along Mobile Bay's main channel did not sit well with many in that city, and that antipathy may have played a part in the story of the Clotilda.

Timothy Meaher, a wealthy Mobile shipbuilder, reportedly made a wager over his whiskey one evening. He said he would outfit a slave ship, dispatch it to Africa, then bring its manacled cargo into Mobile Bay, eluding the agents.

To that end, he sent the Clotilda to the west Africa kingdom of Dahomey. Dahomeyans often skirmished with neighboring tribes and took prisoners whom they later sold to slave traders.

Capt. William Foster, Meaher's agent, purchased 116 prisoners. Most of them were members of the Tarkar tribe.

Returning to U.S. waters, Foster dropped anchor off Petite Bois Island in the Mississippi Sound and sent word to Meaher of his arrival. Under cover of darkness, a steam tug moved the Clotilda into Mobile Bay. Its human cargo transferred to a steamboat, the ship was scuttled and set afire near Twelve Mile Island.

The Tarkars disbursed throughout the bay area.

"My people were the people who took care of the African-Americans who were on board the Clotilda," Williams recalled of his grandparents. "They helped feed them and get them settled in the community."

Although most of the newly arrived Tarkars quickly assimilated within the broader African-American community, a clannish 30 remained together in the Plateau area.

Gradually, they traded their Tarkar names for Anglo ones -- Manobee became Kitty Cooper, Abache adopted the name Clara Turner. Kazoola would be remembered better as Cudjoe Lewis.

They were Christianized, although they retained a strong adherence to the tribal codes by which they had lived in Togo. The avuncular Lewis was the group's unofficial spokesman. In his final years, he often held court for journalists and historians who wanted to know the stories of Africatown and the Clotilda.

Williams chose to honor Lewis with a sculpture crafted and erected outside Africatown's Union Baptist Church.

In 1982, descendants of those who came to America on the Clotilda began sponsoring the Africatown Folk Festival, an event to honor the heritage of Mobile's Plateau area.

Several attempts have been made to raise Africatown's visibility, to promote it as a tourist venue. One man has even talked of locating the ship's burnt wreckage at the bottom of Mobile Bay and salvaging what remains.

Truth is, there is nothing much in Africatown to satisfy the theme-park mentality of today's tourists, nothing to pull them off the interstate or hold their attention once they arrive.

There is just an old cemetery, its headstones and crypts defaced by time and the elements.

And there is Henry Williams, who knew Cudjoe Lewis and who has heard all the accounts of the Clotilda's voyage. He doesn't understand why history today can't be sold without snack bars and interactive exhibits.

Rustling Beanies

May 26, 1999

William "Billy the Kid" Bonney is doing a slow turn in his grave as I write.

When there was yet some wild left in the West, the mere mention of Bonney could cause a shudder that rippled the length of the Chisholm Trail. Those were the days when cowboys such as Mesquite Bill and Wyoming Pete were driving cattle and the Kid was stealing as many of them as he could.

Rustling was a bold and dangerous profession. Get caught and you'd get a bullet through your last meal or be strung up like a cheap wind chime from the nearest oak tree.

When cattle ranchers finally had had enough of sharing their herds with Bonney, they hung a sheriff's badge on the chest of a former bartender named Pat Garrett and told him to go after Billy.

Billy went to his reward when rustling was still roguishly noble, before the era of -- OK, I'll say it -- Beanie Baby rustling.

I learned all I care to know about Beanie rustling while my sister and her husband were houseguests last weekend. Mary and Jim, you see, are today's equivalent of the last century's cowboys. They drive Beanies to market along the Illinois trail to Ohio.

I don't know whether they sing to the herd as cowboys once did. Kind of difficult to imagine a good Beanie-driving song:

Rollin', rollin', rollin'.
Keep those Beanies rollin'.

They visit Columbus about one weekend a month with a vanload of Beanies to be herded to the stockyard (a sprawling flea market at the Ohio State Fairgrounds).

It's not a business for the faint of heart.

Last weekend, during a power outage at the fairgrounds, they had to keep the Beanie herd together and safe from rustlers with nothing more than dim auxiliary lighting.

I don't know how many head of Beanie they lost, but when they made camp for the night at my place, the talk drifted to Beanie rustling.

A rustler took them for about $3,200 of prime stuffed animal a couple of months back.

You see, Mary and Jim have a collectibles shop at a mall in Normal, Ill. In the business of driving Beanies, it is the equivalent of a cattleman's ranch. I suppose that is where they do the branding and the sorting.

The rustler who made off with their goods dropped by that shop earlier this spring with a boxful of autographs of sports figures.

"He had Cal Ripken, Bret Favre, Mark McGwire," Jim remembered. "Said he was an ESPN sportswriter. That's how he got the autographs."

In truth, the closest he ever got to ESPN was watching SportsCenter.

He said he was looking to deal his autographs for some top-shelf Beanie.

He didn't want Doby, Twigs and Bongo. He wanted Grade A Beanie on the hoof -- a wingless Quackers and the purple bear minted in honor of Princess Di.

I've tried to imagine this rustler leaning up against the counter, his stetson pulled down, chewing on a foxtail stem and haggling over the trade.

The stranger with the autographs moseyed out of town without making a deal, but the autographs were merely the bait he used in rustling.

A day or so after he appeared, he telephoned the Beanie shop and said he was ready to deal. He wanted the Beanies shipped overnight, said he would do the same with all of his high-priced John Hancocks.

The rest you can guess.

Beanie rustlers have all kinds of tricks. Some bring bootleg Beanies -- made in China and shipped to Canada -- across the border into Detroit. Once they've smuggled in the counterfeits, they take them to swaps and shows and use the fakes as barter to rustle the genuine article.

The rustlers offer a trade that seems too good to be true and is always proved so once it's too late.

There's a lot of despair on the trail of the lonesome Beanie when the sun goes down, the coyotes are howling and some poor fool is sitting there stuck with a couple of worthless fakes of Trap the mouse or Humphrey the camel.

The White House has been strangely quiet on Beanie rustling. I keep expecting to see a joint news conference with Clinton and Reno announcing a zero-tolerance crackdown.

Until that happens, my sister and her husband will have to sleep with one eye open, watching the dozing Beanies as they settle in for the night.

I tell you, it's a tough business.

News on Page 2

July 21, 1999

The business card attached to the luggage that washed ashore on Martha's Vineyard Saturday identified its owner as Lauren Bessette.

At the time, the import of the discovery seemed to be its suggestion that John F. Kennedy Jr. quite likely was dead. It appeared almost incidental that the discovery indicated that Lauren Bessette and her sister Carolyn also had perished.

Such is the nature of fame.

America did not spend the weekend wondering whether the Bessette family was "cursed," though two beloved daughters apparently were snatched from them on the same evening.

It started me thinking about J.D. Tippit.

Not many people recall J.D. Tippit. He was simply the other person Lee Harvey Oswald killed in Dallas on Nov. 22, 1963. A Dallas police officer, husband and father, Tippit was attempting to question Oswald when the assassin shot him.

Only Tippit's widow has a different reason for remembering precisely where she was and what she was doing on Nov. 22, 1963.

I am naive neither to the weight of celebrity nor the inadvertent cruelties inflicted by news judgments. Rather, it was simply that the soggy piece of luggage in the surf and the fate of the woman who owned it reminded me anew of what it means to be an incidental victim.

Lauren Bessette was a bright and talented 34-year-old woman, a vice president at Morgan Stanley Dean Witter. Her star, like that of John F. Kennedy Jr., clearly was in ascension. Yet there seemed to be no great public hunger to know the particulars of her life. Viewers were too consumed watching old footage of a bare-kneed 3-year-old saluting his father's passing casket.

Lauren Bessette is a footnote.

Not surprisingly, when John Jr.'s plane disappeared, news outlets reprised the chronology and particulars of tragedies that have befallen the Kennedy clan. In addition to the assassinations and deaths in accidents, the catalog of misfortunes also included the close calls.

In 1973, Robert F. Kennedy's son, Joseph, was driving a Jeep when it flipped. He survived, though a female passenger was left permanently paralyzed from the waist down. Her name was not provided in news reports I scanned following the disappearance of JFK Jr.'s plane. But then, she was merely an incidental part of the story.

Nine years earlier, Joseph's uncle, Ted, was injured in a plane crash in western Massachusetts. An aide was killed in the crash. No one seems to remember his name.

A few hundred yards from Martha's Vineyard is Chappaquiddick Island. Political analysts have said that's where the presidential aspirations of Ted Kennedy died. They say it as though oblivious to the more fundamental fact that Chappaquiddick is where the life of 28-year-old Mary Jo Kopechne ended.

But she was just the incidental victim.

The morning after the accident occurred, Ted Kennedy finally showed up at the Edgartown police station to file a report. Kennedy identified Kopechne only as "Mary." He couldn't recall how to spell her last name.

At the approximate moment that Ted Kennedy was wrestling with Mary Jo's last name, a scuba diver labored to remove her body from the overturned Chrysler submerged in a channel near Poucha Pond.

Kennedy later would concede that a preoccupying thought in the hours after the accident was "whether some awful curse actually did hang over all the Kennedys."

To listeners, it seemed that he was more concerned about his diminished political future than the victim of his obvious recklessness.

But then, she wasn't the real story. Kennedy was the real story.

It is a terrible thing that John Kennedy Jr. should die so young. He was bright and gifted and said to be the most compassionate and considerate of men.

It is no less a terrible thing that Carolyn Bessette Kennedy and Lauren Bessette are gone.

But that seems to be Page 2 news.

Hemingway's House

Jan. 8, 1999

KEY WEST, Fla. "That is Jack Dempsey," guide Trevor MacWilliam said, nodding toward a rust-and-black cat slaloming through tourists' ankles in the uncommon chill of a Key West morning.

"We have everyone here from Ava Gardner to Mark Twain," MacWilliam continued. He claimed that the Hemingway House grounds are home to 56 cats descendants of the brood that first occupied the premises when its most famous occupant moved in.

That was in 1931. The blocky limestone home on Whitehead Street was built 80 years earlier by a man who would make his fortune designing Civil War fighting ships for the South.

In 1928, writer John Dos Passos, who lived close by on Pretonia Street, enticed Hemingway to come to Key West.

"Hemingway didn't like celebrity," MacWilliam said, explaining the appeal to "Papa" of this end-of-the-road coral rock.

"He liked to be one of the guys, one of the boys," he said, "and here he could be that."

For a few years, Hemingway and Pauline took an apartment on Simonton; in 1931, her Uncle Gus gave her $8,000 to buy the place on Whitehead.

Someone said that every great writer, sooner or later, sells out everyone he knows. If Hemingway didn't start that trend, he went a long way toward perfecting it. His was, as the title of one Hemingway biography suggests, *A Life Without Consequences.*

Pauline, who had her own career as a Paris fashion writer for *Vogue*, gave that up for Hemingway. She used her money to make him comfortable enough to write while resigning herself to the exacting and thankless role of Mrs. Ernest Hemingway.

In Hemingway House, the walls are hung with photographs of the writer's four wives. Only Martha Gellhorn (for whom he eventually left Pauline) rejected his attempts to subordinate her through matrimony.

Gellhorn went off to become a respected war correspondent during World War II, her marriage to Hemingway lasting only a brief five years.

Key West tub thumpers point out that "The Rock" has been home to nine Pulitzer Prize winners; they love to remind tourists that it was here that "Papa" wrote *Death in the Afternoon, The Green Hills of Africa* and *To Have and To Have Not.* He also wrote several short stories during his Key West years, not least among them *The Short Happy Life of Francis Macomber* and *The Snows of Kilimanjaro.*

Truth be told, the longer Hemingway was here, the more he was gone off on safari, off to the Spanish Civil War, off to the West to shoot bear and elk, off to Cuba to court Martha Gellhorn.

When at home in Key West, Hemingway wrote in a studio converted from a haymow on the second floor of an old carriage house out back. His writing room was connected to his upstairs bedroom by a catwalk. The span eventually was knocked out by a hurricane some time after the writer abandoned Key West and claimed he would rather eat monkey dung than ever return.

Pauline stayed on; she died in 1951.

Joy Williams, an author and authority on Key West history, recalled that when Tennessee Williams inquired of Hemingway how Pauline had died, he was told bluntly, "She died like everybody else and after that she was dead."

When Mary, Hemingway's fourth and final wife, came to Key West to claim the possessions her late husband had stashed around town before fleeing to Cuba, she discovered the manuscript for an unfinished novel.

Working with Scribners' editors, she trimmed, polished and finished the work, eventually published as *Islands in the Stream.*

Hemingway purists thought it scandalous and mercenary. They might also think it scandalous that Key West charges $7.50 a head for tourists who want to see Hemingway House and maybe carry away a laminated bookmark (another $5.95).

Yet it would be difficult, at least with a straight face, to argue that Hemingway is being anymore ill-used in death than he ill-used those in life whose only mistake was to love him.

A Country Called Ralph

June 4, 2000

Not long ago, I received a packet from a local elementary school class. The envelope was filled with suggestions for a new state motto to replace the contested "With God, all things are possible."

The youngsters' offerings employed the adjectives *pretty* and *neat* far too often for my liking.

I wanted the slogans to reflect individual preference in the manner of the motto suggested by one child for inscription on the back of the proposed Ohio quarter.

"The state that loves chihuahuas," a girl had recommended in her submission to the Ohio Bicentennial Commission. I doubt her offering will make it all the way to the U.S. Mint.

The business of mottos and slogans was before me when there landed on my desk information on "the official Web site of the principality of Sealand."

Sealand, according to its promoter, is a flyspeck off the coast of England, just beyond that nation's territorial limits.

Although the information is sketchy, Sealand appears to be a former military defense post built during World War II, abandoned afterward, then claimed in 1967 by a retired British major named Roy Bates.

Bates may be the product of an overactive imagination, his principality more imagined than real. Still, the whole thing started me thinking about finding my own country. It would be somewhere on an abandoned niche of terra firma lost to all but me and a handful of citizens who cast their lot with my new republic.

The way I see it, there are islands in the South Pacific that no one knows about. Some of these peaceful little hideaways may have last been sullied by footprints when visited briefly by a missionary during the Coolidge administration.

No one would object, I contend, if I would borrow one such island.

I will call it the Principality of Ralph. I will announce as much when I stride boldly onto the shore and plant the official zucchini. A flag would be much too militant; someone might step on one of those cocktail umbrellas. With zucchini, the entire population will have something to eat (and leave on neighbors' porches) for the first Thanksgiving.

Why call it Ralph?

I want the nation to remain undeveloped, uninvolved in global politics, unable to wage war. If I call it Ralph, no one will want to provide foreign aid or military hardware.

Can you imagine a Capitol Hill secretary to a U.S. senator interrupting her boss to announce, "I've got Ralph on the line. Can we spare 24 cruise missiles?" It could be the only time a U.S. senator says no.

Tourists wouldn't be a problem. Who would want to reveal to bridge partners: "Us? Oh, well, this winter we're going to spend a week in the South of Ralph."

That would be fine. Our national motto would be, "Move along, folks. Nothing here to see."

The government of Ralph would be jointly run by a Lower House and a Crawl Space. There would be no elections, thus avoiding big-business politics and lobbyists. Citizens would learn that they had been selected to serve by checking the inside of caps on 12-ounce cola bottles, which would be inscribed, Lower House, Crawl Space or Sorry, try again.

Term limits would not be a problem. No one would ever want to submit a resume revealing that they had spent 18 years in Ralph's Crawl Space.

Service in the Crawl Space would be simplified by the government's minuscule size. Outside of water and sanitation operations, the only civil employee would be an island constable. He or she would be authorized to use force only on people who play their car stereos too loud.

Government operations would be funded by nuisance assessments such as cellphone surcharges and temporary visa fees for visiting cults.

Ralph would be a peaceful place. No malls. No shock radio. No orange construction barrels -- there wouldn't be any freeways.

Ralph would not have an official flag. However, for those citizens who might feel unpatriotic by not pledging to die for some cloth symbol, the nation would have an official hammock.

It would be embroidered with the nation's motto: "Move along, folks. Nothing here to see."

I like that.

Waiting at the Rio Grande

Nov. 14, 1999

EL PASO, Texas -- Manuel Rodriguez made it across the Rio Grande River to the American Canal spillway ledge before an officer of the U.S. Border Patrol caught him.

It was Rodriguez's third attempt of the day. Within an hour, he would be back in Juarez, Mexico, where he most likely would begin to ponder a fourth try.

He had come north to the border from Durango, he said, where he worked on a farm when there was work to be had. His pay was $6 a day.

Rodriguez has a brother in San Antonio who is serving time on drug charges in a federal corrections facility. He said he was trying to visit him.

A smuggler in Juarez had offered to get Rodriguez to San Antonio, but he did not have money to pay the man.

Agent Mont Fyffe watched as Rodriguez joined several other detainees about to be transported back across the border.

Fyffe observed, "They know that if you behave yourself, you can go back and try again in two hours."

Fyffe hoped that if Rodriguez tried again, he would stay clear of the canal.

"We were lucky this year," the agent said. "We've only had four or five drownings in the canal. Usually, we have eight or nine. This time of year, if a body goes in the canal, it usually takes four or five days for it to build up enough gas to float."

Those who make it across the Rio Grande and the canal still must run the gauntlet of freeway traffic on I-10.

"We've had three people killed in the last year on I-10," agent Rick Lucio recounted. He motioned toward a trestle across the river. "Puerte Negro Railroad Bridge," he identified. "In this area, this is a big crossing place."

They come across hanging from freight cars or hidden in the undercarriage.

"Trains are not forgiving at all," Lucio commented, recalling that, in 1987, 18 people died when they became trapped in a locked boxcar that they had hoped would be their ticket out of Mexico.

Despite the risks, they continue to come.

Lucio pointed across the border to a shantytown on the edge of Juarez and observed, "That's Colonia Anapra. When you're over there, you have no electricity, no running water, no sewage system. And you look over here in west El Paso and see all of this. Tell me you're not going to try to cross."

Many of those who live in Juarez work in U.S.-owned assembly plants. In Mexico, there are approximately 2,900 foreign-owned manufacturing plants. They pay, according to sources, between $27 and $40 a week for 50-55 hours work.

Lucio, whose great-grandparents came to Texas from Mexico, said he often is lectured by the detainees. He said, "They ask you, 'How can you do this to your own people?' " Lucio responds that he is a Texan, and that so far he has never sent a Texan back to Juarez.

Lucio and Fyffe made the rounds up and down the north bank of the Rio Grande. In the bushes on the other side, they could see shadowy forms just waiting for the chance to make a break for it.

Greg Lambert, a native of Powell, Ohio, and an agent at the border, nodded across the river and observed, "A lot of the people you see here during the day are scouting us. They're watching, just watching. As soon as it gets dark, it gets wild."

Sometimes, a decoy or two downriver will pretend to sneak across the Rio Grande. The idea is to draw the patrol away from an area long enough that a dozen or so of their comrades can cross.

Fyffe's radio crackled, "There's about seven of them crossing the river by the paper plant."

The infrared unit had picked up the forms moving north. By the time Fyffe reached the site, four of the seven had crossed back over into Juarez. The remaining three were hiding somewhere among the salt cedars in the riverbed.

Lucio said El Paso had been averaging from 200 to 250 interceptions a day. He added, "A busy night is going to be 700. That's just the people we catch."

Fyffe, his headlights switched off, studied the Rio Grande riverbed with the area dimly lit by overhead searchlights.

Somewhere out there, Manuel Rodriguez quite likely was biding his time, waiting for just the right time to make his move.

Birmingham Sunday

April 15, 1998

BIRMINGHAM, Ala. -- I stood in the basement of the 16th Street Baptist Church, a house of prayer that some consider the mother church of the civil rights movement.

In the sanctuary upstairs, a volunteer recited the history of the edifice for a small knot of tourists. The basement was eerily still.

It was easy enough to close my eyes and hear again the soft strum of a guitar caressing a dirge in three-quarter time:

Come 'round by my side, and I'll sing you a song
I'll sing it so softly it'll do no one wrong.
On Birmingham Sunday the blood ran like wine,
And the choir kept singing of freedom.

On a Sunday in September 1963, an estimated 15 sticks of dynamite blasted through the eastern wall of the church.

Four girls, 11 to 14, perished.

A memorial room, dedicated to them, is situated not far from the wall where the explosion stopped the church clock at 10:22 and blew out the stained-glass countenance of Jesus.

The 16th Street Baptist Church was the last stop on my recent journey through the South's major civil rights landmarks.

To blacks North and South, many of the sites of marches and martyrdom are like Stations of the Cross. For some Southern whites, those haunts are abiding vexations that unsettle them only a little less than an inquisitive Northern columnist. They don't want to be reminded, thank you.

A few years ago, when *Ghosts of Mississippi* hit theaters across the nation, a prominent Jackson, Miss., businesswoman was asked whether she had yet seen the film about Medgar Evers and his killer.

The woman replied, said Mississippi writer Willie Morris, "My husband and I are sick of nigger movies."

When former Mississippi Gov. William Winter was appointed by President Clinton to the administration's freshly launched Advisory Board on Race last year, he recalled being asked by some, "Why are you bringing that up? Why don't you just let it alone?"

He replied, "Because, left alone it festers and grows, and soon enough we are at one another's throats."

But racial attitudes are imprinted on the marrow of the psyche. Many will contend that attempting to change them by creating a national dialogue is as much a fool's errand as trying to change gravity through a series of town meetings discussing Isaac Newton.

Many believe that what has changed in the tenor of race relations--North, South, East, West--since the death of Dr. Martin Luther King Jr. is that we have gone from overt to covert, from audacious to insidious, from compassionate to resistant.

Paradoxically, "resistant" is where we started.

A visitor can spend a fair amount of time listening to native Southerners, black and white, wax eloquent about how far we have come since 1968.

The consensus seems to be that we have made much progress. From that wide thoroughfare of common agreement, though, dozens of tiny roads meander off in widely divergent directions. Some whites will tell you that we have made epic strides since King, but that some blacks have alienated formerly compassionate whites by wearing legal safeguards as chips on their shoulders.

Some blacks will allow that much has been achieved since the marches, but that everything from glass ceilings to welfare reform, from white flight to the deterioration of urban schools, has made those civil-rights achievements seem more and more like Pyrrhic victories.

An elderly Southern black man described, with a down-home pithiness, how the whole issue of white attitudes toward blacks turns simply upon the twin issues of social standing and social interaction. He observed, "In the South, they don't care how close you get as long as you don't get too high. In the North, they don't care how high you get as long as you don't get too close."

In the memorial room of the 16th Street Baptist Church, Bertha Godfrey, a visitor from Camp Hill, Ala., studied the news photos on the wall, the pictures of the four girls killed on "Birmingham Sunday."

"Terrible," she whispered. "Those poor children."

Making her way out of the basement, she paused on the stairs that front the church.

Down those stairs, 35 years ago, mere children marched two-by-two into Kelly Ingram Park across the street to face the snarling dogs and high-pressure fire hoses of Birmingham's police commissioner, Eugene "Bull" Connor.

"People were beaten and fire-hosed for no reason," Godfrey said.

As soon as Connor's men would arrest a platoon of young people, fresh replacements would march down the church stairs and into the park, where arrest was the least of their fears.

At the head of the park, Godfrey could easily see the statue of Dr. Martin Luther King Jr.

"What happened to the dream of Dr. King?" she was asked.

"It is with us," she said evenly, "and it always will be."

Over in Ingram Park, groups of preschoolers played blissfully among statues that depict another generation's children staring through jail bars and battling police dogs.

A noon sun peeked down through scattered clouds. It was easy to get the impression that this spring would be a splendidly calm one.

But weather is strange. Appearances can deceive. Predictions and long-term forecasts often miss their mark. And even when ominous portents suggest certain calamity, some folks miss or ignore the sirens.

In that way, the weather is actually a little like race relations.

Twelve hours after I pointed the rental car north on I-65 and departed the Birmingham area, the snout of a force-5 tornado dropped out of the clouds just west of Birmingham.

Georgie Blount

Nov. 14, 1993

Who were you, Georgie Blount?

You sit with such prim grace upon your pedestal of graying marble that you seem almost regal.

The cap that crowned your towheaded countenance is gathered between fingers that rest in your lap.

With your left leg crossed under your right, you let the high-button shoe of the latter dangle just over an inscription that reveals precious little about the five years you walked Earth:

"George A., son of E.J. and S.A. Blount. Born Sept. 26, 1867. Died Feb. 14, 1873."

As might be expected, the records in the office at Green Lawn Cemetery offer few clues about your life or the circumstances of your death. An organization that tends the graves of more than 137,000 of Columbus' dead ought not be expected to know much about a little boy gone sixscore years.

"Accident," Green Lawn's Angie Thompson read from a card upon which a few terse notations keep track of your death and burial, and those of the seven kin who followed you, in the small family plot in Section X of the cemetery.

Your death was Page 1 news in the *Columbus Daily Dispatch* on Valentine's Day 1873.

"Terrible Accident!" the headline shouted, and, beneath it: "A little boy falls over stair banisters at the American House and is fatally injured."

The only child of Eli and Sarah Blount, proprietors of the American House Hotel, you toppled headfirst from the banister onto an ironstone hearth at the base of the stairs and died a week later.

In the mildly stilted and occasionally florid manner of journalism in the era of your death, the week you lingered before succumbing, alternately convulsed by seizures and tormented by deliriums, was chronicled in detail.

The obituary noted that your funeral was to be in the hotel parlor.

Your father, Eli, lived 27 years after he lost you. When he died in October 1900, his grave was marked by a homely, military-issue headstone that his government provided to pay homage to his service as a colonel in the 60th Ohio Infantry during the Civil War.

Your mother, Sarah, died in 1908. No headstone marks her grave.

Your grandmother, an uncle, two cousins and a woman named Lydia Tucker (not identified by her relationship to you) round out the family plot.

One grave remained unoccupied after the last family member, your cousin William, was buried in 1932.

Over time, even the heartiest of stone and the best of a sculptor's intentions yield a little to the elements. Not surprisingly, the finely etched outlines of your irises have almost vanished, giving you the appearance of a waif whose unseeing eyes are fixed on the western rim of the cemetery.

Though the last occupant of your small limb on the family tree has been gone for decades, someone has been taking you toys, Georgie.

Perhaps captivated by your sad, stone likeness, an anonymous mourner placed a basket of flowers near the edge of your stone pedestal.

A stuffed yellow duck sits beside it, and, on the other side of the stone, a plastic dump truck rests in the grass.

In the crook of your right arm, someone placed a pink, flop-eared bunny bearing an expression as goofy as yours is somber. A ribbon is tied in a bow at its throat.

The differences in wear on the toys suggest that they may have been deposited on successive visits.

Thompson has asked the grounds superintendent and his assistant about the matter.

"They have no idea," she said. "It is really kind of strange."

No one on the grounds crew recalls seeing anyone around your grave, which is right by the edge of a road used often in carrying out maintenance chores.

Christmas is coming. The twin oaks flanking your stone have spread a grave blanket of sorrel over the grass beneath which you sleep.

The holiday might draw your benefactor back, for the flower basket at your side holds a pair of bright-colored, plastic Easter eggs.

Though nagged by curiosity, I promise not to do anything to discourage the apparent lone, anonymous heart you have touched 120 years after your death broke so many.

"Stinking Catfish"

Aug. 3, 1998

In these doldrum days, when even the most passionate devotees of base-ball weary of jawboning about the Maris Derby or how far out of first the Indians would be in another division, it is cheering to find distraction in a quirky, obscure event.

Minor-league pitcher Ken Krahenbuhl was swapped by the Pacific Suns to the Greenville Bluesmen several days ago for cash, the proverbial player to be named and 10 pounds of catfish.

The fish portion of the deal likely had less to do with cash-flow problems in Greenville than with the enterprise of the Mississippi team's public-rela-tions flack. A *Dispatch* story on the trade noted that, last year, the Bluesmen acquired a second baseman from the Northern League's Sioux Falls team for a mint-condition Muddy Waters LP and 50 pounds of pheasant.

Krahenbuhl was none too happy about the "stinking catfish."

From where I sit, he should be grateful.

Over its long and colorful history, baseball has seen a number of bizarre trades involving everything from golf clubs to prunes. My cursory inspection of the records of the players involved indicates that most did quite well after the humbling experience.

Pitcher "Oyster Joe" Martina got his nickname after being traded by a minor-league team in Dallas to one in New Orleans for two barrels of oys-ters.

Did it hurt him? Not according to *The Baseball Encyclopedia.* He got his cup of coffee when Washington brought him up to the majors.

Hall of Fame baseball announcer Ernie Harwell recorded the particulars of a number of strange swaps in his book *The Babe Signed My Shoe.* No broadcaster more than Harwell deserves the right to chronicle those curious exchanges. In 1948, he was traded from the Atlanta Crackers' announcer's booth to the Brooklyn Dodgers', for a minor-league catcher.

Long ago, a pitcher for a minor-league team in Martinsburg, W.Va., was traded to the Baltimore Orioles (then an International League team) for an outfield fence. Martinsburg owed money for construction of the fence. Baltimore owner Jack Dunn needed a pitcher. Thus did Robert Moses "Lefty" Grove take his first step toward the big leagues, where he notched 300 wins in a career that would earn him a spot in Cooperstown.

Denton T. "Cy" Young, who recorded more victories (511) than any other pitcher in major-league history, was traded, as a rookie, by Canton to Cleveland for a suit of clothes.

Grove and Young may have been humiliated by the goods for which they were bartered, but it must have put some gravel in their guts.

Nashville traded catcher Charlie "Greek" George for a set of golf clubs. He went on to spend five years in the majors

I look around baseball and can see any number of players whose major-league egos might not be so inflated had they been swapped sometime early in their career for, say, a truckload of cantaloupes or a gross of athletic cups.

Writer Mike Blake's *Baseball's Bad Hops and Lucky Bounces* reminds us that a left-handed pitcher named Tim Fortugno was traded by the independent Reno Silver Sox to the Milwaukee Brewers in 1989 for $2,500 and 12 dozen baseballs.

Fortugno went on to play for the California Angels, among others. If his career was not stellar, well, the baseballs Reno received for him weren't, either. They were American League issue and couldn't be used for official minor-league play.

Former major leaguer Euel Moore was said to have once been traded for a plate of beans. Jack Fenton went to Memphis for a box of prunes. Unlike Moore, Fenton never made it to the big leagues. To be humbled is one thing, but to be traded to help correct a team owner's irregularity apparently was crushing.

Fenton seems to be the exception in a string of minor-league trades whose principals came up to the majors only after an early comeuppance.

Too bad it never happened to Albert Belle or Jose Canseco.

By the way, in case you didn't read the story about the Greenville Bluesmen's new hurler Ken "Catfish" Krahenbuhl, on the day after the "stinking catfish" swap that so incensed him, he pitched a perfect game.

Isle of Tears

Sept. 26, 1999

NEW YORK -- *Well, I came to America because I heard the streets were paved with gold. When I got here, I found out three things: first, the streets*

weren't paved with gold; second, they weren't paved at all; and third, I was
expected to pave them.

Time has misplaced or forgotten the name of the Italian immigrant who
uttered that wry appraisal of his introduction to the United States. His
words, however, are preserved on the Ellis Island Immigration Museum wall
in New York Harbor.

From 1892 to 1954, the building served as the main processing site for 12
million newly arrived immigrants to the United States.

On the cusp of a new century, we all might do well to visit Ellis Island.
Except for those whose ancestors were robbed of this land or brought here
in the shackles of slave ships, many genealogies -- at one point or another
-- pass through this small slip of land in upper New York harbor.

Almost one-half of this nation's citizens are descended from ancestors
who made their way through the human cattle chutes of the sprawling Great
Hall on what became known as the Isle of Tears.

The day I left home, my mother came with me to the railroad station. When
we said goodbye, she said it was just like seeing me go into my casket. I
never saw her again.
Julia Goniprow
Lithuania

The visual vernacular of our history invariably includes the visages of an
immigrant couple -- he in porkpie hat or derby, she in babushka -- looking
out from the deck of a steamer toward the Statue of Liberty.

For many of those catching their first glimpse of Liberty and hauling suit-
cases and steamer trunks onto Ellis Island, the worst of their journey was
over. They had spent from two weeks to a month in steerage during passage to America. In the dark, cramped and filthy holds of ships, one in 10
of those coming to the United States died during the crossing.

Anyone who made it was confronted by physicians who chalked "short-
hand" findings of their hasty inspections on the clothing of new arrivals. An
"H" indicated a heart problem, a "P" pulmonary symptoms. A circled "X"
denoted symptoms of an ailment that might be contagious.

My middle sister, who shared the room with me, was running a terrible
fever. She was so hot I couldn't sleep with her. We tried not to let anyone
know she was sick. Finally, she started to break out with measles. We were
terribly afraid they would keep us on the island. The day we were to leave
the nurse noticed she was running 102 fever, and she took Rosalie, my sis-
ter, away from us. This child was absolutely petrified. She thought she was
leaving us forever. They took her to the hospital and put her in quarantine.
We had to leave without her.
Barbara Barondess
Russia

Most immigrants completed their processing at Ellis Island in three to five
hours, yet some were detained because of illness or the suspicion of sickness. In this case, they fell into the category of "undesirable aliens" (con-
victs, anarchists, prostitutes, polygamists and the mentally ill).

Regrettably, some of those who passed inspections were victimized by
corruption that sometimes plagued the immigration process. Inspectors

extorted bribes or sexual favors. Crooked clerks lied about monetary exchange rates. Railroad tickets were sold at rates exorbitantly higher than face value.

Public service posters in Germany warned young women considering immigration that the promise of American jobs as domestics often were enticements to lure them into prostitution.

Despite corruption, the human tide continued. The prospect of beginning life anew in the proverbial land of opportunity easily outweighed any fear of profiteering or abuse.

I wish you to come to America, dear brother, because up to the present I am doing very well here, and I have no intention of going to our country, because in our country I experienced only misery and poverty and now I live better than a lord in our country.

Adam Raczkowski

Poland

The names of some who passed through Ellis Island would become household words in their adopted country: Irving Berlin, Claudette Colbert, Frank Capra, Rudolph Valentino, Marcus Garvey, Knute Rockne, Felix Frankfurter, Bela Lugosi, Kahlil Gibran, Issac Asimov and Edward G. Robinson.

Two-thirds of those processed on the island settled, at least temporarily, in the New York City area. The composition of entire neighborhoods changed as one immigrant group supplanted another -- from Irish to German to Italian to Hispanic to Chinese.

The overlapping mosaic is everywhere apparent today. In Lower Manhattan, Korean jewelry vendors ply their wares throughout Little Italy. In Chinatown, Vietnamese merchants sell produce to Jamaican customers from stores once owned by Germans and Irish.

At the high tide of U.S. immigration in the first decade of this century, as many as 7,000 new arrivals were processed each day on Ellis Island, more than 1 million in 1907 alone. Of the millions who came, 240,000 were denied permission to enter the United States. For many, rejection proved too much to bear. An estimated 3,000 suicides were recorded on the island.

The daily bustle of human traffic through Ellis Island fell dramatically when the United States began imposing strict immigration quotas in the 1920s. Eventually, in 1954, the U.S. Immigration and Naturalization Service ceased operations at the facility. Today, people desiring to immigrate to the United States typically apply through the U.S. Embassy or consular office in their home country. Once they are approved and have established a permanent residence status in the United States, they may apply for citizenship after five years.

Ellis Island, after many years of neglect, eventually became a museum. Today, some think the island is haunted. Barry Moreno, a librarian at Ellis, has cataloged tales of ghostly voices in the Great Room, the apparition of a weeping woman clad in white. Others claim that dogs brought to the island become agitated and bark ceaselessly without provocation.

No doubt it is all the product of overactive imaginations.

Still, it is difficult to pass through the Isle of Tears without sensing something that is at once both ethereal and eerie.

Walter took sick and was admitted to the hospital. He was there six weeks and died on February 9, 1921. We were confined on Ellis Island those six weeks. Our days were very long days and only one of us could go visit our sick boy for five minutes once a week. We had to put on a gown as we were not allowed close to him. Our boy died at ten minutes after 11 p.m. and we had to spend the night there. After all these years, the picture in my mind is so clear when they took him down the hall wrapped in a sheet.

Writer unknown.

Behold a Pale Horse

Oct. 3, 1999

WASHINGTON -- Chill and wind-driven, the autumn rain peppered the face of the black granite chevron, droplets sliding into the recesses and coursing down the half-moon and hairpin of engraved letters.

An occasional tourist passed, stopping to ponder the tokens left that day at the base of the Vietnam Veterans Memorial: a ball cap, a pair of prisoner-of-war bracelets, an artificial rose attached by a ribbon to a small American flag.

Robert Harkin, a National Park Service volunteer, sat in the dry shelter of a small kiosk overlooking the wall. He watched visitors come and go. In time, Harkin would stroll down and gather tributes left at the memorial.

"You run into a half-pint of whiskey," he said of the objects he has encountered, "along with a note: 'This is the drink we were going to have when you came home.'"

Harkin handles all of the items as though the face value were equal to the pain that put them there. Then he ships everything to a National Park Service warehouse in nearby Lanham, Md., for photographing, cataloging and storage.

"You may have a pair of combat boots, a can of Spam, a letter," said Duery Felton Jr., curator of the Vietnam Veterans Memorial collection. "People leave all their experiences here. We try to share the collection with the public, especially that segment on whom the Vietnam experience had a major impact."

Felton's expertise proved invaluable to the Smithsonian Institution's National Museum of American History in putting together a display representative of items left at the memorial.

The remembrances include everything from marbles to medals to Mickey Mouse ears. Dozens of dog tags and campaign ribbons are showcased, as well as numerous notes and letters:

"To Pat Mooney. Remembering a sweeter, gentler time. We never dreamed serving the people would end this way."

Felton said, "A lot of the letters will be marked 'Do not open.' Those letters remain sealed. We try to be sensitive; we're dealing with the dead."

Thus did he leave sealed two letters from a woman to a soldier in Vietnam. The letters were found at the memorial alongside an opened and much-handled letter from the Department of the Army to the woman:

"Occupant

"1812 33rd St.

"Auburn, Wash.

"The enclosed mail, addressed to Pvt. 1st Class Stephen Busby . . . bears your return address.

"I regret to inform you that Pvt. Busby died on 4 April 1970.

"Please accept my deepest sympathy over the loss of Pvt. Busby. I am truly sorry that it was not possible to have delivered this mail.

"Sincerely,

"Thomas C. Adams

"Lt. Col."

An artificial Christmas tree graces a display case; not far away are a menorah, a carton of Marlboros and a small golf trophy with the attached note:

"It's a beautiful day. We'd be playing golf. I'd be beating you by two strokes, sucker."

The custom of leaving objects began even before the granite wall panels were installed. By one account, while a construction crew was laying the memorial's foundation, a visitor stopped and asked a worker for permission to bury his dead brother's Purple Heart in the newly poured concrete.

That was 1982. Since then, Felton (a Vietnam veteran who served with the Army's 1st Infantry Division) has cataloged more than 65,000 objects left at the wall.

The collection has become so extensive that the National Park Service is moving it to a larger warehouse.

Felton has been called upon to advise groups across the United States on preserving and displaying items left at the sites of recent tragedies.

"I spoke to the Oklahoma City bomb blast committee," he said. "And Columbine. I flew out to Colorado to speak to them."

The bestowal of mementos or remembrances at those two sites was, for many, an attempt to come to terms with unspeakable tragedy.

So it is at the Vietnam Veterans Memorial.

One visitor left a small, tattered photograph of a North Vietnamese soldier and his daughter. Accompanying the old snapshot was a note:

"Dear Sir,

"For twenty-two years I have carried your picture in my wallet. I was only 18 years old that day we faced one another on that trail in Chu Lai, Vietnam. Why you didn't take my life, I'll never know.

"You stared at me for so long, armed with your AK-47, and yet you did not fire.

"Forgive me for taking your life. I was reacting just the way I was trained . . . So many times over the years I have stared at your picture and your daughter, I suspect . . . I have two daughters myself now.

"I perceive you as a brave soldier defending his homeland. Above all else, I can now respect the importance that life held for you. I suppose that is why

I am able to be here today . . . It is time for me to continue the life process and release my pain and guilt.

"Forgive me, Sir."

Wedding rings have been left here. So, too, a newspaper clipping bearing the headline:

Vet Kills Self at Memorial
Divorce Papers Found in Hand

The clipping is among the items displayed by the Smithsonian. Not far away is a letter to a hospital corpsman, a medic, whose name is engraved on the wall:

"Dear Allen,

"It took me 20 years to contact your parents. I couldn't find a way to say your son died saving my life. I know you understand. I finally did, though. I talked to your father on the phone. It was difficult for both of us, but my load is so much lighter now."

Beyond the Smithsonian -- closed for the day -- dusk had begun to gather at the memorial. The rain had let up.

Those who know the wall say that it belongs to the tourists by day. At night, the wall belongs to the kin and comrades of those whose names it bears.

They are the ones who leave the tokens and tributes:

A six-pack of beer. A mailed and unopened box of homemade cookies returned from Vietnam to a woman whose son was killed in action. A note scribbled with a quotation from the Book of Revelations: "Behold a pale horse and his name that sat on him was death and hell followed with him."

Oklahoma City

April 30, 1995

OKLAHOMA CITY, Okla.--In a city where situation, chance and mere seconds either killed or spared, the family of Christi Jenkins took the full measure of treachery's random scythe.

Jenkins, a 32-year-old mother of four, was at her station as a teller in the Federal Employees Credit Union on the third floor of the federal building when the bomb went off. A cousin of Jenkins, Woodrow Brady, had just strolled into the credit union to apply for a car loan.

Two floors below, another cousin, Calvin Battles, had entered the Social Security office. A wheelchair-bound stroke victim, Battles had come to apply for disability. His wife was pushing the wheelchair.

"I had four to die," Delores Briggs, Christi's cousin, said yesterday afternoon.

Three cousins and one of their spouses perished.

At Jenkins' funeral at the Greater First Deliverance Temple, pastor Vanuel Little gripped the edges of the pulpit overlooking a flower-shrouded ivory casket and conceded, "We're down, but you can help us, Lord. Such devastation has come to fruition in our city. It has paralyzed a city and maimed a nation, but you can lead us, Lord."

In the first pew, Jenkins' husband, Aldo, nodded slowly at those words. Four children, aged 11 through 16, stared mutely at the casket.

Christi Jenkins had not been a member of the Greater First Deliverance Temple where her funeral was held, but the pastor of her home church in nearby Edmond feared his church might not hold all of those who wanted to say goodbye.

He was right. More than 300 mourners filled the sanctuary and its balcony and spilled into vacant choir seats rimming the pulpit from which four ministers would speak.

The pianist hammered out a rambunctious rendition of *I'll Fly Away.*

A gray-haired woman in the balcony picked up the thread of the beat and, almost in a whisper sang:

"When I die, hallelujah, bye and bye,

"I'll fly away."

Christi Jenkins' pastor, Dan Baldridge, recalling the day after the bombing, told the assembled throng, "We still didn't know if Christi was dead or alive. We were hanging on the edge of our world."

Four days later, her body was found in the rubble.

Before the funeral, Baldridge's wife confided, "Christi loved her job, but she knew her kids needed her."

She and her husband had decided to move to a less expensive home so she could quit her job at the federal building and be with her children.

"I admired her for being willing to sacrifice an income to be home with those children. At the last service she attended, she said that she had set a goal. She wanted to be home in three months."

Only two of those 90 days had passed when a Ryder rental truck pulled into Oklahoma City, its driver pausing only long enough to ask, "How do I get to Fifth and Harvey?"

No one paid much attention when the yellow truck eased into a recessed, pickup-and-dropoff section of curb 15 feet from the north face of the Alfred P. Murrah Federal Building.

At Christi Jenkins' funeral, the Rev. Wesley Norris read, "But the day of the Lord will come as a thief in the night; in which the heavens shall pass away with a great noise, and the elements shall melt with fervent heat, the earth also and the works that are therein shall be burned up."

The service over, Christi Jenkins' mother, Elcena Cummings rose, daubing at tear-polished cheeks, and pressed a palm to a corner of the casket.

Aldo Jenkins draped a steadying arm around her.

The hearse, glistening in the Oklahoma sun, led the procession to the cemetery. Trailing mourners could not have missed a sign erected a mile from the burial site, a board inscribed, "Stop the violence."

Linda Dieckman, a secretary at Christi's church watched Aldo Jenkins bite his lip and bow his head at the grim clicking of the gears as the vault was lowered into the yawning grave.

"What is so sad," she said, "is that it didn't have to be."

Briggs, Christi's cousin, turned from the gravesite and walked numbly to her car.

In the past week, she had buried two cousins and was still not finished with funerals.

Big Joe Bezilla

July 15, 1994

PITTSBURGH - On a July day designed more for the beach than the cemetery, the hearse eased up Franklin Road past the home of its chief passenger and nuzzled against the curb beside Nativity of Our Lord Church.

Six youthful pallbearers, squinting at the reflection of the midmorning sun off the casket lid, carried their departed loved one, Joe Bezilla, up the church steps and into the sanctuary.

An old gypsy proverb reminds us: "You have to dig a deep grave to bury your daddy."

Joe Bezilla was not my daddy, although, for the better part of two decades, we shared a father-son relationship refreshingly free of the turf wars and minor insurrections that colored the years with my dad.

Joe's daughter and I were married for 16 years, during which he and I spent much time in the company of each other.

He was a man who could not have been accused of living timidly. In a manner befitting a fellow with the build of a middle linebacker, he embraced his days with a breathtaking bearhug.

He was only 7 when death claimed his father. Bristling at the compensatory protectiveness of his mother and sisters after the loss, he toughened himself to the rough-and-tumble realities of life on the working-class streets of the Steel City.

He played semipro baseball (second base for a scrappy team christened the Pleasant Valley Smilers), earning two Depression-era dollars a game and a stunning collection of suture scars that gave his shins the look of an aerial photo of a switching yard.

He never made a champagne salary as an athlete, but then Joe Bezilla was a boilermaker man.

He drank Iron City.

He sang baritone.

He gave the prime of his working life to a company that made barges and towboats on Pittsburgh's Neville Island. He gave his money to Nativity of Our Lord. He gave his love to two daughters and a wife whose lifelong battle with severe depression cast a shadow over many of their years together.

His pleasures were simple: an occasional game of poker with the guys in the parish men's club, an annual summer trip to stroll the boardwalk at Ocean City, N.J.

Joe never met a stranger. He would've made a terrible hangman, forever holding up the business of the state to show pictures of his grandchildren to the condemned.

I last saw Joe alive a year ago.

The advancing years and a gathering of assorted infirmities had conspired to draw in the boundaries of his world. His wife had died a few years earlier, and many of his friends and contemporaries were gone, too.

He spent a good portion of his mornings by the living-room window that looked out onto Franklin Road, waving to neighbors passing on the sidewalk and children on their way to school.

For the past several months, he gamely battled the cancer that eventually claimed him a week ago.

A man who--to paraphrase Will Rogers--never met a meal he didn't like, Joe shrank from 250 pounds to 124.

Despite a ferocious will to live, the cancer finally battered him to the point that he grudgingly accepted the certainty of a fast-approaching end.

Taking his daughter's hand in his own and holding it to his cheek, he consoled, "We sure had some good times, didn't we?"

A steady stream of people who shared many of the good times with Joe filed past the casket. I stopped counting after 200.

A long train of cars trailing the hearse snaked through north-side streets beneath a cloudless sky.

The late Roger Miller once observed that no matter how important we become, the size of our funeral will more or less depend on the weather.

The weather was spectacular.

But I know Joe Bezilla.

He could have brought them out in a blizzard.

The Utes

Oct. 1, 1997

FORT DUCHESNE, Utah -- The tawny loam is soft underfoot in Fort Duchesne Cemetery. A rumor of wind slowly twirls a stars-and-stripes pinwheel planted on a grave next to a government-issue veteran's marker.

Not far away, Lester Mountain Lion sleeps beneath a small statue of Jesus, a rosary draped in the manner of a bandoleer across the chest of the plaster icon. A prairie dog has burrowed into the side of the grave, a transaction of nature that would not have displeased the plot's main occupant.

The most striking feature of the cemetery on the Ouray Uintah Reservation of the Uncompahgre Utes, though, is the vast number of soldier's graves.

"Who better to fight for the country than warriors who have been fighting for their own land for more than a century?" asked Larry Cesspooch.

Cesspooch, a 46-year-old Ute, Vietnam veteran and editor of the reservation's newspaper, said that a strong warrior fraternity exists among Utes who went off to fight at Belleau Wood and Guadalcanal, Heartbreak Ridge and Hue for a nation by which they had been ill-used.

When whites began settling in the Colorado-Utah area, 12 different tribal bands of Utes called the area home.

Ouray the Arrow was considered chief of the Utes by the encroaching whites, perhaps more than anything because of his peaceful solicitousness toward U.S. government officials.

It was with Ouray that the United States forged a treaty that herded the Utes into eastern Utah. In exchange, Ouray was given a lifetime pension, a home and a farm.

"He was a sellout," Cesspooch said.

When the Utes in Colorado were assembled for enrollment on the reservation in Utah, Cesspooch's ancestors resisted.

Indian agents, baffled by long Ute names, rechristened many of the members of the tribe.

On his mother's side, Cesspooch's older relatives were issued the surname Cuch.

Cuch is the Ute word for "no."

It was the answer Cesspooch's family gave to each of the Indian agent's questions:

Do you want to be removed from Colorado?

Cuch.

Do you want to enroll on the reservation?

Cuch.

What is your name?

Cuch.

Thus were they branded by their own resistance.

The land ceded to the Utes for their reservation was not particularly well-suited for agrarian use.

"The government saved the best land for white homesteaders," Cesspooch said. "What they didn't know was that they had set us on one of the biggest oil deposits in the West."

When the energy crisis hit in the '70s, the Ute oil wells finally began exacting a curious form of reparations.

Though 134 years have passed since Ouray signed the treaty with the government, the Utes are still battling the whites.

Hunters enter reservation lands to poach game, ever feigning ignorance that the property and its wildlife belong to the Utes.

The reservation has been in and out of litigation with the nearby town of Roosevelt for 20 years.

Roosevelt was homesteaded by Mormons on Ute property late in the 19th century. Though the Ouray Uintah Reservation has its own police force, Roosevelt exists as an odd sort of jurisdictional doughnut hole in the middle of everything.

Cesspooch says Roosevelt police officers are capricious in misdemeanor enforcements, singling out Utes for minor traffic infractions for which whites are not held accountable. All the while, Roosevelt merchants benefit from Ute business.

So now the Utes are boycotting Roosevelt.

"If all we are to them is a dollar sign, we'll take our business someplace else," Cesspooch explained.

He said that plans are under way to establish on the reservation a bank and several other necessary commercial institutions for which the Utes had previously traveled to Roosevelt.

At this point, the project is somewhere between pipe dream and blueprint. But Cesspooch says he believes he will see it come to fruition.

In the cemetery not far from Cesspooch's office, sagebrush forms a stunted palisade around the graves of Mary Medicine Man Jake, Tecumseh Murray, Denver Sixkiller and Calvin Unca Sam.

Do not look for the grave of Ouray among the Utes who proved their warrior mettle from the beaches of Normandy to those of the South Pacific.

After Ouray negotiated the removal of his people to Utah, he stayed in Colorado on the farm the government had given him, spending his government stipend and, as one American Indian put it, living and eventually dying like a rich white man.

Actual Size Not Shown

March 15, 1996

I was accorded the Mount Rushmore of journalistic veneration this week when my likeness suddenly appeared on the side of a COTA bus.

Perhaps suddenly is not an apt adverb, suggesting as it does an association with mystical sightings of weeping religious statues and Shroud of Turin shadows on silos.

Truth be told, I knew several weeks ago my mug was about to be plastered on a bus. What I didn't know was how large it would be. Ear to ear, I match the wheelbase of a '69 Coupe DeVille. My chin runs from the curb to the roof.

Blemishes and pimples the size of Frisbees and pie plates leap out at innocent bystanders. Nostrils the size of manhole covers bring small children to tears. The crow's feet fringing my eyes resemble an aerial shot of the tributary basin of the Snake River.

As much as an actual-size image of my face frightens me in the morning when unexpectedly glimpsed in the medicine cabinet mirror, I shudder to think how unsettling it will be to sleepy commuters at 6 a.m.

Don't get me wrong.

I am flattered that the paper would want my face on a rolling billboard. It is just that such heady distinctions tend to bring out the pessimist in me.

Each time a gully-washer leaves 5-inch puddles along the curbs of major thoroughfares, my face will smile at fist-shaking pedestrians who have just been drenched by a 4-foot cascade of muddy water.

Every time a running commuter fails to catch up with a departing bus, he will see my grin as he pauses to catch his breath and wonder why he is suddenly having chest pains.

No longer will angry motorists grouse that they were cut off by the No. 8 Frebis Ave. bus. Now they'll blame it on the Mike Harden Express.

I am the one cursing motorists will think about each time the bus pulls away from a stoplight, leaving a pungent plume of exhaust and making a sound reminiscent of Godzilla floating air biscuits in Tokyo Bay.

Commuting citizens may come to look upon it with great antipathy. Pranksters recently blackened the front teeth of a local TV news personality pictured on a bus, thus giving her the look of a color commentator for the ESPN monster truck competition.

My sleep will now be troubled by dreams in which TV news minicams pan the side of my bus before zooming in on the body under the sheet near its rear tires.

Aghast TV anchors will read from the TelePrompTer: ``The 90-year-old victim was delivering homemade cookies to local orphanages when she was struck by the Mike Harden Express. Witnesses claim she was in the crosswalk." And there I will be, grinning as if I had good sense, for all the rolling cameras.

I feel gnawed by the urge to drop in at the COTA garage now and then to check tire tread and brake linings. Suppose this behemoth loses brake power while bearing down on a stalled '74 Pinto full of nuns and Sunoco high-test.

I am possessed of an almost-visceral conviction that if anyone is arrested for flashing commuters on a COTA bus in the next 12 months, it will be on ``my bus." And when, after such an unfortunate episode, swooning spinsters are led off the bus by paramedics, they will debark from my side.

Travel Writer Lisa Reuter is on the bus' port side; Outdoors Writer Tom Porch is on top. I am on the side with the doors, through which will step the handcuffed exhibitionist in the London Fog trenchcoat, waving at the cameras.

This could be really bad.

I'd rather not think about the vast number of news stories that might all begin, ``A disgruntled former bus driver . . . "

It will be a long time before I again have the urge to rent the film *Speed*.

Sam Perdue, Columnist

Dec. 20, 1995

``You're still young," Sam Perdue told me last month, a final avalanche of sand hurrying through the waist of his hourglass.

``You don't see it now, but one day you'll retire and the phone will stop ringing. All those years you thought they adored you, it was really the column that kept them calling -- not the columnist. It can get lonely."

Neither meanness nor self-pity colored the pronouncement. It was simply Sam dispensing the wisdom of the years as dispassionately as the house deals a round of five-card stud.

His voice sounded like a cross-saw drawn slowly through an old cedar. Disney would have given such pipes to a curmudgeonly crocodile trying to hide a 24-karat heart.

That was Sam.

He was 27 when he was hired as a copy boy at the *Cleveland Press*. A Purple Heart in his sea bag, a little gimp in his gait from the shrapnel he picked up in the South Pacific, he was doing the gofer work of a college intern just to get a foot in the door of newspapering.

When a job opened up at the old *Columbus Citizen* a few years later, he jumped at the chance. He was green, but he had grit and a gift for the craft. To some it might have seemed that Sam had more rough edges than a grappling hook, but he was simply as bluntly honest about the gravy stains on his own personality as about those he wrote of on the police beat and in the courts.

By the time I graduated from college in 1973, he was city editor of the *Columbus Citizen-Journal*. As a copy editor there, it was my job to prune the stories his reporters turned in, to try to shoehorn them into a stingy news hole.

Boisterously demonstrative, Sam was the perfect opposite of his boss, a cheerless, dyspeptic fellow with all the warmth and charm of a bank examiner.

I didn't stay long at the *C-J,* certain that Sam's boss liked my witty headlines (``Council Eyes New Probe") too much to ever let me write.

When I returned, eight years later, Sam was a columnist, trying to keep Ohio government honest and state cars out of Dunkin' Donuts.

``You can't do it if it isn't in your heart to do," he liked to say of the craft we shared. It wasn't that he romanticized the profession so much as he believed that journalism ``called" its best practitioners while suffering the half-hearted labors of those better suited for poultry science.

No confusion obscured his appraisal of the responsibility of journalism. More than once he told me, ``If you don't like people with funny last names or people who talk in a funny way or people who smell bad or are about to be evicted -- the losers -- then you are in the wrong business. The establishment has easy access to the media, but those people don't."

His heroes were a blend of muckrakers, literary greats and some who had been both. Their commonality was the stunning clarity with which their work depicted the time in which they moved. Writing with unflinching honesty about that often unsavory world won them no friends at the chamber of commerce.

``A few had it," he wrote me once. ``Swift, Dickens and Hugo. Their legacy passed to Twain and Jake Riis, who left it to Lincoln Steffens, Ida Tarbell and Upton Sinclair. From them were begat Steinbeck, O'Neill. Their inheritors were Kempton, Fast, Seeger and a lot of minorities not mentioned in the white culture of schoolbooks."

Because Sam never lost his soft spot for the underdog, his intolerance of duplicity or his abiding suspicion of the motives of the monied few, his death last Saturday left intact a reputation whose light was not for self-glory so much as to better allow us to inspect our own work and motives.

On the day before Sam died, I was stopped at a traffic light on my way to work when a woman trudged across the street in front of me. She clutched a long green coat together at her belly where the buttons were gone. Her eye was puffed out from a blow, almost closed to the brittle chill.

She looked like she didn't have enough stomach for life left in her to make it through December, I thought. That was when I saw the bank sign cheerily reminding, ``Snow may be falling, but our deposit rates aren't.''

I will never be convinced that wasn't Sam Perdue's way of saying goodbye.

The Driving Lesson

Jan. 24, 1997

For all the family dysfunction addressed by the courts and social welfare agencies today, the emotional apocalypse created by parents teaching children to drive remains beyond the pale of the law.

A few nights ago, I was the back-seat witness as 16-year-old Jennifer took the wheel of the Honda to engage real traffic (Sunday parking-lot forays don't count). Her mother was beside her.

It was close to midnight on Hard Road. Traffic was sparse.

Conditions seemed perfect for a calm, reasoned and productive driving lesson.

Forget it.

The car hadn't gone 100 yards before I had the sensation of being in a roller-coaster car directly behind a pair of blowheads going through serious cocaine withdrawal. They were like a pair of overwrought Chihuahuas when the doorbell rings:

"Watch the berm! You're drifting."

"I'm trying to watch the yellow line."

"You're real close to these mailboxes."

At this moment I suggested that Debra get a door-hanger route until Jennifer gets her license. There wasn't much tolerance for humor in the front seat.

"Watch your speed."

"I'm going 25. How can I watch the speed and the mailboxes and the yellow line at the same time?"

"I'm just trying to help you. You're drifting toward the berm because you're not used to incoming traffic."

"Oncoming traffic," I corrected. "It would be incoming if Toyotas were falling from the sky strapped to Scud missiles."

"She knows what I mean."

"Would you two be quiet so I can drive?"

I leaned back in the seat, peering out the side window, recalling my father's driving lessons.

He taught me how to drive in a '57 Cadillac whose square footage was about the same as a double-wide mobile home's.

Sitting next to me on the front seat, he would momentarily pretend not to notice a misstep, then draw pensively on his Pall Mall before saying, "Do that again and I'll knock you halfway into next week."

He had a way of focusing the mind marvelously.

Debra prefers to intimidate Jennifer by conjuring up the specter of police cruisers lurking behind every billboard, and sour-faced judges just waiting to throw the book at teen-age drivers.

"If you get a ticket, it costs you points on your license," Debra explained while, beside her, her captive audience was trying to balance the requisite driving skills of speed, tracking, object avoidance and feigned deafness.

"And if you get a speeding ticket, the court may make you go to special classes."

"Where?" Jen demanded.

"San Quentin," I said. "You might have to be a bad man's wife for a while."

"I'm trying to make a point," Debra hissed.

I shut up. After all, I'd had my day helping teach my three how to drive. I had lived to retire with the title, despite the fact that one of them might be the only driver Sharon Township police ever clocked at 58 mph through a BP carwash.

I couldn't recall which of my older children had so much trouble mastering the standard transmission, but, for months, anyone along for the ride looked like an ashen baby boomer rocking back and forth on the dance floor to *YMCA.*

"Slow down, there's a hill," Debra ordered, though her daughter had many seconds earlier spotted a bright yellow sign the size of a Frigidaire, lettered: HILL.

I kept quiet, thinking of G.K. Chesterton's quote, "The only people who seem to have nothing to do with the education of children are the parents."

"Watch your speed, Jennifer!"

"I'm going 12."

"The speed limit is 10."

Can't be too cautious. The Hard Road hill is a 90-meter ski jump whose terminus is marked by a wicked left turn and 25 feet of tortured guardrail.

I fought the urge to scream, "We're all gonna die!"

Jennifer pulled the Honda into the driveway and sighed sullenly.

"I'm just trying to teach you what I know, Jennifer," her mother protested.

"Try to look at the bright side, Jennifer," I consoled. "When you get a marriage license, you won't have to take her along on the honeymoon."

Aunt Gracie: On Viagra

July 5, 1998

My Dear Nephew Mike,

I am writing to tell you, before you hear it through the grapevine, that your Uncle Ott and I have separated.

He made up a bed for himself in a back room down at the Gas-N-Go and is taking his meals at the Blue Moon Cafe. I suppose he is doing OK on money because I hear he's ordering from the right side of the menu.

We've been getting some counseling from the minister down at the Two Pig Run Church of the Risen Lord.

We'll see what happens.

For 54 years, I cooked for that man, picked up after him, listened to him snore. You get used to each other's little habits and quirks, and you go on.

Funny thing. when I told Verniece Mudgett that we had been married for 54 years, she said, "Gracie, you only have to do nine in Ohio for murder."

Of course, things are a little tense for her and Dewey, too, down at Mudgett's Funeral Home and Bed & Breakfast. A couple of weeks ago, she took to setting up a cot in the Celestial Rest visitation room just so she could get some sleep.

"Don't it bother you to be sleeping in the same room with the deceased?" I asked her.

She said that was pretty much what she had been doing until Viagra came along, and she had gotten to the point that she really didn't mind.

Verniece is the one who started up the support group down here called ViagrAnon.

We had our first meeting last week down at the Grange hall.

Verniece started it off by reading aloud from a prescription insert all of the side effects of that damned little blue pill:

Migraine, colitis, tremors, vertigo, depression, insomnia, abnormal dreams.

I interrupted, "Verniece, we already know what it's doing to us spouses. What are its side effects on the men?"

She said that Carl, the pharmacist down at Geezenslaw's Serv-U-Well, told her he can't keep the stuff on the shelves. He said he got so tired of being asked when the next batch would arrive that he finally just took a magic marker and changed a line on the sign on the front door. It now says, "No shirt. No shoes. No Viagra."

Last week, the mayor said he was thinking about declaring the town a Viagra-free zone.

Several days ago, I was down at Dillman's Pick-N-Save looking over the melons when something almost knocked me off my feet. I thought I had been maced with Aqua Velva. It was the widower Owen Mooney. He was wearing a wild Hawaiian shirt unbuttoned halfway down his chest and a hairpiece that looked like roadkill with earflaps.

The man is 84 years old.

He said, "Hey, good lookin', I hear you and Ott split the sheets. There's a dance Saturday at the senior center." Then he rattled a prescription bottle in his pants pocket just in case I missed the message.

It was a little pathetic. Old geezer with a pencil full of lead and no one to write to. Well, I sure wasn't interested in a pen pal.

Sure enough, he was at the senior center dance Saturday. I had volunteered to do refreshments, and there wasn't any good way to get out of it.

He had one of the Nutter sisters, Ruth and Iny Rae, on each arm.

Wert Hoover had given his band a break and was playing a slow-dance number, what we call backseat music, solo on the saw. I tell you, Percy Sledge wasn't intended to be played on a saw.

Anyway, right in the middle of the dance, Owen, who was draped around Iny Rae Nutter like kudzu, went down like a sack of bricks.

Just like that, he was gone. Doctor said he was probably dead before his hair hit the floor, which was about two seconds before he did.

Dewey Mudgett picked up the body. Verniece moved her daybed out to the garage. Said she wasn't spending the night in the Celestial Rest visitation room with anyone on Viagra, dead or alive.

The minister from Two Pig Run preached a short eulogy that included a short religious poem he'd written for the occasion. I can't remember it all, but it did rhyme Gomorrah and Viagra without being too tacky.

I felt a little low after the service. Thought I would drop by the Gas-N-Go to see how your uncle was getting on. "Beefy" Kirwin was looking after business said your uncle had gone up to Chillicothe to pick up a fuel pump for Wandalene Lusk's Subaru.

I looked in on your uncle's room in the back. In the wastebasket I spied a couple of *Penthouse Forums* and about half a bottle of Viagra.

Kinda sad, but we may be able to work things out after all. At least, after the drug wears off.

My best to your momma.

Love,

Aunt Gracie

Three Pigs Revisited

June 9, 1999

A fable for our age.

Once upon a time, in a glade deep in the forest, there lived three little pigs.

There was nothing particularly remarkable about them, as pigs go. One worked in a video store, another was a systems analyst, and the third had a small-engine repair shop. They were as happy as pigs have the capacity to be.

The oldest of the three, the systems analyst, was considered the wisest and most prudent. He worked hard, invested wisely and saved enough

money to build a sturdy, if modest, brick ranch on the edge of the woods.

His younger brothers, impractical and a bit wild, spent foolishly, partied hard and cared little about the concerns and responsibilities that seemed to consume their older sibling.

When it came time to build their homes, one of the younger two cobbled a shanty out of sticks and twigs he had gathered from the floor of the forest. The other fashioned a flimsy cottage of straw and thatch. Neither of the structures appeared sturdy enough to withstand the first strong gust that came along, and one was not long in coming.

When the police composite of the big, bad wolf appeared in the local daily, the two younger pigs paid scant attention. Their older brother installed deadbolts and floodlights and refused to answer the door after dark.

The straw cottage went quickly when the youngest pig refused the wolf's demands, and its occupant might have been eaten in a minute had he not fled out the back door an instant before the walls collapsed.

The frightened porker pounded on the door of his brother's stick house, wailing, "Yo! Let me in, man. That wolf has gone crazy and he's headed this way."

It took the wolf a little longer to blow down the stick house, but not much.

When the oldest pig caught sight of his brothers hot-footing it up his driveway, a small and gloating part of him wanted to let them sweat a while as the wolf closed in. Instead, he ushered them in with a sigh of exasperation and ordered them to help him stoke the fire under a huge black kettle suspended in the hearth. The older pig knew the wolf's MO and wasn't taking any chances.

Sure enough, after the wolf had wearied of huffing and puffing, he shimmied up the side of the house to the roof and leaped down the chimney.

The forest ranger who read the wolf his rights as the scalded beast was being loaded into an ambulance assured the three pigs, "You boys won't have to worry about this one for a long, long time."

But the wolf copped a plea on a lesser charge and, at the sentencing, his lawyer made an impassioned case for leniency based on his client's troubled childhood and difficulty gaining acceptance in a society that tended to prejudge wolves.

After a month in the slammer, the wolf was released on shock probation. Then he went straight to the personal-injury lawyer who had handed him his business card during a break in the trial.

The lawyer brought suit against the oldest pig, contending that his negligence in failing to install a safety grating over the chimney had caused his client to sustain grave and disabling injuries, crippling emotional anguish and a loss of his professional livelihood. He further stated that said negligence was compounded by the pig's "unconscionable refusal" to come to the aid of his client after the wolf had landed in the cauldron.

The wolf asked for $38 million in actual and punitive damages plus attorney fees.

The pig spent most of his life's savings fighting the case, becoming so disconsolate and preoccupied by the battle that his employer was forced to let him go.

The wolf's attorney knew how to work a jury. He had made his bones winning a $16 million settlement in an earlier case (Goldilocks vs. Bears) bringing that jury to tears with his closing arguments about the constant pain his client suffered.

Nodding toward her wheelchair, he said her budding career as an exotic dancer had been snuffed out in an instant all because of a homemade chair and the reckless negligence that permitted it to go unmarked with proper warnings about its weight limit.

He was a smooth one, that lawyer. In the end, the wolf won. The court attached the pig's house and possessions.

His life a shambles, forced to live on the streets, he was sleeping under a bridge the night he was set upon by three hungry bears (yes, those bears) and eaten.

Dental records were required to identify the remains, which his youngest brother buried in the yard near the satellite dish. He would have taken more time with the grave, but the wolf was on Montel talking about his new book and he didn't want to miss the interview.

Heloise Rejects

Aug. 29, 1999

I was reading Heloise last Sunday when it dawned on me: She must get an incredible number of suggestions that she simply cannot use.

Wonder what she does with all those rejects?

Dear Heloise: I was sorting through some old clothes the other day when I came across a panty girdle. I almost threw it in the trash before I realized that if I sewed the leg holes closed and filled it with dirt, I could use it as a hanging planter.

It is now filled with geraniums and never fails to draw comments from everyone who sees it hanging from the front porch ceiling.

-- Onie Foonman, Possum Breath, Mo.

Dear Heloise: Please tell your readers not to throw away those used tea bags. I dry mine in the sun, snip off the string and let the cats use them as pillows. They are just the right size.

-- Marcilene Snopes, East Natural, Idaho

Dear Heloise: I am the sort of person who can gain 5 pounds just looking at the candy dish, so I am always searching for new and different low-calorie snacks to help me keep my "girlish figure" (as Duane calls it).

Not long ago I received a large box in the mail containing a Wayne Newton commemorative dish that I had ordered from Wayne's fan club.

To protect it from breaking during shipping, the dish was packed in those funny little foam plastic peanuts. Just out of curiosity, I sprinkled a little salt on one and tried it.

They are not bad, and the best thing is they contain zero calories and no

saturated fats. Duane likes them with salsa.

-- Rayette Blorchman, Landfill, Ga.

Dear Heloise: Not long ago I buried my grandmother and was shocked to discover that the cemetery throws away any dirt leftover after filling the grave.

The way I see it, that dirt has been bought and paid for and ought to belong to the family. You can use it for potting plants or filling in low spots in the yard. What's more, most gravediggers don't mind shoveling it in the hatchback if you ask them real nice.

-- Wanda Fussmucker, Resume Speed, Wyo.

Dear Heloise: My husband suffers from dry and itchy skin, particularly during the winter months. Lately I have taken to spraying him with Pam (you can use any nonstick cooking spray) when he gets out of the shower. His skin is now smooth as silk and he smells so much better than when we were using lamp oil.

-- Verniece Mudgett, Methane, Ohio

Dear Heloise: Last week, I was visiting a neighbor when I happened to comment on the bright and colorful throw pillows in her family room. That was when she let me in on a neat secret. The throw pillows are actually vacuum sweeper bags. When a bag is full, she simply removes it from the sweeper, seals it with duct tape and spray paints it a nice accent color to match the couch.

-- Arnetta Samples, Lost Caboose, Ind.

Dear Heloise: I nearly panicked when my Tuesday bridge club arrived and I discovered that I was almost out of that handy cheese spread that comes in an aerosol can. I was afraid I was going to have to serve them plain old Ritz crackers. Then I remembered the tube of denture adhesive in the medicine cabinet. Blend it with a couple drops of yellow food coloring and I dare you to tell the difference.

-- Cora Mae Pfeffernoose, Lower Altoona, Pa.

Dear Heloise: My husband Harley Ray and I were at the hardware store last week and were shocked at the price of bug zappers.

We thought it was going to be another miserable summer on the patio with the mosquitos and gnats until my sister informed me that she and her husband use their pop-up toaster as a zapper. Just put the setting on dark, press down and the light from the toaster coils draws bugs like a magnet. Make sure you shake the dead bugs out every week or so. Otherwise, the Pop Tarts develop a funny aftertaste.

-- Congolia Wildermuth, Roadkill, Nev.

The Pool Nazi

June 5, 1998

The guy in line in front of me at McDonald's was in the tertiary stage of Fife's Syndrome.

I tried not to stare, but those afflicted with the condition are difficult to ignore. Moreover, Fife's Syndrome victims don't want to be ignored. It is part of the disease.

Blame me for the name. I decided to call it Fife's Syndrome after *The Andy Griffith Show's* annoyingly overzealous deputy, Barney Fife.

Fife's Syndrome is what little people get when they are given a badge or a modicum of official authority over others and then become tyrants.

The guy in line at McDonald's was making life miserable for a minimum-wage clerk. He carped about prices, sluggish service, the fast-food industry in general and McDonald's in particular.

A walkie-talkie hung from a holster on his belt. For a few moments, I thought he might be pondering calling in an airstrike on the place.

Fife's Syndrome victims gravitate toward "gatekeeper" jobs. They're not doctors; they're the people you must get past to see the doctor. They don't own the corporation; they run its parking garage.

"The pool Nazi!" said a co-worker of mine, describing a Fife's Syndrome flunky who manages the swimming pool in the apartment complex where he lives.

The sole job of the pool Nazi --let's call him Sergei -- is to check pool passes and remove dead, chlorinated bugs from the water.

Sergei is not even a lifeguard. But the pool is his little empire, a Barney Fifedom of his very own.

"No swimming for you today," is an expression he turns over in his mind with near-orgasmic ecstasy, just waiting for the hapless tenant foolish enough to have left his pool pass back in the apartment.

He struts about in a pair of those odd, skintight double-knit shorts favored by some high school football coaches and male prison inmates nicknamed "Trish."

"You must use your thighs when you leg-kick," the pool Nazi sneers at swimmers he doesn't know and who haven't asked his advice.

Not only does the pool Nazi check passes when tenants enter the pool area, he does routine spot checks afterward to make sure no one has tried to sneak a pass over the fence to a non-tenant.

Two weeks ago, Fife's Syndrome ruined a district track meet for an Olentangy High School athlete named Misty Spring. Spring had posted a long jump of 17 feet, 4 1/2 inches, good enough to qualify for the regional until the head judge noticed that the young woman's sports bra, instead of being a solid color, was sky blue with white piping: disqualification.

In the regional, Spring was lined up to run the mile relay when a referee noticed that the numbers on the backs of a couple of Olentangy runners' uniforms were in different typefaces, and that the colors had faded slightly.

The girls were ordered to change uniforms or be disqualified. Frantic, Spring was in tears, running around looking for a number in the right font when she should have been trying to concentrate on the relay she was about to run.

Fife's Syndrome. Pool Nazis. Fine-print experts. Dyspeptic bureaucrats. Impoundment-lot clerks.

Fife's Syndrome is everywhere. Some of those afflicted fall victim to the clutches of the disease while trying to get even with the world. I think a good number of those saber-rattling, nuke-loopy demonstrators in Pakistan have Fife's Syndrome. I honestly believe they never would have decided to develop a nuclear capability if not for all of those years of 7-Eleven jokes.

Just what the world needs: a Third World Barney Fife with a 50-megaton warhead and a chip on his shoulder.

The Tug Captain

Sept. 24, 1999

PORTSMOUTH, N.H. -- Lawson Doughty nosed his tugboat against the salt freighter and began shifting the St. George A. Valletta to a new mooring along the Portsmouth harbor docks.

With calm seas and only a whisper of wind, he made quick work of the chore, nuzzling the freighter's hull in the manner a seasoned sheep dog turns the flock to pen.

Job finished, he cut an easy arc around the harbor and brought the 108-foot Fells Point tug to berth beside her sisters, the E.F. Moran and the Eugenia Moran. Waving from the wheelhouse to the dockside office of Moran Towing of New Hampshire, Doughty secured the tug for the day, then made his way to the wharf.

"I've always been on the water. All my life," said Doughty, a trim, graying, 57-year-old tug captain.

Pilot boats, tugboats. He's done 'em all.

Doughty was born to a Portland, Maine, clan whose family tree might be more appropriately drawn as a mainmast and yardarms.

Within Doughty's immediate family, his father, Sidney, and all five of his sons took to the sea.

Lawson is the only one the sea hasn't claimed.

"My father was a fisherman," Doughty said. "He and my two older brothers were lost at sea in 1942. They were on a 50-foot fishing boat, the Marlene, named after my next oldest sister. They were after haddock."

No one knows what happened. The Marlene could have been run down by a large ship or taken by a squall. Their bodies never were recovered.

"Mother was three months along with me when it happened," Doughty said. "Six months later, I was born."

Doughty recalled of his mother, "She was always worried about anything we did on the water. But we all ended up on the water. And she respected that."

Listening to him, one recalls the lines of Melville's *Moby Dick:*

There is, one knows not what sweet mystery about this sea, whose gently awful stirrings seem to speak of some hidden soul beneath.

Doughty had his salt-water baptism in the Navy, serving four years as a boatswain's mate. He pulled a tour on the USS New, a destroyer posted in the Gulf of Tonkin off the coast of Vietnam.

Returning to Maine, he worked as a deckhand and captained pilot boats. In time, he landed a spot as a tug captain.

In 1971, he lost his brother Charles.

"They found him between the dock and the boat. He had to have fallen off the boat into the water or off a ladder while getting on the boat."

It was winter. Weighted by his fishing garb in the near-freezing water, Charles was unable to save himself.

Nine years later, Manley, another brother, would perish in a similar circumstance:

"He was going onto a fishing boat and the rail gave way. He went in the water and hypothermia got him. He was up under the dock. By the time they got to him, it was too late."

Doughty bore Manley's pall when the body was carried over to a cemetery on Casco Bay's Chebeague Island off the southwest coast of Maine.

Yet, the accident did not dissuade Manley's son and namesake from taking to the Atlantic waters in a 70-foot trawler.

Lawson Doughty understands. He could never have worked in an office or on an assembly line. Too predictable for his blood.

"It's never the same -- the wind, the tide, the current, the size of the boat," he said of the sea.

Neither of Lawson's two offspring has followed the Doughty tradition. One became an assistant buyer for a department store chain; the other is manager of a delivery service.

"It's up to them," Doughty said of their chosen careers.

To be sure, he is grateful that he doesn't have to worry about them when the skies turn leaden and the seas run high.

With rue and respect, he ackowledged, "The sea can take anything, anytime it wants."

Amish Vice

June 26, 1998

In light of reports this week in Pennsylvania about two Amish men being accused of buying cocaine from a motorcycle gang, I'm submitting my script for a revival of the old TV series *Dragnet*.

Sgt. Troyer: My name is Troyer. Levi Troyer. I'm a cop. I was working the day shift in narcotics trying to get a lead on a cocaine trail that seemed to connect a motorcycle gang called the Pagans with a couple Amish gangs, Heck's Angels and the Quilters. That's how I ended up here at the Yoders' Troyer knocks on door.

Edna Yoder: Yah.

Sgt. Troyer: (flashing his badge) I'm Sgt. Troyer. Intercourse Police.

Edna: Twelve kids I got with my Jacob. Now you say there's a law.

Sgt. Troyer: Ma'am?

Edna: Intercourse.

Sgt. Troyer: That's the name of the town, ma'am. Intercourse, Pa.

Edna: Yah. So it is.

Sgt. Troyer: Is that your buggy out in the drive, ma'am?

Edna: It's my boy Onan's.

Sgt. Troyer: Don't see too many Amish lowriders.

Onan Yoder: Who is it, Ma?

Sgt. Troyer: Are you Onan, son?

Onan: What's it to ya?

Edna: Is my boy in some kind of trouble?

Sgt. Troyer: We're investigating a 358.

Edna: A 358?

Sgt. Troyer: Cow tipping, ma'am. We think it might be drug-related.

Edna: No!

Sgt. Troyer: We found traces of cocaine on 20 overturned Holsteins up at the Miller place this morning.

Onan: I was here all night.

Sgt. Troyer: An outhouse was pushed over, too. We dusted it for fingerprints after we got the widow Miller out, of course.

Onan: I told you I was here all night.

Sgt. Troyer: Sure you were, son. Do you know this woman? (holds up photograph)

Onan looks away.

Edna: Isn't that Rachel Stoltzfus? What is she doing?

Sgt. Troyer: They call it a "wet bonnet" contest. Big turn-on for buggy druggies, right, son?

Onan: I don't know nothin'.

Sgt. Troyer: We hear she is a real snuff queen.

Edna: Rachel dips snuff?

Sgt. Troyer: It's a figure of speech, ma'am.

Edna: Oh.

Sgt. Troyer: Son, we got a witness who says you were there at the Heck's Angels clubhouse for gang initiation the night Rachel pulled the buggy.

Edna: What buggy?

Sgt. Troyer: Figure of speech, ma'am. She had to do it to become a buggy mama. (He removes a crack pipe from his pocket.) Ever see this before, son?

Onan: It ain't mine.

Edna: Can't get much tobacco in that.

Sgt. Troyer: We found it in your horse's feedbag, son.

Onan: (beginning to break down) I didn't mean to hurt nobody.

Sgt. Troyer: We know you didn't, son, so why don't you do yourself a favor and lead us to Mr. Big? The judge might go easy on you come sentencing.

Onan: (sobbing) I'm sorry, Ma. I don't know what happened. I didn't know what I was getting into. The guys said, "Here, try this, kid." It looked safe corn silk dipped in udder balm. Next thing you know, we were out in the dairy barn huffing methane. Then cocaine.

Edna: Where did you get the money?

Sgt. Troyer: You want to tell her, son?

Onan: I fenced goats.

Edna: Goats?

Sgt. Troyer: Goats.

Onan: Ever try to score a rock of crack with a goat?

Sgt. Troyer: Can't say that I have, son.

Edna: (choking up) Is my boy going to prison?

Sgt. Troyer: For a while, ma'am.

Edna: (wailing) God help us. I know what happens to young boys like him in prison.

Sgt. Troyer: Ma'am?

Edna: Television.

Sgt. Troyer: Yes, ma'am.

Mother of Martyrs

Oct. 18, 1998

HOI AN, Vietnam-- Dang Thi Khi lifted her gray head from the palm mat of her deathbed. Like an ancient sea turtle, she appeared to be mustering the last of her dwindling reserves to take bearings in a world no longer familiar.

From the open doorway fronting her spartan, one-room house, a quilt of rice straw had been spread upon her yard and the abutting roadway. Chaff from the year's third and final harvest, it dried beneath an unrelenting sun.

Before long, the monsoon would be upon Hoi An.

Before long, after the fits and starts of her 91 brutal and grievous years, Mrs. Khi would die in the house where she was born. And she would be buried on the edge of the rice paddies her neighbors tend.

When the first U.S. combat troops waded ashore at nearby Da Nang in March 1965, Mrs. Khi was 58.

Her husband, Vo Quat, was the chief of the local Viet Cong contingent. The couple's four sons all were part of the guerrilla force.

Two months after U.S. Marines landed, Mrs. Khi's eldest son, Vo Nhu Hung, was killed in fighting at Phuoc Son.

Another son, Vo Nhu Sanh, died in combat in 1967. She was told only that his remains had been buried by his comrades somewhere in the mountains.

Not long after, she was arrested and questioned concerning the whereabouts of her husband and two surviving sons.

When she refused to disclose the location of their base camp, her interrogators broke her arm.

Her husband and a third son, Vo Nhu Truoc, were killed south of Hoi An during the Tet Offensive of 1968.

A year later, her last surviving son died in a firefight at Dien Nam.

When South Vietnam fell in 1975, she was informed by the government in Hanoi that her losses in the cause of the North officially qualified her as a "mother of martyrs."

The distinction entitled her to a small pension and a few government concessions and amenities.

She was accorded priority status on waiting lists for government-administered housing, though she never had a desire to leave the home in which she reared her sons.

On national holidays, the government occasionally sent her gifts or invited her to Hanoi. There she was posed for photographs on the steps of Ho Chi Minh's tomb with other "mothers of martyrs" and top government officials.

She made her last trip to Hanoi two years ago to be presented with the remains of her son who was killed in the mountain fighting in 1967.

A photograph of that ceremony is tacked to the wall near the doorway of her home.

In late summer, sensing her time was near, she bought her casket. It rested beneath a plastic tarp on a pair of sawhorses across the room from her bed.

Mrs. Khi's sister-in-law, Nguyen Thi Son, kept a vigil at her bedside.

Mrs. Son said that when her sister-in-law last spoke, she told her, "I have survived rockets, shells and mortars. I have tried to hide my deep sorrow in my heart, but life has been very harsh."

All across Vietnam, as the mother of martyrs lay dying, the nation was hanging flags and banners in preparation for the celebration of Independence Day.

Most of the banners were lettered with quotes from Ho Chi Minh.

They recalled his words on the inestimable worth of freedom and independence. They quoted his observations on the unity of the people and the nobility of the cause.

None of the banners celebrated his oath that, even though he might lose a dozen to each of the enemy's dead, he would continue to press on until his adversary lost heart for the fight.

In Hoi An, the most conspicuous living hostage to Uncle Ho's pledge tried once more to raise her head and, failing, closed her eyes against the wall hung with framed government proclamations saluting her distinction as a mother of martyrs.

Baseball Advertising

April 4, 1999

Baseball fans have been cussing and discussing reported talk of selling advertising space on player uniforms ever since the story broke last week.

Dispatch sports columnist Bob Hunter sank satirical fang deep in the major-league sport's tender parts on Friday. He even mused over further options to help line the owners' pockets and keep player salaries high enough that potential Hall of Famers such as Willie Greene don't have to find more gainful work.

I love baseball. I just can't help adding my two cents' worth of doggerel about what might happen when the day comes that the Chief Wahoo patch on Cleveland uniforms can no longer be seen for the ads pitching everything from Chi-Chi's to Charmin.

'Twas spring again in Cleveland,
And the umpire cried, "Play ball!"
The boys were in the dugout,
The fans were wall to wall.
There was huge anticipation
In the city by the lake,
Hope rode on the April breeze,
Excitement filled the Jake.

The hometown nine took the field,
The crowd let out a yell,
That echoed through the countryside,
Off every hill and dell.
Then just as quick, a deathly pall
Swept over all the throng.
'Twas clear to every Cleveland fan
That something grave was wrong.

There was something strangely different
About the tribe's attire.
Why it looked as though the boys
Were clad in uniforms for hire.
As Nagy took his warm-ups,
Fans glimpsed upon his arm,
One patch for Ballpark hot dogs,
Another for State Farm.

He stepped to toe the rubber,
And discern the catcher's sign,
Then touched a cap emblazoned
With an ad for Gallo wine.
From saddened fans the players heard
A deep collective groan,
Vizquel wore an ad for Kwell

And Thome Coppertone.

Shuey wore a sleeve patch
Recommending Autozone,
A Snicker bar graced Alomar,
Colon Old Spice cologne.
Lofton wore a shirt-sleeve patch
Touting Dewar's Scotch.
An ad for Preparation H
Was sewn in Hargrove's crotch.

How sad to see the hometown boys
Humiliated so.
How could baseball sell its soul
To turn a little dough?
A grumbling fan turned to his mate
And said, "Do tell me, please?"
Would DiMaggio have been a shill
For Birds Eye frozen peas?

"Would the Babe have worn a patch
Endorsing soup or pantyhose?
Would Mantle let 'em sew an ad
For Alpo to his clothes?"
"This ain't the game I used to know,"
One fan was heard to rue.
"The players are just sandwich boards
For Ford and Subaru.

"They stiff you for the ticket price
And gouge you for your brew,
And make you look at ads for Tide
Right next to Chief Wahoo."
A human wave of sadness
Then swept throughout the stands,
And slowly out the exits
Moved an exodus of fans.

The goose that laid the golden egg
Had met its sad demise.
Just goes to show it doesn't
Always pay to advertise.

It Shouldn't Happen Anywhere

March 29, 1998

JONESBORO, Ark. - Passing half-mast ensigns that rippled and shivered in the gusts of late March, the burnished hearse shed its motorcycle escorts where the paved road gave way to a puddled clay trail that led through flanking scrub pine to Kellers Chapel Cemetery.

The pallbearers shouldered the metal box beneath the winter-bare branches of a catalpa and started uncertainly down the hill. The strewn confetti of dog violet and white clover marked their way to the mourners' tent, just beyond the grave of a stillborn whose headstone was carved with the image of a drowsing shepherd boy over whose shoulder a lamb stood lone sentinel.

"Come on in here," the Rev. Alvin Swan told mourners huddled in small knots beyond the flapping canopy shading Stephanie Johnson's casket.

Jonesboro was burying the last of its slain children, and Swan had been charged with the daunting task of plucking solace from faith's deep pockets for a family whose grief no words could assuage.

He spoke of the Bible's long-suffering Job while a few outside the tent cupped palms around Marlboros they needed more than Genesis.

Now and then, a muffled keening issued from under the canopy, causing the assembled women to daub reddened eyes and the men to stare at their shoe tips.

Swan, pastor of the Bolivar Full Gospel Pentecostal Church, knew a thing or two about the demons with whom Stephanie's parents wrestled. He had lost a 13-year-old son to an auto accident and bristled with uncomprehending rage when the minister at the funeral invoked, "All things work together for the good of them that love the lord.

"I didn't see what good God was getting out of this," Swan remembered of that moment.

He was not long into his eulogy at Emerson Funeral Home before he realized the folly of trying to reconcile theodicy and tragedy and wrench comfort from the two.

"About halfway through the message," he conceded, "it started to get to me some. There was a part of the message where I became aware of the reality that what I was saying wasn't easing the pain. But you can't close the book."

He rode out to the cemetery determined to ease the grief, yet knowing there was precious little he could say.

"Miss me but let me go," he recited at graveside.

It is the last line of a poem he hoped might bring comfort to the family. After he had recited it, the cemetery workers moved tentatively toward the canopy and began to seal the vault and lower the casket.

The grinding click that dropped Stephanie to her rest stirred something in her mother, who rose and reached for her daughter only to be pulled back by her husband. The whine of the burial gears screeched like fingernails across a chalkboard.

"We're not a people with a forgiving heart," Swan allowed after the committal service. "There is a side of us that is bitter. The Bible says we are forever bitter and never come to the knowledge of the truth."

He swept a palm over hair chestnut going ashen, knelt to say goodbye to Stephanie's mother and started up the hill to his car, sidestepping ruts in the sienna clay.

The hearse driver gunned the engine and steered the vehicle back to the main road.

Had he not another funeral for yet another shooting victim to attend, he might have noticed the Methodist church guidepost with its fluttering white ribbons, a sign whose recently amended message had been altered from some forgotten scriptural axiom to confess, "Things like this shouldn't happen anywhere."

Queen of the Bodice Rippers

May 24, 2000

Dame Barbara Cartland, dowager queen of romance reading fare, died Sunday in her sleep, at 98. During her lifetime, she had written 723 romance novels.

On that fine Sunday morning when Sir Cyril, the Viscount Frothingslosh, rang the bell at Dame Cartland's estate at Hertfordshire, his ear caught the distant, excited yipping of his inamorata's Pekingese.

A smile crossed the ruggedly handsome face with sad gray-green eyes. A quiver of desire rippled through the bulging biceps beneath the tunic of a lieutenant in the Queen's Orchardmen (royal gatherers of road apples from Her Majesty's steed).

"I'm here to see Dame Cartland," Sir Cyril told the maid.

"Don't know if that's such a good idea today, sir," she demurred. She averted her eyes from the bouquet-bearing suitor. "She had a bit of a funny turn this morning."

"Oh, come now. She's just playing the shy one isn't she?" Sir Cyril dismissed, pushing past the maid as sweat beads of passion formed on his firm upper lip.

He mounted the stairs two at a time, the breathless maid in tow as he tore open the boudoir door.

"Aren't you coy?" he bubbled as he approached the motionless figure propped on bed pillows. "Pretending to be dead to the world, are you, my pet?"

"Quite," the maid muttered.

Sir Cyril threw the bouquet toward the maid and commanded, "Put these where she can see them."

"That'd be in a casket," the domestic grumbled.

"I beg your pardon?"

"I said, 'I'll get a basket.' "

"My sweet, sweet, Barbara," Sir Cyril gushed, pulling a chair to the bedside and taking her hand in his.

"Gawd, blimey, what a plonker," the maid groused of the blissfully ignorant suitor. "Thick as two short planks."

Twi-Twi the pet had begun sniffing the visitor's trouser leg.

"How cold your hand, my dear," Sir Cyril whispered. "She thinks it's so cute to ignore me. Maybe I should just post her a letter."

"If you can get the groundhogs to deliver it, sir," the maid said.

Yielding to his searing unspoken need, Sir Cyril passionately kissed his love's fingertips.

"Relax," he murmured, nibbling at Dame Cartland's earlobe. "You're stiff as a board."

The maid rolled her eyes.

Twi-Twi cozied up to Sir Cyril's pant leg.

"Bad dog!" the maid chastened. "I told her ladyship she should have something done about that mutt a long time ago."

Sir Cyril did not seem to hear. The flames of his passionate ecstasy had transported him to love's Mount Olympus. His ears were deaf to the silly and mundane world above which ardor had so elevated him. Nor did he notice the undertaker standing in the bedroom doorway.

"Over there, love," the maid instructed the mortician, "if we can get Casanova away from her."

"Sir, I have come for Dame Cartland," the newcomer announced.

Indignant, Sir Cyril demanded, "And just who, sir, might you be? Barbara, is there something you've been keeping from me? Who is this vile, vain swain? Is he the reason you have seemed so distant? Tell me, my love, am I coming on too strong? Do you need some space?"

"About 6 feet of it, if you're askin' me," the maid interjected.

"Dame Cartland is coming with me," the undertaker said firmly.

Drawing his sword from its scabbard, Sir Cyril stepped forward, warning, "Unhand that woman."

"She's dead, sir," the exasperated maid bellowed.

Dazed by the shock of that dawning awareness, Sir Cyril sheathed his sword and slinked from the room.

Puppy Kindergarten

Dec. 9, 1996

MONDAY, DEC. 2 -- Dear Diary: 6 p.m. Arrive at puppy kindergarten with Molly. Dog seems too old for puppy kindergarten. Sixteen weeks. Paws big as ham hocks. Head large as pumpkin. Bladder the size of thimble. Deep chestnut eyes. Nothing behind them.

Dog wets when frightened. Dog wets when excited. Dog wets when door-bell rings. Doorbell sticks. Lots of paper towels.

Kindergarten teacher named Amy Jewett-Sadler. No-nonsense trainer. Gives canine students five minutes to socialize before class. They form a nose-to-rump conga line and circle the classroom.

"There's a lot of butt-sniffing at the beginning," trainer says. Seems strange. Never thought I'd hear kindergarten teacher say that.

Trainer teaches that pet owners must assert authority over dog --must become "alpha dog" while puppy becomes "subordinate dog." Irish setter puppy yawns at this.

Pet owner worries about puppy dirty-dancing with her ankle, dirty-dancing with furniture, dirty-dancing with Barbie dolls.

Trainer says, "Don't worry about your dog being oversexed at this point." Says that it is only "dominant behavior." Nothing to do with sex. Tell that to Barbie.

Trainer moves on, reminds class, "I talked about `ouch' last week. How is that going for everyone?"

"Ouch" training involves yelping like dog when dog nips. Have tried this. Everyone in house doing high falsetto "Yow! Yow! Yow!" when Molly nips. Sound frightens dog. Dog wets floor. More paper towels.

Trainer notes that owner should be able to touch puppy without puppy bit-ing. She advises to touch dog all over: "Touch each individual toenail. Lift up their ears, and stick your fingers in their ears." Pull up muzzle. Touch gums. No fun. Dog mouth is great pit of slime and unflossed cat litter.

Trainer says she will teach us "alpha roll." Move is like WWF takedown. Flips puppy onto back and into submissive position. Lets puppy know who's boss. Shows puppy that owner is "Great Alpha, king of the wolves."

"You need to stare him down," trainer explains. Must look dog in the eyes until dog looks away. Molly seems bored with this activity. Looks away quick-ly. Maybe training is working. Maybe dog has just noticed intriguing pattern in wallpaper. Can't tell.

"They have the attention span of a gnat," trainer consoles.

Staring session ends.

"No more free treats," trainer orders. "No more free treats just because they're cute." Cute puppies seem offended, especially dog resembling fuzzy bedroom slipper. Owners of cute puppies act like trainer must be talk-ing about someone else.

Must teach dog "down" or "lay," trainer explains.

Puppy owners seem confused about which of two choices to call this com-mand.

Trainer says, "You can call it `booger' if you want."

Wonder if trainer thinks some puppies are smarter than their masters.

Last lesson of day is to teach puppy "Be mellow." Owners must take down puppy with "alpha roll," pin dog's hip while gripping paw and massaging shoulders all at the same time. "Be mellow" very difficult. Easier just to give puppy a joint and say, "Here, hit this. Be mellow."

Trainer decides to demonstrate "Be mellow" on worst-behaved puppy in class. Asks pet owners to vote. Molly is unanimous choice. Am embarrassed. Dog thinks it is high honor.

Sulk out of puppy kindergarten. Still many more weeks to go.

On drive home, dog begins to nip. Daughter wails, "Yow! Yow! Yow!" Wife yells, "Yow! Yow! Yow!" All go, "Yow! Yow! Yow!" Driver of other car at stop-light gives disgusted look. Pretend we are singing Christmas carols.

"Yow! Yow! Yow!" has worked. Puppy startled. Must remember to get seat covers Scotchgarded.

Dear Diary: Babysitting Christian

Aug. 16, 1999

Dear Diary,

Thursday, Aug. 12: Grandson Christian arrives at house. I greet him at front door. He wails. Not a good start. Son-in-law hands me diaper bag. Weighs 67 pounds. Contains everything Christian needs for Mount Everest expedition. Holds one gross of diapers, powder, food, formula, inflatable playpen, collapsible stroller.

I take Christian. He screams after departing father. Cats flee. Dog crawls under bed. It will be a long day.

I try to soothe grandson. Point out framed photos of family on foyer wall. He smiles at photo of mother -- is frightened by others. Try to place Christian in bouncer seat. He cries. Spock says OK for babies to cry. Grandson cries at 114 decibels. Neighbors will call Children Services.

Remove grandson from bouncer seat. Hold on lap. He wants to stand. Does flamenco dance in lap. Hard feet. Very painful. Am now soprano.

Grandson working on pacifier. Spock says too much pacifier not good. Baby will develop buckteeth. Will be able to eat a pineapple through a tennis rack-et. I remove pacifier. Bad move. Did not know that pacifier suction creates vacuum. Vacuum holds things inside baby. No vacuum -- baby fills diaper.

Diaper change no picnic. Must hold baby flat with one hand, unfold diaper with other, while leaning way back. Baby boys sometimes like Old Faithful, though not as predictable.

Baby powdered and changed. Person who invents dipstick for checking diapers will become very wealthy.

Baby still cranky. Perhaps hungry. Many jars of baby food in diaper bag. Pureed chicken and beets. Sounds revolting. Pureed turkey and pumpkin with cranberries. Thanksgiving in a jar. Go with that.

Place baby in bouncer seat. Baby yelps. Show him baby food. Baby quiet. Dog smells food. Stands next to bouncer.

Grandson likes to eat. Swings arms to show happiness. Arm hits spoon. Turkey, pumpkin, cranberries end up on dog. Baby amused. Opens mouth to laugh. Turkey and saliva run down chin.

Baby grabs dog's upper lip and pulls. Elasticity amazing. Dog not amused.

Continue feeding. Baby bored. Tell baby spoon is airplane. He must open hangar so plane can land. Try to make jet noises. Baby looks away. Tell him plane low on fuel. Will crash. All 237 passengers and crew will die. Long investigation. NTSB will trace cause of crash to baby. Many lawsuits. Baby opens mouth, grabs foot. Sticks toes in mouth.

Perhaps grandson wants dessert. Open jar of blueberry and apple goo. Spoon into baby's mouth. Baby sneezes. Pause to clean glasses. Wipe blueberries from beard.

Baby finished eating. Rubs eyes. Good sign. Perhaps tired.

Give baby bottle. He drinks. Eyes close. Place baby in crib. He screams. Try to rock baby. Closes eyes. Try crib again. Nothing doing.

Perhaps TV will make baby tired. Hold baby on lap. Punch remote control. Afternoon TV strange. Show called Montel. Small man. Handsome. Guests as large as Volkswagens. All screaming at once. Show is about parents who have traded children for pickup trucks. Good program for grandson to see. Maybe teach him respect. He whines.

Switch to Oprah. Guest is crying. Oprah is crying. Grandson begins crying. Do not feel so good myself. Turn off TV.

Daughter says baby will nap if she lies next to him. Will try that strategy.

Make fort of pillows so baby will not roll. Lie next to baby. Tell baby to sleep. Sing *You Are My Sunshine*. Sing *99 Bottles of Beer* (twice). Sing aria from *La Boheme*. Grandson still awake. Grandfather falling asleep.

Awaken to sudden pain. Baby has grabbed nostril. Small hands. Able to fit three fingers in nostril. Did not know babies have fingernails so sharp. Pain so bad eyes water. Try to remove baby's hand. Baby laughs.

Baby grabs hair at top of chest, near throat. Yanks. Baby studies hair ripped from grandfather. Seems amused. Perhaps baby will be professional wrestler, become famous for nostril hold and hair removal.

Baby finally nods off. Gently lift baby and carry to crib. Must not awaken. Doorbell rings. Dogs bark. Baby screams.

It is baby's father. Time for baby to go home. Son-in-law takes baby. Tells baby to wave "bye-bye." Baby waves. Baby exits.

Grandfather exhausted. Must nap. Fall into bed. Absently lick mustache. Taste blueberries. Taste turkey. Taste beets.

Sleep.

The Orchardman

Nov. 10, 2000

MALTA, Ohio -- Childish whimsy and the promise of a new $10 bill inspired Marion Hickerson's children to christen their father's orchard operation the Never Never Fruit Farm.

The toil and frustration of tending 600 apple and peach trees straddling both sides of Stockport Road gave breadth to Hickerson's tongue-in-cheek explanation of the name:

"You never get rich. You never run out of work."

He waited until he had ushered his visitor into the cool of his apple room before adding to the mix a third absolute:

"You'll never find better apples anywhere."

The bouquet wafting through the stash room would turn the most celebrated of Paris perfumers Granny Smith green with envy. Intoxicating, the scent is the accumulation of an orchardman's winter worry and spring sweat ripened by nature's alchemy to a heady incense.

The growing season has been a good one for the 83-year-old man. Brisk fall trade has left only a small inventory of crates filled with fruit so large that it's difficult to palm three apples to a hand.

From the brow of the hummock rising behind his modest house 85 miles east-southeast of Columbus, it is possible to take in the vista of the land he has groomed for 60 years. Far from smooth, the rounded crowns of hills -- in hues of jade, moss and olive -- are bunched together like throw pillows arranged against the headboard of the horizon.

To behold it all from the postcard-shaped window that fronts his living room, Hickerson must look past the rude homestead across the road. That is where three of his five children were born after he and Mae set up housekeeping in 1940.

A large sign on the prow of the old place carries a list of names, saying, "Stewards who have held title to this farm."

The word steward was not carelessly chosen. Hickerson believes to his marrow that he is merely Providence's custodian.

"I don't own this land. I just have title to it. It's up to me to make it better for the next generation."

To some, such an overwrought sentiment might carry the taint of false modesty. They never saw the place in 1940.

Riven with gullies and farmed fallow, its allure and potential resided only in the vision of a man willing to close one eye and squint with the other.

When he led a team out to slopes fractured by ruts, he explained, "I'd put one horse in the gully and one on the bank, and gradually plowed it smooth."

Electrification did not make it to the far reaches of Hickerson's place until 1947, two years after he had purchased his first tractor.

To make ends meet, he taught night classes in farm management to local veterans fresh home from World War II. Mae, who died 12 years ago, was a registered nurse.

Hickerson is plain-spoken in the manner that a city cynic who worked in central casting would be too easily tempted to resist parodying.

Fielding questions that beg philosophical expansiveness, he has a habit of hooking his thumbs under the breast sides of his bib overalls and prefacing responses, "Well, now, sir . . ."

At such moments, he is the most engaging of men.

Waxing pensive on his contention that one's faith fits better as armor than plumage, he said, "You should speak where the Bible speaks and remain silent where the Bible is silent."

Striding up the slope behind his house, with English shepherd Tippy at his heels, he inspected the rows of apple trees for signs that interloping bucks once again had skinned off bark with their seasonal rutting.

Pointing out a broad hillside where he once bulldozed 1,000 peach trees that had become winterkill's casualties, he suggested visiting a spot across the road where he had planted replacements.

Tippy hopped into the back of the pickup and -- as the truck jounced up the grade to the orchard -- braced himself like an unseasoned sailor trying to find his legs.

At the crest of the rise, when Hickerson switched off the ignition, his passenger drank in the view and asked: "How does it feel to behold stewardship from such a pleasant perch?"

In answering, the older man's first three words came as no surprise.

"Well, now, sir . . ."